Raku Recipes

A Problem-Solution Approach

J.J. Merelo

Apress®

Raku Recipes: A Problem-Solution Approach

J.J. Merelo
Granada, Granada, Spain

ISBN-13 (pbk): 978-1-4842-6257-3   ISBN-13 (electronic): 978-1-4842-6258-0
https://doi.org/10.1007/978-1-4842-6258-0

Managing Director, Apress Media LLC: Welmoed Spahr
Acquisitions Editor: Steve Anglin
Development Editor: Matthew Moodie
Coordinating Editor: Mark Powers

Cover designed by eStudioCalamar

Cover image by Vincent Guth on Unsplash (www.unsplash.com)

Distributed to the book trade worldwide by Apress Media, LLC, 1 New York Plaza, New York, NY 10004, U.S.A. Phone 1-800-SPRINGER, fax (201) 348-4505, e-mail orders-ny@springer-sbm.com, or visit www.springeronline.com. Apress Media, LLC is a California LLC and the sole member (owner) is Springer Science + Business Media Finance Inc (SSBM Finance Inc). SSBM Finance Inc is a **Delaware** corporation.

For information on translations, please e-mail booktranslations@springernature.com; for reprint, paperback, or audio rights, please e-mail bookpermissions@springernature.com.

Apress titles may be purchased in bulk for academic, corporate, or promotional use. eBook versions and licenses are also available for most titles. For more information, reference our Print and eBook Bulk Sales web page at http://www.apress.com/bulk-sales.

Any source code or other supplementary material referenced by the author in this book is available to readers on GitHub via the book's product page, located at www.apress.com/9781484262573. For more detailed information, please visit http://www.apress.com/source-code.

Printed on acid-free paper

Dedicated to my family, for their understanding, encouragement, and support, and to the late Jeff Goff, for introducing me to Raku

Table of Contents

About the Author

J.J. Merelo is a professor at the University of Granada, where he has been teaching since 1988. He has been using Perl since 1994, and Raku intensively since December 2016. He is currently in charge of Raku documentation, and he trains, teaches, and consults on Perl and Raku projects. He likes to take pictures of sunsets, to look up at buildings and wonder who made them, to practice a bit of yoga on the side, and to meet new students and see them grow in the classes he teaches.

About the Technical Reviewer

Moritz Lenz is a software engineer and architect. In the Raku community, he is well known for his contributions to the Raku programming language, the Rakudo compiler, and the related test suite, infrastructure, and tools. He is also a prolific Perl and Python programmer.

Acknowledgments

Again, to Apress for trusting me on this second book about Raku and the team that helped me get through it: Mark Powers, Matthew Moodie, and Steve Anglin. Moritz Lenz has been immensely constructive in his comments and taught me lots of things in little blue pills at the margins. He also started the Raku documentation project, so undoubtedly I wouldn't be here (for several dimensions of the world here) without him.

I'd like to specially dedicate this book to Jeff Goff. I probably heard first about Raku from one of his talks; the last section of the last chapter of this book uses his distribution, `Grammar::Common`. His knowledge of the language and his enthusiasm for it really helped the community, where he was a positive force. He will be missed.

Again, I need to thank the Raku community, whose support and answers to StackOverflow (and other) questions helped me solve many conundrums; their encouragement has never faltered. I know them by their nicks, and this is what I will use here; they're listed in no particular order. Raiph, jnthn, alexdaniels, altai-man, wendyga, lizmat, ugexe, patrickbbkr, tbrowder, xliff, jonathanstowe, and many, many others. Their enthusiasm makes Raku possible and improves the (programming) lives of a great (and undoubtedly larger in the near future) community.

Also, to my family. Charo, Charete, Ceci, and Elena have put up with me talking about obscure features of the language as well as with my cooking. I love you.

Introduction

This book is about Raku, and when it's published it will probably be the first book with the Raku name in its cover, Although the name of the language is barely one year old, the language itself goes way back. Raku's functionalities are a superset of those found in most other modern languages. This book tries to show you how to use, in practice, the most common but also the most outstanding of these functionalities.

In order to use this book properly, you need to have some knowledge of how to program, at the least. I wrote the recipes to be self-explanatory, but if you get lost in the syntax or in the capabilities of the language, it might be better if you read a basic textbook like my *Perl 6 Quick Syntax Reference,* published by Apress. Having the documentation at `docs.raku.org` handy will also help.

The main objective of this book is to give you a series of patterns you can reuse to build your own Raku modules and applications. Many recipes include direct code, but others walk you through the process of creating, checking, and improving them, so that you get in the groove of how to program using Raku. The book attempts to be comprehensive in that effort: it helps you not only with the syntax and semantics, but also with the tools that are used with Raku.

You can read this book in any order; different chapters cover different parts of the language, so it's not required that you follow it in sequential order. It's true, however, that in some of the later chapters, we build on previous chapters, so following the original order will not hurt. You can start wherever you like and follow cross-references to other chapters if you feel like doing so. Within a chapter, it's a good idea to you read them in order, since recipes sometimes build on each other within the chapter. That's not a rule, and again you can simply follow references when they appear if you prefer.

## CHAPTER 1

Putting Raku to Use in a Real-World Environment

Before solving any problems, you need to prepare your environment to edit, test, and run your Raku programs. This chapter will propose solutions to the problems that you will face. Raku can be used as a first language (and, in fact, I encourage you to see it that way), but you can also use concepts from other languages straight away.

Let's say that you like cooking, and you have decided to create an app with recipes you created, as well as others from content providers and the public at large. People will be able to see, upload, comment, and rate recipes. The back office will be written in Raku, since that will allow you to leverage all its capabilities.

You will need to perform a range of different tasks related to processing, handling, rendering, and applying all kinds of operations to these files.

But before you do that, you need to have your tools ready. You will start to do that immediately in this chapter.

Recipe 1-1. Get Your Tools Ready

Problem

You need to create a program, module, or script in Raku.

Solution

Install Rakudo Raku and the Comma IDE and start using them.

© J.J. Merelo 2020
J.J. Merelo, *Raku Recipes*, https://doi.org/10.1007/978-1-4842-6258-0_1

How It Works

Raku is a compiled language that uses a virtual machine that runs bytecode assemblies created by a compiler. This is similar to the way that Java creates `.class` and `.jar` files that are then run in the Java Virtual Machine or the way that C# creates assemblies that are run in the CLR.

The Raku compiler, then, is actually a stack of different programs.

- The lower level is occupied by the virtual machine that runs the bytecode assemblies. Raku is not committed to a single virtual machine, and in fact there are currently three virtual machines available: MoarVM, the JavaScript Virtual Machine, and the JVM. In general, MoarVM is the reference VM and, unless stated otherwise, the one that will be used in this book.

- The next level is occupied by NQP (an acronym meaning Not Quite Perl or possibly something totally different), a simplified language that generates the bytecode via translation to Java or MoarVM bytecode.

- The top level is occupied by the compiler(s). An interpreter will parse the Raku code, leaving the job of generating bytecode to NQP. Using an intermediate language means that the Raku interpreters can be written in Raku. A program is considered a Raku interpreter as long as it's able to pass all the tests in the roast suite. Instead of opting for a reference implementation, like Perl (the sister language) or a specification like ECMAScript, Raku opts for a reference test suite, which gives the implementers much more flexibility when creating interpreters/compilers. As of today, however, there is a single implementation, which is called Rakudo Raku or simply *Rakudo*.

Installing Raku in this case assumes you are installing this full stack, with at least one virtual machine, usually MoarVM.

Raku is open source, and you can simply clone all three repositories and create your own version of Raku by fiddling with the compiler options. The Raku community encourages you to do this, if what you want is to hack and learn using Raku. However, the advice of the community is to install Raku in one of the two following ways.

Use the rakudobrew Version Manager

This will get you the full stack, compile MoarVM if needed, and create a `perl6` executable that, after configuring it correctly, you can run from the command line. This also downloads the `zef` module manager, which you can install afterward. Download `rakudobrew` and follow the instructions in its repository (`https://github.com/tadzik/rakudobrew`). Be sure to include the installation of any prerequisite that is not present and make it available from the command line.

These commands will download the version manager, select the version that has been downloaded, and build `zef`, as well as make it available to you:

```
rakudobrew build moar-2019.11
rakudobrew global moar-2019.11
rakudobrew build zef
```

You can run these commands:

```
raku -version
zef -version
```

You will obtain something like this, showing what has been installed and the stack of versions that it includes:

```
This is Rakudo version 2019.11 built on MoarVM version 2019.11 implementing
Perl 6.d. and v0.8.2
```

The output indicates the versions of Rakudo and MoarVM; generally they will match (if you use `rakudobrew`), but you can of course mix and match them. In general, our advice is to use the last versions. The `implementing` bit refers to the version of the language specification that is being used. The first production-ready version was 6.c, the one developed at the time of this writing is 6.d, and 6.e is currently in the works.

Note   Versions of Rakudo/MoarVM/Raku follow a *year.month.version* scheme. Several versions are produced every year. You can keep updated on the latest releases (and other Raku-related news) by following the @raku_news Twitter account.

3

If you develop modules or need to check your code against several versions, this is probably the best option.

Use Rakudo Star

Rakudo Star is a *distribution*, that is, a package that not only includes Raku, but also zef, the documentation, and the most fundamental modules. It's a *batteries included* download that you can use straight away to start your own programs. Packages are prepared for the three most widely used operating systems: Linux, Windows, and OSX. You can download them from https://raku.org/downloads.

Rakudo Star releases are (usually) made shortly after the corresponding Rakudo releases and have the same numbering system. They are tested for stability, and they include fixes for the included packages. They are easier to install and are highly encouraged by the Rakudo developers. You can't go wrong if you use them for this book and for your development environment.

Source Control Tools

Using source control is no longer optional in professional or homebrew software development. Using Git with any of the online hosting sites, GitLab and GitHub, is convenient every step of the way. We will assume from now on that your programs are created in a repository. Additionally, you might want to install the GitHub or GitLab CLI to take advantage of extensions to the basic Git tool.

So, for starters, we'll create a repository in our favorite Git hosting environment, GitHub, GitLab, or BitBucket. For the time being, GitHub does not allow you to select Raku as a language in the drop-down menu to create an appropriate .gitignore, so just leave that blank and we'll do that later. After creating the repository, clone it locally. Alternatively, you can just create an empty folder and initialize it with git init.

Comma, the Raku Integrated Development Environment

The IDE of choice for Raku is called *Comma*. Edument, a Swedish-Czech company, created it based on IntelliJ IDEA. It's released in a Community edition, which is free, and a Comma Complete edition, whose license can be purchased from the company. The Community edition includes an incredible amount of tools to develop, run, and debug Raku programs.

We will use the Comma Community edition to solve the first problem. In the recipes-related startup we created, we need to count the total number of recipes, which are spread over all the different directories.

Recipes will be structured in a tree, just like the one shown in Figure 1-1.

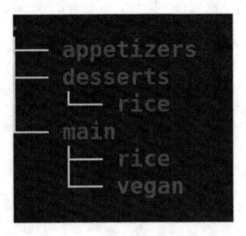

Figure 1-1. *Initial subdirectory structure of the recipes repository*

No matter what the structure, the program will be able to determine how many recipes there are by descending recursively into the files and counting them. These files are in the Markdown format and have a certain structure, but we are not going to take that into account for the time being. We just count the number of files—a relatively simple endeavor.

However, projects can and do evolve, and Comma understands that it's going to be working within a repository and is aware of the status of the files in that repository. So the first thing you are going to do is choose File ➤ New ➤ Project from existing sources. You'll get a dialog like the one shown in Figure 1-2.

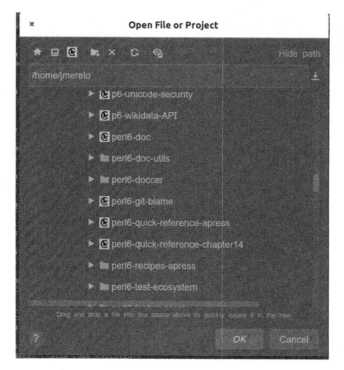

Figure 1-2. *The list of projects, prompting you to select one. The ones already controlled by Comma have the butterfly icon*

Among the grayed-out folders, we will see `perl6-recipes-apress`, which is where the cloned repository resides. Select that folder to host the project and let Comma manage it. You'll get a pop-up like the one in Figure 1-3, where you'll be prompted to select the project name, which by default is the directory name (and it's reasonable to leave it exactly that way). By clicking Next, you can then select the SDK. You can just skip that step for the time being. By choosing File ➤ Project Structure, you can set both at any time.

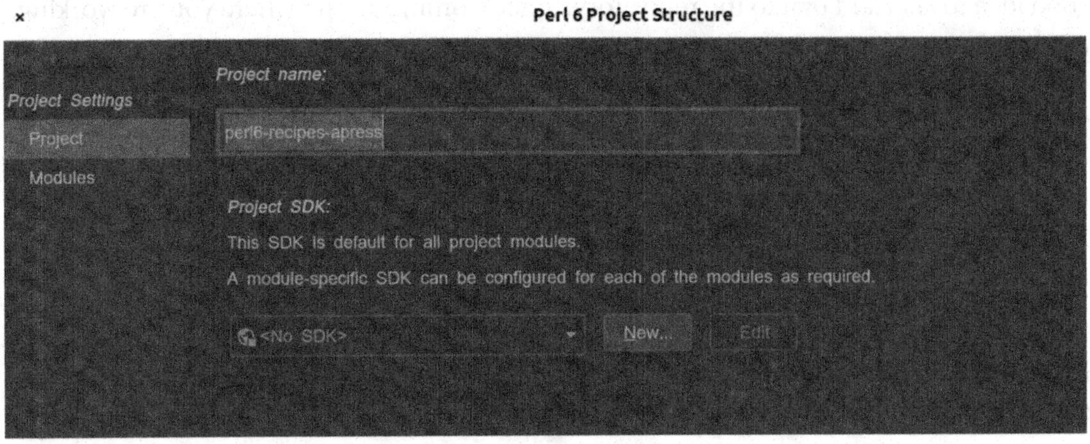

Figure 1-3. *Select a project name and, later on, an SDK*

You need to select the SDK, or software development kit. In IntelliJ IDEA-speak, that's tantamount to selecting the Raku compiler you are going to use from within the IDE. This is not necessary until you actually run something, but you can do it now. By clicking New, you'll be able to select from the versions of Raku that have been installed, as shown in Figure 1-4.

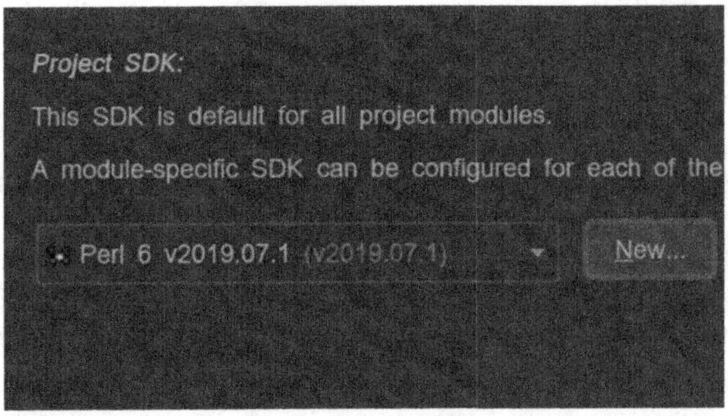

Figure 1-4. *Select the SDK, or version of Perl, you are going to use in the project*

The combo will show all the versions you installed via rakudobrew or using any other method. In this case, select the current version of Raku.

Before you actually create the script, you can do an additional bit of configuration. Comma creates a series of files that track your local repository configuration, including things such as the two choices you made before. They are saved to a series of XML files in a directory called .idea, as well as an .iml file in the repository root. It's probably a good idea to also add that to the repository. Since Comma knows where you are working, you'll be prompted to add them to the repository, as shown in Figure 1-5.

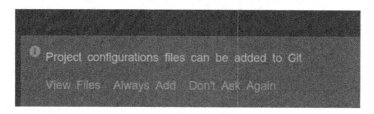

Figure 1-5. *Comma prompt to add Comma configuration files to the source control system*

This adds a series of files to Git. From the console, you can write git status and you'll get an answer like the one shown in Figure 1-6.

```
nuevo archivo: ../.idea/codeStyles/codeStyleConfig.xml
nuevo archivo: ../.idea/modules.xml
nuevo archivo: ../.idea/perl6-recipes-apress.iml
nuevo archivo: ../.idea/vcs.xml
nuevo archivo: ../Chapter-1/count-files.p6

Archivos sin seguimiento:
  (use «git add <archivo>...» para incluir en lo que se ha de confirmar)
```

Figure 1-6. *git status showing all Comma configuration files added to Git*

The .idea/workspace.xml file contains the layout of the workspace; that is, how your Comma IDE is laid out, the open files, and so on. It probably makes sense to keep it local and off the repository. For the same reason, keep it off your local status by writing the following

echo workspace.xml > .gitignore

Which, at the same time, will create the workspace.xml file. Wrap it up by committing and pushing all the changes before you create the file.

Choosing File ➤ New will open the dialog shown in Figure 1-7. Select Raku Script (Perl 6 Script), since you are going to create a simple script. The menu allows you to create all kinds of things, from undetermined files, to test files, to Raku Modules (which you will do later in this book).

Figure 1-7. *Create a Raku script from the Comma IDE*

The file you create, whose name you're prompted to enter, will have the basic structure of a Raku script, including the pound-bang line, as shown in Figure 1-8.

Figure 1-8. *Boilerplate for a script created by Comma (we added use v6;)*

The template for the script includes a sub MAIN. We will add use v6; which is only needed if you also have Perl interpreters ready and available, because it produces an error with them. I also added the $dir = '.' argument, which will hold the top-most directory of the recipes repository you'll be processing.

The typical pound-bang line is as follows

```
#!/usr/bin/env raku
```

This line uses a system utility to look for the raku binary in the current environment; that includes the one installed with rakudobrew as well as the one included with Rakudo Star, and it allows you to use any of them.

Caution   This does not work in Windows, where instead you have to run raku from the command line. It does work in Linux-like environments like the Linux subsystem or msys.

You need to add use v6; as the next line, which will prevent the perl5 interpreter from erroring and will produce an error indicating that you should switch to Raku to run it.

You can fill in the rest of the program like this:

```
use v6;

sub MAIN( $dir = '.' ) {
    say tree( $dir )».List.flat.elems;
}

sub tree( $dir ) {
    my @files = gather for dir($dir) -> $f {
        if ( $f.IO.f ) {
            take $f
        } else {
            take tree($f);
        }
    }
    return @files;
}
```

The gist of this program is in the subroutine tree, which recursively descends into all subdirectories and creates an array with all the files. That array is converted to a list, which is flattened, and the number of elements is counted.

We can directly commit this file from Comma, as shown in Figure 1-9.

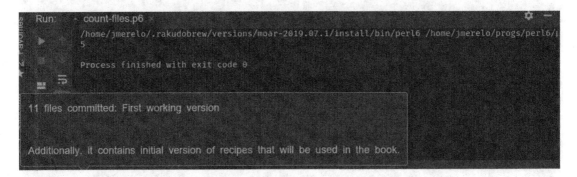

Figure 1-9. *Checking in a change from Comma by clicking the clouded area on the top right*

The IDE will prompt for a commit message, and you will get a system message like the one shown in Figure 1-10.

Figure 1-10. *Comma reports on commit done and shows the commit message*

If you click the Commit button, you get the option to commit and push at the same time. You can also push from the command line if you prefer to do so.

After this, we need to run the script. Comma lets you open a console on the work directory by clicking Terminal in the bottom bar. You will get all the goodies if you add a run configuration, including the possibility to debug it. By default, you have no Run/Debug configurations created, since Comma does not assume that you will be creating a particular kind of project. You need to click Add Configuration and you'll get a dialog like the one shown in Figure 1-11.

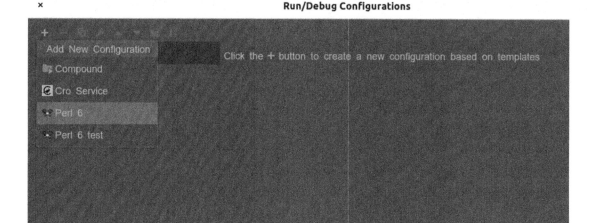

Figure 1-11. *Run/Debug Configurations dialog, with Perl 6 selected*

Perl 6, as selected in Figure 1-11, refers to a Raku script. You'll get that dialog when you click +, to select the type of script you will be using. When you select that, a dialog will open, and you need to select the path to the script, as well as give it a name, something like Count Recipes. Since the script needs the top-most directory where the recipes reside, add recipes as a Script parameter. That name will appear then, instead of the previous Add Configurations name.

You can click the green Play sign to the right of the script to run it. The result of running the script will appear on the console, in a window tagged with the name you've given it.

With this, you've managed to run your first script from the Comma IDE. In general, Comma is ready to run and debug all your Raku code, from simple scripts to complex, concurrent modules, for which it's especially prepared. So we strongly advise you to use Comma for all your Raku projects.

Recipe 1-2. Put Concepts from Other Languages to Use in Raku

Problem

Since Raku is not your first language, you know how to do most things in another programming language. Therefore, you want to hit the road running with Raku.

Solution

Raku is a multi-paradigm language; it's functional, concurrent, and object oriented. If you know any language that follows one or any of those paradigms, you can apply what you know to Raku by simply Googling the syntax or using the language documentation.

There are also specific documentation pages that compare Raku to other languages. Consult them for particular examples and for direct translations of function names and constructs.

How It Works

The official Raku documentation at `https://docs.raku.org` includes a set of migration guides for the following languages:

- Perl. There are several pages devoted to migrating from Perl to Raku. They are totally different languages, but a sizeable part of the community is skilled in that language, so the six pages cover operators, functions, and most of the specific syntax used by Perl for regular expressions, for instance.

- Node.js/JavaScript

- Ruby

- Python

- Haskell. The first Raku compiler was written by Audrey Tang in Haskell, so these languages are closer than you might think.

Searching for "how to do *X* in Raku" will take you to the right place in the documentation, the StackOverflow answers, or online tutorials. In some cases, Raku gives specific names to certain commands or data structures. Table 1-1 provides a short translation guide of Raku names to names in other languages.

Table 1-1. *Raku Names Compared to Other Languages*

Raku Name	Other Languages
Range	Python, Go: A function, not a data structure Ruby: Range Haskell: Range
Seq	Ruby: Range (not lazy) Haskell: Seq (not lazy) Clojure: lazy-seq
Traits	Elixir: @behaviour
Roles	Called traits in almost every language Kotlin: Interfaces JavaScript: Traits and Mixins Ruby: Mixins
Sink context	Void context
Phasers	Some languages, like Python, use specific files like `__init__.py` for running code at some specific phase of program or module loading. Perl has similar `BEGIN`, `END` and other blocks. Kotlin has `init` blocks in classes.
Multi-dispatch	Multiple dispatch in most languages
Proto	Elixir: Protocols
Subset	In general, this corresponds to the concept of refinement types, for instance in TypeScript or Liquid Haskell. Ada: Subtypes or constrained types

In general, Raku incorporates many paradigms, data structures, and constructs found in modern programming languages; it's very difficult to find a language that has such a wealth of them. If you know any language, especially functional languages such as Haskell or Scala, it will be very easy to map the data and control structures you know to Raku by using Table 1-1 or a search engine.

Of course, there are many control and data structures that are unique to Raku: Junctions and Grammars, for instance. I strongly encourage you to check out the *Perl 6 Quick Syntax Reference* book, from Apress and the same author, to get acknowledged with them.

When books and reference fail, you will need a helping hand. We'll get to that next.

Recipe 1-3. Get Involved in the Community

Problem

You need help with the finer points of Raku, and/or you want to get to know other people who are working with Raku.

Solution

There are several Twitter accounts you can follow, as well as some StackOverflow tags and several IRC channels.

How It Works

A community is essential to the health of a programming language or technology. They are places where you can pick up nuances about new languages and learn about any new developments and patterns.

The Raku community uses IRC, the Internet Relay Chat, extensively. It's the predecessor of Slack, with different hosts divided into channels, every one of which uses # as a prefix. The main channel is #raku in Freenode, which is indicated with this URL: `irc://irc.freenode.net/#raku`. When clicking or typing that URL, your browser will ask you to open an IRC client, of which there are many. I favor weechat, a console client, but there are console-oriented as well as more window-oriented ones for any operating system. You can also use a pre-installed web client from this URL: `https://webchat.freenode.net/#raku`.

In addition to the people who hang out there, #raku is populated by a series of bots that will help you evaluate Raku expressions as well as navigate the code and its history.

Other channels that might be useful are the following:

- #raku-dev is where the core developers hang out.

- #whateverable is a channel where you can consult with the friendly bot Camelia, which will evaluate your Raku expressions for you. You can do this also in any of the other channels. If you intend to use it heavily, it's better if you move aside to this channel, so that you don't disturb the flow of conversation there.

There are several mailing lists you can also subscribe to; these can be useful for seeking advice. See https://raku.org/archive/lists/. The perl6-user list is probably the one you should be subscribing to. It does not have too much traffic, and you can help and be helped by other users.

The "extraofficial" official Raku Twitter handle is @raku_news, with weekly news curated by Liz Matijsen and other Raku related events, tutorials, and trivia. There are other Perl6ers with varying degrees of activity on Twitter and Raku-related tweets. An interesting one, even if it's not Raku exclusive, is @perlwchallenge, a weekly challenge that can be solved using Perl 5 or Raku. It points to blog posts that feature how to solve the challenges in both languages. It's a very interesting way to learn new things and to challenge yourself by solving these problems.

Finally, StackOverflow gets a few Raku related questions a week in the [raku] tag. Becoming part of the community implies not only checking it out for helpful answers to your questions, but also voting up helpful questions and answers, and checking it out from time to time just in case you can help someone else.

It's also very likely that there's a Perl (and Raku) meeting in your country or nearby. There are major Perl conferences in the US, Asia, and Europe every year, and they feature Perl and Raku talks, developers, and users. Nothing beats meeting face to face, and you can always learn new things about the language and its libraries.

Recipe 1-4. Install Some External, Useful Modules

Problem

You need to create a program, and you need a library or module that is not included in the core library or is part of the Rakudo Star distribution.

Solution

Use zef to install the modules you need, search for them, and automatically install all their dependencies.

How It Works

Raku comes with a few "batteries" included in the form of standard libraries. These include all the basic classes and types, as well as additional modules for working with native libraries (NativeCall) and Rakudo-specific modules and classes.

The Rakudo Star distribution packs a few more libraries in its bundle—for instance a few libraries that deal with JSON, some testing libraries and scripts, HTML templates, and HTTP libraries and utilities. That is more than enough for basic applications, with the added value that they have been extensively tested against the Raku version they are bundled with.

There are many more libraries in the Raku ecosystem, around 2,000 by the end of 2019. You can access them at https://modules.raku.org, where they are organized by tags and names.

In your case, you want to process the recipes in the library to extract their titles. They are written in Markdown. You can search for modules that include Markdown in their names or descriptions by simply using zef, the Raku module manager.

```
zef search Markdown
```

This will return a list of modules that implement Markdown, or somehow do something related to it. From the (shortened) description, Text::Markdown seems to be what we are looking for. You can install it with the following:

```
zef install Text::Markdown
```

This will also install all needed dependencies, if there are any. All modules use Pod6, the Raku markup language, to describe what they do. You can check out their repository for the APIs they publish. In some cases there will be additional tutorials. For instance, this module is featured in a Raku Advent Calendar article at https://perl6advent. wordpress.com/2017/12/03/letterops-with-perl6/.

You can then use that module to write this program, which will take one file and take care of its main header:

```
use Text::Markdown;
sub MAIN( $file ) {
    if $file.IO.e {
        my $md = parse-markdown-from-file($file);
        say "Recipe title: ", $_.text
                for $md.document.items
                .grep( Text::Markdown::Heading )
                .grep( { $_.level == 1 } );
    }
}
```

The first line (after the shebang, which we will stop featuring from now on) includes the sentence that imports Text::Markdown into the current program and makes all its exported functions available. One of these functions is parse-markdown-from-file, which takes a file and converts it into a complex object, an array of Text::Markdown::* objects. You can print just the name of the recipe by taking all items in the document ($md.document.items) and filtering only those that are a heading (* ~~ Text::Markdown::Heading), and again filtering only those headings that have a level equal to 1 ({ $_.level == 1 }).

While this module is useful for this particular problem, there are several other modules that you might be interested in downloading. These modules have a high *river* score, which means that they are used very often, and at varying depths, by other modules in the ecosystem. They add interesting functionality to Raku, and thus it's a good idea to get acquainted with them.

- Template::Mustache: A module for rendering data structures into templates.

- URI: A module for handling universal resource identifiers.

- Cro: A module for creating distributed applications, including microservices and many others.

- File::Temp: A module that creates temporal files in an OS-independent way.

In general, the Raku ecosystem will contain the tried and mature module that you need to complete your application. Just use `zef` and/or `modules.raku.org` to search for it, and `zef` to install it into your coding environment.

Recipe 1-5. Detect the OS Environment and Change the Program Behavior Accordingly

Problem

Your program might eventually run in an unknown operating system. You need it to be aware of its environment.

Solution

Use `$*DISTRO`, `$*SPEC`, and other dynamic variables to determine specific characteristics of the operating system and write code specific it it.

Also avoid direct references to operating system paths; use `IO::Path` instead to access those paths in an OS-independent way.

How It Works

In your `recipes` site, you need to create a simple catalog of all the files in a directory in order to check them. This can be solved idiomatically using directories and globs, but you opt for a more direct approach by issuing the corresponding call in the operating system. This program will do that for you.

```
class Recipes {
    has $.folder;
    has $!is-win = $*DISTRO.is-win;

    multi method show( $self where .is-win: ) {
        shell "dir {$self.folder}";
    }
}
```

```
    multi method show( $self: ) {
        shell "ls {$self.folder}";
    }
}
```

```
Recipes.new(folder => "recipes").show
```

In Raku, there are many ways to do anything, and *idiomatic* methods are not something you will hear about often. Using the OS-specific command issued from the Raku program is as idiomatic as using the `dir` subroutine or the `sub` method of `IO::Path`. In this case, we also use two idiomatic Raku constructs: including the invocant in the signature via the colon:

```
multi method show( $self: ) {
```

And using `where` in the signature to determine which version of the method we are going to call.

All in all, this recipe does the following: it initializes the `is-win` attribute of the `Recipes` class as soon as an object is built and it receives as a default value the result of calling `is-win` on `$*DISTRO`. The `multi` indicates that, if `is-win` called on the object itself (`$self`) is `True`, the first version of the method (which uses `dir`) will be called. Failing that, it will go to the second version, which uses `ls`, a command that works in Linux and OSX. Multiple dispatch acting on the object itself is an interesting pattern that can be applied in Raku, and is peculiar to it.

This variable is a *dynamic scope* variable, which is denoted by the twigil * following the sigil $. These all-caps variables are initialized by the compiler, so their values depend on a series of heuristics (and compile-time set variables) that detect the operating system the script is running in.

By default,

```
say $*DISTRO
```

will return something like `debian (9.stretch)`. That is the result of calling the `gist` method on the variable. However, the variable contains more information about the operating system:

```
say $*DISTRO.perl
# OUTPUT: «Distro.new(release => "9", is-win => Bool::False, path-sep => ":",
```

```
#      name => "debian", auth  => "https://www.debian.org/", version =>
       v9.stretch,
#    signature => Blob, desc => "Debian GNU/Linux 9 (stretch)")ˣᴸ»
```

The most interesting pieces of information are the path-separator used in the shell, which is : in Debian, and the release numbers, which might be useful when adapting code to different versions of the specific OS.

Another variable, $*SPEC, is specifically related to the way the files are specified, and it contains a class that will be used to work with files. There are four classes available in Raku: IO::Spec::Cygwin, IO::Spec::QNX, IO::Spec::Unix, and IO::Spec::Win32. Since these are used internally by the IO::Path class, it's always better to use them (instead of the name of the file directly) to build a path, so that it's guaranteed to work in any operating system. As a matter of fact, this was not considered in the previous version of the class, so we will modify it this way:

```
class Recipes {
    has $.folder;
    has $.folder-path = IO::Path.new( $!folder );;
    has $!is-win = $*DISTRO.is-win;

    multi method show( $self where .is-win: ) {
        shell "dir {$self.folder-path}";
    }

    multi method show( $self: ) {
        shell "ls {$self.folder-path}";
    }
}
Recipes.new(folder => "recipes/desserts").show
```

As long as there's a slash in the path, we might need to adapt that to the specific operating system. IO::Path does that for you. Previously we were using the name directly, now we're using an IO::Path object, which will stringify to an OS-adequate path when we insert it into the command to list the files. Since this path is not going to change, it's created automatically with the object.

CHAPTER 2

Input and Output

Most programs need to interact with the filesystem and the network to obtain data and to produce a result. Input/output routines and classes, or I/O for short, group that functionality. In this chapter we include several recipes that will help you work with files of different kinds in different ways.

Recipe 2-1. Read Files Handled as Arguments

Problem

You need to process a series of files, but you don't know in advance which files you are going to work with, so it's better if the script works with the files you provide as arguments.

Solution

The dynamic variable $*ARGFILES is an alias to a pseudo-file that includes all files whose names have been provided in the command line. Use it in your script.

How It Works

You need to compute the weight of your recipes site, which is the gross number of sentences that are there. Or, you need to compute that number by directory. Either way, it's an operation that you need to do on a set of files, and it will treat the content of the files uniformly. So let's create a script that prints the number of sentences (separated by a period, or a double line separator, as in headers).

This can be done, as a matter of fact, with a single line of code:

```
say "Sentences → ", $*ARGFILES.lines.join("\n")
    .split( / [ '.' | \v**2 ] / ).elems;
```

© J.J. Merelo 2020
J.J. Merelo, *Raku Recipes*, https://doi.org/10.1007/978-1-4842-6258-0_2

$*ARGFILES behaves as a single file handle with the files already open. You don't need to worry about opening or closing every file handle in turn; as long as you call the script with a list of files, Raku will collate them and make them available under that single variable. You can perform different operations on this file, such as read it line by line. This allows you to collate lines using whatever you want, for instance, a carriage return. The regular expression used by split will divide the resulting string either by a literal period ('.') or two vertical spaces (\v ** 2).

You can run this script this way, for instance:

```
perl6 Chapter-2/count-sentences.p6 recipes/desserts/*.md
```

And it will return 5 as the version that's currently in the repository.

Note   I also encourage you to run this script from Comma, at least to get used to it. In this case, it's a single file and there's not much to debug, but multi-line scripts and more complex modules will really profit from the tools and tips provided by Comma. If you want to do so, you will have to include a configuration, with the script name and working directory (the top of the repository, for instance). The only thing you have to take into account is that Comma does not understand globs, so as script parameters you will have to flesh out the names of the files, this way: `recipes/desserts/buckwheat-pudding.md recipes/desserts/ guacustard.md`

This is, in fact, equivalent to doing this:

```
say "Sentences → ", $*ARGFILES.slurp.split( / [ '.' | \v**2 ] / ).elems;
```

The set of files is simply *slurped*, that is, swallowed whole to a single string, carriage returns and all. Separating by lines and then joining using whatever you like gives you a bit of more flexibility; you might, for instance, want to eliminate lines that act as headlines. The splitting expression above could create empty "sentences" (if there's a period followed by two vertical spaces, for instance), and, besides, we want to eliminate headers (which start with a #). This version will take care of that:

```
say "Sentences → ", $*ARGFILES.lines.grep( /^<:L>/ )
        .join("\n").split( / [ '.' | \v**2 ] / ).elems;
```

By using grep to select only those lines that start with a letter (<:L>), we eliminate headlines, which start with a hash mark, empty lines (provided that there are no lines that start with a space and are followed by any other letter, which we will take care not to use), and headings. All that's left are lines that start with a letter. But there might be some cases where there are empty lines at the end of a section or file, and we might have forgotten to add a period that ends a sentence there. We'll mark this also as the end of a sentence, which explains the double vertical space in the split. Finally, we count the number of elements of the created array, which will indicate the number of sentences.

The script will work the same with a single file instead of several. If you want to find and process files individually, you can of course do so. In the next recipe, we will see how to deal with them asynchronously.

Recipe 2-2. Read and Process Files Asynchronously
Problem

You need to read files with an unknown size without blocking the program.

Solution

Raku includes many facilities for asynchronous operation. You can work either with asynchronous input/output or using taps for event-driven operation.

How It Works

Asynchronous programming is a powerful, if not exactly popular, way of working with tasks whose duration is not known in advance. Synchronous programs start the task, and the rest of the program waits until that task is finished. This kind of behavior is quite inconvenient when a response needs to be given in a timely manner, such as on the web.

Asynchronous programming started to be popular with JavaScript. Designed originally for web interfaces, JavaScript works with events that are processed in order, but that do not block the UI. When the server-based version Node was created, this kind of behavior extended itself to all kind of events. The interpreter runs an event loop, with some tasks creating events and *callbacks* that are invoked when the event is activated.

This is quite convenient in input/output. Instead of synchronously waiting for the whole file to be read, a reading task is initiated, and a callback function is called when that task is finished. Reading proceeds in the background, while the rest of the program is left to its own devices, processing other things, or creating other events, that will be processed in turn.

Let's assume that you need to check all files in the recipes database, and then perform some operation on them, such as extracting their titles as we did in the last chapter. These files might have different sizes, or be at different depths in the filesystem, which means all operations will be delayed if one of the files takes longer than usual.

Use this script:

```
use Text::Markdown;

sub MAIN( $dir = '.' ) {
    my @promises = do for tree( $dir ).List.flat -> $f {
        start extract-titles( $f )
    }

    my @results = await @promises;
    say "Recipes ⇒\n\t", @results.map( *.chomp).join: "\t";

}

sub tree( $dir ) {
    my @files = gather for dir($dir) -> $f {
        if ( $f.IO.f ) {
            take $f
        } else {
            take tree($f);
        }
    }
    return @files;
}

sub extract-titles ( $f ) {
    my @titles;
    if $f.IO.e {
        my $md = parse-markdown($f[0].slurp);
        @titles = $md.document.items
```

```
    .grep( Text::Markdown::Heading )
    .grep( { $_.level == 1 } );
  }
  @titles;
}
```

The `tree` routine, which is the same one we used before, runs recursively over the directories to collect all files. That should not take long, although we could also run that part asynchronously, and even in parallel. What we will do in an asynchronous way is open and then process the content of the files.

The main part of the program runs over the list of files and creates a promise for each. The `start` command does precisely that: It creates a promise out of the block it receives as an argument. In Raku, the `for` loop returns a list of the results of the last sentence of every iteration. The single sentence here, `start`, will return a promise; we assign that array of promises to a variable, effectively called `@promises`.

Within every promise, there's a plain vanilla block of code that checks for the existence of the file (who knows, it might have disappeared on its way from the `tree` routine, it's always better to err on the safe side). Blocks cannot use the `return` keyword, but they will return whatever the last statement produces. So that promise, which will be *kept* when finished, will return that value.

However, that value is not assigned to anything for the time being. It's stored in the promise, but you will not know what it's worth until the promise is actually kept. The `await` statement does precisely that: it waits until all promises in its argument are fulfilled and returns their value; `@results` will contain those values, which are then printed, in a synchronous way, in the next step.

Reading files this way is going to be marginally to noticeably faster than doing it synchronously. The increase will depend on how big the files are and the amount of processing that needs to be done in each. But there's still a part of the script that's not asynchronous. We might as well go async all the way using supplies.

A *supply* is a sequence of objects that can be populated and picked asynchronously, always in the order it's filled. You `emit` to a `supply` to fill it up, and `tap` from it to use its values. The good thing about these taps is that they can occur asynchronously, and there can be as many taps for a single supply as are needed. Check out this script:

```
sub MAIN( $dir = '.' ) {

    my $supply = supply tree-emit( $dir );
```

```
    my @titles = gather {
        $supply.tap( -> $f { take $f.IO.lines.head } )
    };
    say "Recipes ⇒\n", @titles.join("\n");

}

sub tree-emit( $dir ) {
    for dir($dir) -> $f {
        if ( $f.IO.f ) {
                emit $f
        } else {
                tree-emit($f);
        }
    }
}
```

It dives recursively into the directory, emitting the name of the file for every one it finds. Since the tree-emit routine is called from within a supply, that supply will gather all the filenames. The tap that's called with $supply.tap will obtain the first line of every file and gather it in an array, but the code within the supply block will not be run until it's actually tapped. Think about a supply not as buffer, but as a list of tasks that are not run until they are absolutely needed. If we make this alteration to the script:

```
sub MAIN( $dir = '.' ) {
    my $supply = supply tree-emit( $dir );
    say "Now let's rock";
    my @titles = gather {
                $supply.tap( -> $f { take $f.IO.slurp.lines.head } )
    };
    say "Recipes ⇒\n", @titles.join("\n");

}
```

The result will be printed in this order:

```
Now let's rock
Let's emit recipes/main/rice/tuna-risotto.md
```

(and the rest of the files)

This style of operation is also called *reactive* programming; the taps *react* to every object in the supply, in turn. It's an efficient way of working with I/O, since it will reduce the overhead incurred by loops. Many modern languages—from Node.js to Dart through Python in its latest 3.x versions—use this kind of reactive operation for everything from simple file I/O to serving web pages and other services.

Recipe 2-3. Connect Input and Output of External Utilities and Files

Problem

You need to run an external program and process its output, or conversely, you need to provide an external program with text in order to process it.

Solution

The `Proc::Async` class provides all kinds of facilities to interface with external interactive command-line programs.

How It Works

Once the foundations for working asynchronously are set, you can use it for all kinds of things. You can interact with files and with other programs that issue text at unknown intervals. Think about system logs or other kinds of programs that append to a file from time to time. For instance, this script takes snapshots of a process running across the system and appends them to a file:

```
watch "ps -e | tail --lines=+2 >> /tmp/ps.log"
```

The file will look like this:

```
28485 ?           00:00:03 kworker/u8:0
28821 ?           00:00:19 gimp-2.8
28829 ?           00:00:01 script-fu
30976 ?           00:00:00 docker
31001 ?           00:00:00 containerd-shim
31029 pts/0       00:00:00 sh
31189 pts/4       00:00:02 zsh
```

This is a basic structure that includes, as the last two elements in each line, the time the command ran and the short form of the actual statement.

This program will monitor this file and act on it:

```
my $proc = Proc::Async.new: 'tail', '-f', '/tmp/ps.log';

$proc.stdout.tap(-> $v {
    $v ~~ m:g/([\d+] ** 3 % ':') \s+ (\S+)/;
    with $/ {
        for $_.list -> $match {
        my $command = $match[1];
        my $time = $match[0];
        given $command {
                when .contains("sh") {
                say "Running shell $command for $time"
                }
                when none( "watch", "ps", "tail" ) { say "Seen $command" }
        }
        }
    }
});

say "Listening to /tmp/ps.log";
await $proc.start;
say "Finished";
```

It's somewhat long, but its structure is quite simple. First, the asynchronous connection is created, then the monitor is set up, and finally the actual process is run, also asynchronously.

As indicated in the solution, `Proc::Async` is the class that drives all this interaction; it's documented in `https://docs.raku.org/type/Proc::Async`. We use it in the first line, creating a process that is going to run `tail -f /tmp/ps.log`. We need to split it this way to protect it from shell escaping. Proceeding to the last part of the script, we create a promise by starting the process and using `await` to wait for the promise to finish. That will never happen, actually, since `tail -f` runs until it's interrupted.

But the async processing is done in the middle. As we did in the previous recipe, we use taps. `Proc::Async` creates supplies out of every process handle: standard input or `stdin`, standard output or `stdout`, and standard error. We're only interested in `stdout`, so that's the supply we tap. We run every line through a regular expression. The `([\d+] ** 3 % ':'` part is a set of three groups of one or more digits, separated by a colon. That's the time it's been running. The second part is simply the beginning of the command. The parentheses capture the content and we run the loop only if there's actually something captured (with $/). The $_ will be equal to $/ (since `with` topicalizes, making $_ equal to its expression).

As you can imagine, connecting this to the input of another program will work more or less in the same way. You can, for instance, run a program and connect its output to the input of another program. For instance, to count the number of recipes (which are Markdown files) in the repository, we use this:

```
my $find-proc = Proc::Async.new: 'find', @*ARGS[0] // "recipes", "-name",
"*.md";
my $wc-proc = Proc::Async.new: 'wc';

$wc-proc.bind-stdin: $find-proc.stdout;
$wc-proc.stdout.tap( { $_.print } );

my $wc = $wc-proc.start;
my $find = $find-proc.start;
await $wc, $find;
say "✓ Finished"
```

This program uses two asynchronous processes. We will read from the `find` process, which uses a UNIX command-line utility that finds files in the filesystem. It takes as the first argument the starting directory and starts to go deeper from there, until all the subdirectories are checked. We will use a command-line argument for that, but by default it will use `recipes` as the top directory.

The second process is another command-line utility that counts words. It produces a line like this:

```
6        6        209
```

It shows the number of words (6), the number of lines (6), and the total number of characters (209). Since the first program will produce one file for every line, the two first numbers are the same.

The next line uses `bind-stdin` to connect the input of the `wc` utility to the output of the `find` utility, kind of as if you made the following (in UNIX/Linux):

```
find recipes -name "*.md" -print | wc
```

As you probably know, the pipe symbol | connects output from the left side to the input from the right side. Raku will do that programmatically, and also efficiently. Once that is done, you can tap the supply of the `wc` process, which will print the output.

Since we have two processes now, you will have to await until both promises are fulfilled, which you do in the next-to-last line of the program.

These pipelines can be as complicated as you want; you can bind output to several inputs, for instance, and create *glue* scripts that connect different, and readily available, utilities.

These scripts will also work in MacOS and in the Linux subsystem of Windows, as well as in the different bash command lines that are available for Windows. In this case, however, we use PowerShell commands. In any case, Raku will use whatever operating system facilities are available to run the commands you launch.

Recipe 2-4. Read and Process Binary Files

Problem

You need to work with binary files such as images or video.

Solution

Reading binary files is possible with any file-reading command. Its content, however, needs to be stored in special data structures called *blobs*. Depending on the format, there will also be Raku Modules that can deal with them; for instance, modules for images or sound files.

How It Works

Suppose you stored a series of images on your recipe website, and you need to check them for size before they are served so that they can be reduced, adapted to a certain screen, or whatever. You need to know the width and height of an image, anyway.

These are two pieces of data that are stored inside the file. They are part of the header. Specialized tools called EXIF readers are able to collect this data, along with all the rest of the data related to the camera settings, and even GPS data in some cases. Let's keep it simple and obtain just the width and height using Raku. This program will do the trick:

```
my Blob $image = slurp( @*ARGS[0] // "../recipes-images/rice.jpg", :bin);

# From here https://stackoverflow.com/a/43313299/891440 by user6096479
my $index = 0;
until $image[$index] == 255 and $image[$index+1] == any( 0xC0, 0xC2 ) {
    $index++;
    last if $index > $image.elems;
}

if ( $index < $image.elems ) {
    say "Height ", $image[$index+5]*256 + $image[$index+6];
    say "Width ", $image[$index+7]*256 + $image[$index+8];
} else {
    die "JPG metadata not found, damaged file or wrong file format";
}
```

Despite its many numbers, it boils down to these steps: get the data (in binary form), look for a marker (that indicates the chunk of the file where the data starts), and then get the data and print it. Let's break this process down:

- First, we use a blob to store the binary contents of a file; slurp will return a blob if it's run with the option :bin, as in binary. A blob is basically a list of bytes (actually, uint8, unsigned integers represented with eight bits). The until loop explores until it finds the marker for that segment: a byte valued FF in hexadecimal, or 255, followed by another whose value is either C0 or C2 in hexa.

- When that marker is found, the height is stored in two bytes in the fifth and sixth bytes, which we convert to decimal by multiplying the first by 256. The width is stored in the next two bytes, and we convert it in the exact same way.

- If a file that has been damaged or has any other format is issued in the command line, those markers will not be found. The loop will end and the script will exit with an error message.

If you need to obtain more information from these images, or simply store them in the self-same form somewhere else, blobs are the way to go.

Recipe 2-5. Watch a File for Changes
Problem

You need to check a file or directory for changes of any kind.

Solution

Use IO::Notification.watch-path, which will return a supply you can tap to check or otherwise act on the changes, which will have the shape of IO::Notification::Change objects.

How It Works

You have already seen how asynchronous code works in Raku. In general, it watches a series of events and runs some code when an event occurs.

In the previous recipes in this chapter, other pieces of code generated the events. However, the system itself also generates events all the time at a low level and we can work with them if we just tap into that stream. Did I say tap? Well, we got taps in Raku, don't we? So you can just write a program that taps into the stream (or supply) of events created by changes in the appropriate file or directory.

For instance, suppose we need to check if new recipes have been added to our collection of recipes in the filesystem, or if something has been done to them. We could, after a new recipe is added, run some checks, or raise an alarm if one that didn't include broccoli was deleted (it's totally justified if it includes broccoli). Let's do that with this script:

```
my $dir = @*ARGS[0] // 'recipes';

my $dir-watch-supply= IO::Notification.watch-path($dir);

$dir-watch-supply.tap: -> $change {
    given $change.event {
        when FileChanged { say "{$change.path} has changed"}
        when FileRenamed { say "{$change.path} has been renamed, deleted or
        created" }
    }
};

await Promise.in(30).then: { say "Finished watch"; };
```

As indicated in the solution to the recipe, we are using the convenient IO::Notification Raku class to check on the recipes directory. This class includes a single method, watch-path, which takes a string representing the path to watch as an argument. This method produces a supply, which we can effectively tap.

The tap will produce change events, objects of the class IO::Notification::Change that have two attributes: the type of event, that is, if it's been FileChanged (changed size, for instance) or FileRenamed (which includes creation or deletion, as well as actual renaming), as well as the path. That is why we check for the value of $change.event, adapting the message about the involved path depending on the type.

However, a supply just creates a stream of events, and a tap asynchronously runs when one of those events is produced. We need something to wait, though, for the events to happen. We need an *event loop* that allows the script to continue execution until a certain condition is met. That is what the last statement does. It creates a promise that is kept after 30 seconds; effectively, this is a waiting loop that will be there for 30 seconds, after which the script will be finished.

Note   It's very likely that the messages produced by the tap are kept in a buffer and will all be printed by the end of the program. This is also why these kinds of event loops must be exited gracefully, so that all the buffers are flushed and the events and the messages produced by them are not lost.

The problem with this is that the event loop can't go on forever. It will be watching for 30 seconds; then, it would have to be restarted again to catch new changes. That might eventually become annoying; a watch should be always watching. The next script will do that:

```
my $dir = @*ARGS[0] // 'recipes';

my $dir-watch-supply= $dir.IO.watch;
my $ctrl-c = Promise.new;

$dir-watch-supply.tap: -> $change {
    given $change.event {
        when FileChanged { say "{$change.path} has changed"}
        when FileRenamed { say "{$change.path} has been renamed, deleted or
        created" }
    }
};
signal(SIGINT).tap( { say "Exiting"; $ctrl-c.keep } );
await $ctrl-c;
```

This script uses an alternate form for the file watch, creating an IO::Path out of the string and putting a watch on it. This is not the main change, however. A new and literally empty promise is created next; we call it $ctrl-c because that is what it will take care of. The checking tap is exactly the same, but it changes right after that.

First, we set up a tap on the supply of SIGINT signals. SIGINT is the system signal that is invoked when Ctrl+C is pressed. We can capture that signal and act on it; in this case, we will print a message indicating that we are gracefully exiting the application, and then we *keep* the promise, that had so far been unfulfilled. Since the program will be kept waiting until that promise is kept, which is what the next statement does, it will effectively get out, flushing the output buffers and generally doing the right thing to exit the program.

CHAPTER 3

Data Science and Data Analytics

Scripting (and other) languages are great resources for getting data from one format to another, or for performing operations on data that has already been massaged. Data science refers to data gathering, data munging, and performing operations to produce a result; data analytics is less mathematically oriented and refers to simple aggregation or performing individual operations on the data.

Some programming paradigms, like functional programming, are used for these kinds of tasks. Thanks to its multi-paradigm nature and its extensive set of native functions, Raku is uniquely suited to these kinds of tasks, as we will see in this chapter.

Recipe 3-1. Extract Unique Email Addresses/User Names from Several Files

Problem

For a set of email addresses that exist across three files, you need to determine which ones are repeated in all three files, and conversely, which emails appear uniquely in only one of the files.

Solution

Use set operations to determine the intersection among all files, or the symmetric difference between two of them.

© J.J. Merelo 2020
J.J. Merelo, *Raku Recipes*, https://doi.org/10.1007/978-1-4842-6258-0_3

How It Works

You have decided to create a newsletter with new monthly recipes on your `recipes` website. The system collects new addresses in files, one address to a line. Unfortunately and provisionally, just files are used instead of a proper newsletter application, which could manage all of this easily. Every person in the office saves the email addresses they receive for the first few weeks. As new sign-on drives occur, you eventually end up with many different emails. These people are often interested in different versions of the newsletter (only desserts, just vegan, and so on). You decide to create a *core* list of email addresses that will receive all the newsletters. You do this by determining which people signed up for all the different versions, through all the different file creators.

The files will be listed like this:

```
one@ema.il
another@electron.ic
yetan@oth.er
```

… and so on. One to a line.

This script can do that for you:

```
say [∩] do for dir( @*ARGS[0] // "emails", test => /txt$/ ) -> $f {
    $f.lines;
}
```

This is a lot of work in what is essentially a single line, so let's break it up. Essentially, this script is reading only the files whose names end with `.txt` from a directory, dividing them up by lines, creating a list-of-lists, and applying a reduction operator to that list-of-lists. That reduction operator takes every member in turn, computes the intersection, and leaves the result to intersect with the next list on the list-of-lists.

Let's break down this expression from bottom to top, right to left.

1. `$f.lines` will create a list with the email addresses, which are placed on different lines. The `slurp` method will read a whole file. The result of this will be returned.

2. `$f` will contain an `IO::Path`, which will be used as the loop variable.

3. The loop will run over a list returned by `dir`; this command will examine the directory that is passed as the first argument in the command line (`@*ARGS[0]`) or, if that's not defined (`//`), `"emails"`. There might be other files in the directory, so we get only those whose name ends with `txt` (`/txt$/`). This is a regular expression, and you could use any expression in principle to filter the files. As a matter of fact, `test` can be any kind of test, including file permissions or type tests. We will be using it on a directory with that name that includes several files—`email-(1,2,3).txt`—which is why we use that pattern for filtering.

4. We use `do` before `for`, which places `for` in a list-creation context. This will create a list with the result of every iteration, which in our case is also a list (of emails in every file).

5. In front of that, the list reduction hyper-operator, `[ ]`, is applied to the intersection operator, `[∩]`; these are called *hyper* because they need an underlying operator to work, combining their semantics. In this case, it combines the semantics of the intersection operator with the apply-in-sequence-to-list semantics of the `[ ]` hyper-operator. Raku supports many Unicode mathematical operators with their implied semantics, but it's not always easy to determine how to type them in a particular editor or operating system. Every one has an ASCII (read: easily typed) counterpart, generally some symbol surrounded by parentheses. In this case it's (&) (mnemonic rule: & means and; intersection selects those elements that are in one set *and* the other). Reduction is a common list operation that sequentially applies an operator to the first two items in a list, and the result of this is operated on the third element, and so on. So in this case, for three files, what it's doing is (`@list[0]` ∩ `@list[1]`) ∩ `@list[2]`. Using reduction hyper-operators means we don't need to know in advance how many items there are in a list.

This eventually results in a very compact script that can run from the command line:

```
raku -e 'say [∩] do .slurp.lines for dir( @*ARGS[0] // "emails", test =>
/txt$/ );'
```

We reduce it even further by moving the loop body in front of `for` and eliminating the loop placeholder variable. We have to make a simple change to extract the emails that appear in a single file:

```
raku -e 'say [(-)] do .slurp.lines for dir( @*ARGS[0] // "emails", test =>
/txt$/ );'
```

The (-) (ASCII equivalent) or ⊖ is the symmetric difference operator. One of the nice things about Raku is its ability to use these kinds of operators on sets. Sets are not only good for mathematical calculations, they also have very nice business use cases, as shown in these two examples.

Recipe 3-2. Create a Weighted Random Number Generator

Problem

We need to create a *cheating roulette* or *loaded die* that yields winning numbers with greater probability than others.

Solution

Use Mixes. This data structure is a set with weights, and the weights of the elements of the set can be used to "load" the result, relative to the others.

How It Works

Mixes are sets of different elements, every one of which has a weight assigned to it. For instance, we want to generate new recipes by throwing a *die* with as many elements as ingredients, but we also want to take into account our preferences for some ingredients. We can *load* onion, and *unload* garlic, for instance, and use this small program to create a list of ingredients we will use.

```
my $ingredients = ( rice => 1, chickpeas => 1,
                    onion => 2, tomatoes => 1,
                    garlic => 0.5, pasta => 1,
                    chestnut => 0.25, bellpeppers => 1).Mix;
```

```
for ^10 {
    say "New recipe ⇒ ", $ingredients.roll( 5 ).unique.join(", ");
}
```

Mixes are essentially hashes or associative arrays with real values, which is why we declare them by creating that kind of hash and calling .Mix on them.

There's not much more to this recipe. Mixes are created exactly for this kind of thing. We are loading the onion and unloading the garlic and the chestnut (it's expensive and not very good if it's not the season). We are actually rolling that loaded die five times, and it will yield the ingredients with the (relative) probability we need. That roll will create a list of five elements, of which we extract the unique components (which will make some of the recipes shorter). Finally, we print the whole thing, resulting in something like this:

```
New recipe ⇒ chickpeas, onion
New recipe ⇒ pasta, bellpeppers, tomatoes, onion
New recipe ⇒ onion, rice, pasta
New recipe ⇒ bellpeppers, onion
New recipe ⇒ bellpeppers, onion, chickpeas, pasta, garlic
New recipe ⇒ onion, chestnut, tomatoes, garlic
New recipe ⇒ tomatoes, onion, rice
New recipe ⇒ tomatoes, onion, garlic, pasta
New recipe ⇒ onion, rice, tomatoes
New recipe ⇒ onion, pasta, rice, bellpeppers
```

There's a lot of onion, which should only be expected, and not many chestnuts. It's obviously random, and some of the time it will have to be eliminated from recipes where it appears twice, but still it's quite clear where the loaded die falls.

Recipe 3-3. Work with a Spreadsheet, Filtering, Sorting, and Converting Data

Problem

We need to access data that is included in an Excel spreadsheet.

Solution

There's a working module in the ecosystem, `Parser::FreeXL::Native`, that can read spreadsheets directly. If the spreadsheet has been saved in the text-based CSV format, it can be read and parsed directly or via the `Text::CSV` module.

How It Works

It's quite normal for businesses to keep structured data in a spreadsheet; the Excel format is widespread and can be produced and read by Microsoft Office products, as well as by open source applications like LibreOffice and online apps like Google Suite. Data in these spreadsheets is distributed in rows and columns, so it's easy to enter it as well as produce charts or apply operations on it.

You have received a spreadsheet of calorie data for the ingredients that you will be using.

Note   As a matter of fact, government organizations such as the FDA produce spreadsheets with useful nutritional information all the time. The one we will use here, however, is created specifically for this purpose.

The spreadsheet we will work with is shown in Figure 3-1. It will have three columns, with the name of the ingredient (which we will use as key), the unit for which we show the calories, and the calories.

Ingredient	Unit	Calories
Rice	100g	130
Chickpeas	100g	364
Lentils	100g	116
Egg	Unit	78
Apple	Unit	52
Beer	⅓ liter	216
Tuna	100g	130

Figure 3-1. *Sample ingredient database*

You need to read that information, contained in a `calories.xls` file, and compute the calories of a nice tuna risotto dish. This script will do that:

```
use Parser::FreeXL::Native;

my %ingredients = %( Rice => g => 350,
                     Tuna =>  g => 400 ,
                     Cheese => g => 200 );

my Parser::FreeXL::Native $xl-er .= new;

$xl-er.open("data/calories.xls");
$xl-er.select_sheet(0);

my $total-calories = 0;
for 1..^$xl-er.sheet_dimensions[0] -> $r {
    my $ingredient = $xl-er.get_cell($r,0).value;
    if %ingredients{$ingredient} {
        my ($q, $unit )= extract-measure($xl-er.get_cell($r,1).value);
        if %ingredients{$ingredient}.key eq $unit  {
            $total-calories += $xl-er.get_cell($r,2).value
                            * %ingredients{$ingredient}.value / $q;

        }
    }
}

say "Total calories ⇒ $total-calories";

sub extract-measure( $str ) {
    $str ~~ /^^ $<q> = ( <:N>* ) \s* $<unit>=(\w+)/;
    my $value = val( ~$<q> ) // unival( $<q> );
    return ($value,~$<unit>)
}
```

In order to run this program, you need to install the module it's using, via the following:

```
zef install  Parser::FreeXL::Native
```

This is a *native* module. This means that it provides a Raku front to a compiled, a shared library, which in this case is called FreeXL. This library can be installed in Linux or the Linux subsystem in Windows via the usual installation command (in the case of Ubuntu):

```
sudo apt install install libfreexl-dev
```

You should follow the usual procedure to install it in MacOS or Windows.

That is a nice feature of Raku; the NativeCall interface provides an easy way to wrap around native libraries, so that you can leverage them in your programs via a natural Raku interface.

This script has two different parts: the first one reads the values in the spreadsheet, the second will use those values to compute the calories in the dish, whose ingredients, units used to measure them, and quantities are contained in the %ingredients variable. This variable uses a pair to represent the quantity; the key of that pair will be the unit (grams, in this case), and the value will be the number of units. In this case, 350 of rice, 400 of tuna, 200 of cheese. Which may be a bit too much for you, but my family loves cheese.

The first part reads the values from the spreadsheet: it reads the file, selects the only sheet in it (index = 0), and starts to run over the rows. It starts with the second row (index = 1), since row 0 just contains the headers.

The second part is a loop that runs over the rows of the spreadsheet, whose index will go to the $r variable.

The *regex*, that is, the regular expression (sometimes the plural is written regexen) that extracts the unit and quantity of measurement from the second column (index 1) is a bit tricky, which is why we have put them in a separate extract-measures routine. But we need to know how calories are counted, and this is a convenient way of determining it. Regular expressions get a bad reputation, but once you get the gist of them they are excellent for the kind of task—getting data from text that has a bit of structure.

Let's try to understand the regular expression. For these ingredients, it says things like 100g, which means that we measure calories per 100 grams (which is the usual way). But we need to break that into the measure (100) and the unit (g). First, we anchor the regex to the beginning of the string via ^^. Right after that, a number, if present, will indicate the measure. We express that via (<:N>*), with the asterisk implying that, in some cases, as when it simply says Unit, it's going to be absent. Parentheses are used to capture the result. Note that we're using `<:N>` here, as opposed to the more familiar `\d`: Unicode property. We have a ⅓ in our set of measurements (for beer, that's close to half a pint and it's one of the ways we measure beer in Spain, *un tercio*), and that wouldn't match `\d`, so we use a character class description that covers it. Then the unit will be separated (or not) by some whitespace (hence again the *) and will be a set of one or more "word" (`\w`) characters.

That regex will get, for the three ingredients we're interested in, the figure 100 into the `$<q>` variable, and g into the `$<unit>` variable. Variables that use angular brackets can be defined and assigned inside regular expressions and used outside them, as we do in the defined routine. However, `$<q>` needs additional processing, once again thanks to *el tercio*. Usual routines converting strings to numbers can't deal with them directly; they will only work with number literals such as 3, 2.3e7, or the ASCII version of the fraction, 1/3. As a matter of fact, this is not going to happen to any of the ingredients in this script, but that does not mean we shouldn't take that case into account.

Note   We could have used this shape, like 1/3, to express fractional numbers in our table. However, that would have created a whole host of other problems in the regular expression. So let's just don't.

If we use `val` over a string containing just "⅓", it will return a failure. But failures are nils in disguise, so we use this fact to assign a value to `$value`. If conversion with `val` fails, `unival` will be applied to it, returning the numeric value, which is what we return.

The routine will return a list of two values: the quantity used to measure calories and the unit. The first could be an empty string.

Once the data has been extracted from the spreadsheet, we need to add it. The lines of the loop do that: first we obtain the name of the ingredient, which is the first column in the spreadsheet. We proceed only if that ingredient is in our dish; only then do we use the regular expression to extract the measurement and unit. Then, if the unit is the same as in our list of ingredients, we do an operation to compute the number of calories based on the weight (in this case) of the ingredients.

The result here will be a whopping 1,231 calories. Not to worry, though, since it's a recipe for four people. You can even splurge on the cheese if you want, just a few calories will be added.

As commented in the solution, we can also read CSV files using an alternative module. A CSV file with the same information is a text file that looks like this:

```
Ingredient;Unit;Calories
Rice;100g;130
Chickpeas;100g;364
Lentils;100g;116
Egg;Unit;78
Apple;Unit;52
Beer;⅓ liter;216
Tuna;100g;130
Cheese;100g;128
```

The semicolon acts as a separator, and there's one row in every line. This script will read and print the contents of the file:

```
use Text::CSV;

say csv(in => "data/calories.csv",  sep => ';', headers => "auto" );
```

You will need to install Text::CSV first, but as you see, it's a single statement. Besides the filename, we indicate which separator to use (if it's not the default comma), and with the auto-headers option, we make it automatically create a hash for every row, using the headers as the keys. The first row, for instance, will become:

```
{Calories => 130, Ingredient => Rice, Unit => 100g}
```

CSV is a format that, along with JSON and other data serialization methods, is used extensively in data science. We will come back to it in the next recipe.

Recipe 3-4. Apply a Series of Transformations and Extract Data from Them

Problem

You have data stored in a list of arrays, and you want to apply one or several transformations to that data, including processing or filtering, and then extract a single quantity. For instance, say you want to compute the total number of calories in a set of dishes and then exclude those dishes with more than 1,000 calories.

Solution

This operation is called map/reduce. In Raku, there are several mapping operators, including map itself, and reduce operators that can be built from binary (infix) operators using the hyper-operator. Additionally, the feed operator allows you to create a single chain of operations that can be easily identified visually.

How It Works

Map/reduce is functional operation where the elements of a list are first mapped to another list (via any kind of operation and/or filtering) and eventually, an operation is applied to the resulting, giving a single, reduced, result.

That is, we initially have something like this:

a1,a2,...,an ==> b1,b2,...,bn ==> c1,c2,...,cm

And then, after the different *map* phases, it's reduced by doing this:

((c1 op c2) op c3).... op cm) ==> X

There are two main functions doing the map part in Raku—map and grep. We have encountered them before. Since they produce another list, they can be simply chained by being applied as a method to the result of the previous operation. This can be visually confusing, so Raku also uses the feed operator ==> (also called the rocket) as syntactic sugar for these kind of (chained) map operations.

For instance, we have to process the CSV files with the calorie data and produce a single map with only the non-dairy ingredients. We will then refer to that map later to compute the calories in the dishes. You can do it this way:

```
use Text::CSV;

my %calories = csv(in => "data/calories.csv",  sep => ';', headers =>
"auto", key => "Ingredient" );

%calories.keys
    ==> map( { %calories{$_}<Ingredient>:delete } )
    ==> grep( { %calories{$_}<Dairy> eq 'No'} )
    ==> my @non-dairy-ingredients;
```

```
%calories.keys
    ==> map( { %calories{$_}<Dairy>:delete } );

say %calories{ @non-dairy-ingredients}.map: { parse-measure( $_<Unit> ) };
sub parse-measure ( $description ) {
    $description ~~ / $<unit>=(<:N>*) \s* $<measure>=(\S+) /;
    my $unit = $<unit> // 1;
    return ($unit,$<measure>);
}
```

In this example, the CSV file is read in such a way that instead of having an array of hashes, we have a *hash* of hashes, with the column indicated by key.

We have two `map` chains in this script. The first works on the keys of the `calories` table, which is an array, so it will eventually return an array. It will first delete the `Ingredient` key, which we already know as the key to the hash. It does not really affect the output, but changes the aspect of the `calories` table. Then `grep` is used to select only those ingredients that are non-dairy. In the next step, we also delete the `Dairy` key from the `calories` table, since we know those selected are non-dairy.

Eventually, we produce a list of units and measures used in the `calories` table. We slightly change the regex from the one we used before, which was able to catch only digits. Since we measure beer by ⅓ liters, we need something that has the Unicode property "N" to capture it too. We will use this subroutine later on, in the next script.

This script was intended as a warm-up and as an introduction to the next one, which actually solves the problem. It will read the recipe ingredient breakdown from the files, add the calories for every dish, filter only those that have less than 1,600 calories (that is, 400 calories per person, which is reasonable) and add that quantity. This program will do all this:

```
use Text::CSV;

csv(in => "data/calories.csv",  sep => ';', headers => "auto", key =>
"Ingredient" ).pairs
    ==> map( {
        $_.value<Ingredient>:delete;
        $_.value<parsed-measures> = parse-measure( $_.value<Unit> );
        $_ } )
    ==> my %calories;
```

```
my @recipes;
for dir("data/recipes/", test => /\.csv$/) -> $r {
    my %data = csv(in => $r.path, headers => "auto", key => "Ingredient").
    pairs
        ==> map( { $_.value<Ingredient>:delete; $_; } );
    push @recipes: %data;

}

say qq:to/END/;
Your non-caloric recipes add up to
{[+] (@recipes ==> map( { get-calories( $_ ) } ) ==> grep( * < 1600 ) )}
calories
END

# sub parse-measure taken from the previous script

sub get-calories( %recipe ) {
    my $total-calories = 0;
    for %recipe.keys -> $i {
        if %recipe{$i}<Unit> eq %calories{$i}<parsed-measures>[1] {
            $total-calories +=
            %calories{$i}<Calories> * %recipe{$i}<Quantity> /
            %calories{$i}<parsed-measures>[0]
        }
    }
    $total-calories;
}
```

It's the longest script so far, even if we eliminate the parsing sub. But it's conceptually simple: it reads the calories table and puts it into a single associative array called %calories, reads the recipes and puts them into an array called @recipes, and then, in a single sentence, maps recipes to their calories, selects those that have less than 1,600, and tallies them up to a single number.

The sub that computes calories is also very similar to the one we've seen before, so we will just focus on the map/reduce operation that is midway through the script. First, the map part: @recipes ==> map({ get-calories($_) }) will map (or convert) the array of associative arrays that contain the recipe ingredients (and quantities) into a list of numbers. This list of numbers will be filtered by `grep` in the next stage: `==>` `grep( * < 1600 ) )`. Just a couple of recipes, whose name we're not interested in now, have that quantity. These recipes' calories will be added in the *reduce* phase, the [+] at the beginning of the map chain. This is wrapped in curly braces to evaluate it before inserting it into the output string, and it uses the *heredocs* syntax to avoid a bit of clutter. The `qq:to/END/` is a quoting construct, with the double q guaranteeing any expression inside is going to be evaluated, and `END` indicating the marker that will be posted at the end of the string.

In general, using map/reduce will save you a lot of nested loops, and will allow you to process data in a functional way. If you have lots of data, it can even be parallelized using hyper or race. So thinking about data flows in this way is a win-win proposition.

Recipe 3-5. Create a Random Data Generator

Problem

For testing and other purposes, we need a random data generator that generates appropriate data structures.

Solution

Use `pick`, which is class-specific and works with many different data structures.

How It Works

When working with labeled data, it is sometimes necessary to create combinations that can be used as suggestions, such as for testing algorithms or simply as an end result. This data needs to have some kind of structure; for instance, a string that follows a certain regular expression or a set of items, every one of them with a certain quality.

For instance, you might need to generate random dishes for your recipes. Most dishes will have a main ingredient (say, rice) and an additional ingredient on the side (say, chickpeas). What? Chickpeas and rice are a delicious Mediterranean dish, same as beans and rice across the Caribbean. Of all the ingredients we have on the table, we can mix and match them to generate new dishes. Let's change our ingredient table to something like this:

```
Ingredient;Unit;Calories;Dairy;Vegan;Main;Side
Rice;100g;130;No;Yes;Yes;Yes
Chickpeas;100g;364;No;Yes;Yes;Yes
...
```

We added two columns to the CSV where we keep the data: the Main and Side columns indicate whether that ingredient can be used as a main ingredient, or added to a main ingredient to create a full dish.

What you want now is to generate a dish with a main and a side ingredient. This script can help you with that:

```
use Raku::Recipes;
my %calories-table = calories-table;
my @main-course =
    %calories-table.keys.grep: { %calories-table{$_}<Main> eq 'Yes' };
my @side-dish =
    %calories-table.keys.grep: { %calories-table{$_}<Side> eq 'Yes' };
say "Your recipe ⇒ ", @main-course.pick, " with ", @side-dish.pick, " on
the side";
```

We created Raku::Recipes for all the utility routines that we keep using in several recipes; in this case, we will use calories-table (which we have used before a couple of times), a routine that reads the CSV, parses the description of measures for every ingredient, and places everything into a hash.

Note   This module is available at the book's GitHub site and the Apress website. After downloading it using Git (git pull JJ/raku-recipes-apress), or downloading it from the URL Apress makes available, change to the directory where it's downloaded and write zef install.

We are just going to use the name of the ingredients: those that act as the main course will go to @main-course and side dishes will go to @side-dish. We use a filter on the keys of the table to select only those keys (ingredients) that have the corresponding field (Main or Side) marked as Yes.

Random generation, after that, is straightforward: we use `pick` on both arrays to select a random ingredient from each one. This will print something like:

```
Your recipe ⇒ Pasta with Chickpeas on the side
```

That's all good and well, but pasta is in both arrays. A dish of pasta with pasta on the side is kind of underwhelming. Let's try to avoid that next:

```
given (@main-course X @side-dish).grep( { @_[0] ne @_[1] } ).pick {
    say "Your recipe → @_[0] with ", lc( @_[1] ), " on the side"
}
```

The two arrays are defined exactly the same way. However, we use a `grep` filter to get only pairs that have different ingredients. `@main-course X @side-dish` will create a list of ingredient pairs that constitute a dish. `grep` checks that the first and the second ingredient are different, so the resulting list will have only proper pairs. By using `given`, we put the pair into the topic variable, `@_`. Finally, we take our pick over the resulting array of (guaranteed) pairs of ingredients; we use `lc` to lowercase the second one to avoid having a capital letter in the middle of a sentence.

We use `given` because it's a topicalizing statement, that is, it puts its argument into a proper topic variable, `$_`, `%_` or `@_`, depending on its type. In general, `given` will be used in the same way `switch` is used in other languages: it will perform checks on the topic and run different blocks of code when there's a match. However, in this case it will simply run the block of code without any further checks. Also, this topic variable is an array, so the block will have `@_` defined with the two ingredients. This variable is used to print the dish directly.

Additionally, you could use the loaded die technique you learned about earlier in this chapter. An additional column with preferences could be used for that, and you would have to store the ingredients in a Mix, instead of an array, and use `roll`. The principle would be exactly the same. With these different options, you can see the "There Are Many Ways To Do It" principle in action, something that informs every design decision in Raku.

Recipe 3-6. Process Big, Structured Files

Problem

Big files contain information that needs to be processed efficiently, possibly with some memory constraints.

Solution

You can either use `.lines` on a file handle, which will create a lazy sequence out of the lines of the file, or use `.Supply` on it to read it in chunks if it's not easily divided into lines.

How It Works

Current computers have a good amount of memory. But it's a law of nature that the size of the files that your computer will need to process will always grow to twice the size of the available memory in no time. So, although in most cases slurping a whole file in memory will do, in some cases that might be too slow, or simply impossible given the available memory. For instance, LibreOffice Calc, the open source spreadsheet, will choke when trying to read a file with a few hundred megabytes. Will Raku be able to keep up with it? Spoiler alert: yes it will.

Let's talk first about the concept of *laziness*. A lazy data structure is simply one that computes its components only when they are requested. A lazy sequence that is generated using a function will only re*ify* its element number *n* when it's requested. Meanwhile, it will be in limbo, but, more importantly, it will not be in memory, gobbling up space, and the resources needed to compute it will be available for the rest of operating system.

The `IO::Handle` objects that take care of input/output in Raku are quite powerful, and among other things, they can be turned into lazy data structures that return lines of a text file only when needed.

For instance, you need to load the nutrients-per-product database that is published by the U.S. department of Agriculture as a 179MB CSV file. As such, you could, in principle, use `Text::CSV` to deal with it. But that will gobble up north of 179MB, and, worse than that, will take a long time before you see results pop up in the console.

(In this case, you could use a line-oriented API, but you've already seen in another recipes how to use it, so let's try a different approach with no dependencies.) Let's use IO::Handle.lines this way:

```
.say for "/home/jmerelo/Documentos/Nutrients.csv".IO.lines.grep: {
    my @data = $_.split('","');
    $_ if @data[2] eq "Protein" and @data[4] > 70 and @data[5] ~~ /^g/
}
```

This script will print only those products that have more than 70 grams of protein (an arbitrarily chosen number). This script will immediately start to print the lines in the console, just like this:

```
"45332602","203","Protein","LCCS","70.59","g"
"45333759","203","Protein","LCCS","77.42","g"
"45333760","203","Protein","LCCS","72.73","g"
...
```

Processing the whole file is not going to take long—28 seconds on my desktop computer. More importantly, the process monitor reveals that the program never uses more than approximately 100MB of the resident memory, substantially smaller than the file size.

The good thing about having these results immediately available is that we could, for instance, create a supply and emit them to that supply. A tap would pick up those lines and, for instance, look up the product code (which is cross-referenced in another file) asynchronously.

A supply can also be used if the file is organized in some other way; for instance, as a text or as a JSON file. IO::Handle.Supply will read chunks of a particular size from it, and then emit them as a string. Text files can be processed by lines anyway and, as shown in the previous recipe, this chunking is a technique better reserved for binary files. It's good to know, anyway, that there is more than one way to do it.

CHAPTER 4

Math

Programming languages are the offspring of mathematics, but they have different capabilities to translate mathematical language and expressions to code. By implementing operators using their Unicode glyph, you will find that Raku code is closer to math than it is to other languages. By its functional nature, Raku functions can also work as pure functions (applications, in mathematical terms) and thus the data flow can be seen more clearly in Raku code.

In this chapter, we will work through several recipes that deal with mathematical objects and apply mathematical operations in sensible ways.

Recipe 4-1. Generate Mathematical Sequences and Extract Random Elements from Them

Problem

A mathematical sequence has an initial value and a generator that computes the next term in the sequence from the previous values. You need a straightforward way to work with these potentially infinite data structures and extract arbitrary elements from them.

Solution

Use Seq together with the sequence operators. Additionally, you can use ready-made sequences from the Math::Sequences module in the ecosystem.

How It Works

Raku includes the built-in (or core) data structure, Seq. The Seq data structure is used to represent a lazy sequence, which can represent infinite sequences and compute every

© J.J. Merelo 2020
J.J. Merelo, *Raku Recipes*, https://doi.org/10.1007/978-1-4842-6258-0_4

term on demand. It goes a little bit further, in that it can deduce the rest of the sequence from the first terms, especially with simple geometric or arithmetic progressions.

You've probably heard the story about the inventor of chess. He was asked by the king to quote his price for such a great game. He wanted to be paid in grains of wheat, to the tune of putting one grain in the first square in the chessboard, and double the quantity of grains in every successive square. "Done deal," answered the king. However, if he had Raku at hand, he could have typed the following and realized immediately how large this number was:

```
say [+] (1,2,4...*)[^64]
```

The (1,2,4...*) is the actual Seq. We need to type at least the first three elements so that Raku knows enough to tag it as an arithmetic progression and can then compute the rest. The … is the sequence operator, a smart operator that is able to generate sequences of any kind of element, including these *infinite* sequences. The square brackets take a slice that goes from the first to the 64th element (excluded), and finally we use the hyper-ed sum to sum everything. The result, as expected, is 18446744073709551615. By the way, you can also compute this in Raku with the following:

```
say 2⁶⁴ -1;
```

say 2^{64} -1;

Note   The king was amused or not amused, depending on who you ask, and either had a good laugh or cut the dude's hair at the neck.

Sequences can be also computed recursively from an operation applied to the previous terms. The one that follows, for instance, combines the two previous elements in the sequence and takes modulo 9.

```
sub digits( $_1, $_2 ) {
    return $_1, $_2, { ($^a ~ $^b) % 9 }  ...  *;
}

for 1..5 X 1..5 -> @_ {
    say digits( | @_ )[^10];
}
```

The $^a and $^b are placeholder variables that will take the value of the previous and next-to-previous variables in alphabetical order. The block they are in will compute the nth element out of the previous two. Instead of using a single pair of numbers to start, we create a sub that returns a Seq. That sub is invoked in the loop that's created next: it creates an array of 25 pairs that are handed to the sub by flattening them. The | will create two arguments out of an array. We eventually print the first ten elements of every sequence, obtaining something like this:

```
(1 1 2 3 5 8 4 3 7 1)
(1 2 3 5 8 4 3 7 1 8)
(1 3 4 7 2 0 2 2 4 6)
```

In many cases, using Seq will save you lots of work in building complicated loops or recursive functions, and its syntax in Raku will be easier to understand.

Recipe 4-2. Program a Divide-and-Conquer Algorithm

Problem

You need to solve a mathematical problem by dividing it into smaller problems that are solvable.

Solution

Use recursion so that the base case, that is, the smallest one, is solved, and you can build up from there.

How It Works

Divide-and-conquer is a technique that is used in many problem domains to convert difficult problems into ones that can be solved with relative ease. A classical example is sorting. Sorting a long list is solved by using a *pivot*. It involves putting all elements smaller than a certain size in a list and those larger in another list. You have therefore divided the problem of sorting into two problems, the problem of sorting those two smaller lists. This algorithm is called *quicksort*, and it's extremely efficient time- and memory-wise.

The same types of problems present themselves in cooking. How can we cook a meal that has the highest protein content, without surpassing a certain calorie level? Or cook one with the highest fiber content without surpassing a certain amount of protein?

Note   You have probably noticed that this is an example of the *knapsack* problem.

Let's use the `calories` table to find a combination of ingredients, in the same dosage as in the table, that optimizes the amount of protein. This time we'll do so without paying attention to amounts or to rules about how to create a good meal. This program will do that:

```
use Raku::Recipes;

# We're using this code from Raku::Recipes:
sub calories-table( $dir = "." ) is export {
    csv(in => "$dir/data/calories.csv",  sep => ';', headers => "auto",
    key => "Ingredient" ).pairs
    ==> map( {
        $_.value<Ingredient>:delete;
        $_.value<parsed-measures> = parse-measure( $_.value<Unit> );
        $_ } );
}

my %calories-table = calories-table;

multi sub recipes( -1, $ ) { return [] };

multi sub recipes( $index,
                    $weight  where
                    %calories-table{@products[$index]}<Calories> > $weight ) {
    return recipes( $index - 1, $weight );
}

multi sub recipes( $index, $weight ) {
    my $lhs = proteins(recipes( $index - 1, $weight ));
    my @recipes = recipes( $index - 1,
                        $weight - %calories-table{
                        @products[$index]}<Calories> );
```

```
    my $rhs = %calories-table{@products[$index]}<Protein> +  proteins(
    @recipes );
    if $rhs > $lhs {
        return @recipes.append: @products[$index];
    } else {
        return @recipes;
    }
}

my $max-calories = 1000;
my @products = %calories-table.keys;
my @ingredients = recipes( @products.elems -1 , $max-calories );
say @ingredients, " with ", proteins( @ingredients ), "g protein";

sub proteins( @items ) {
    return [+] %calories-table{@items}.map: *<Protein>;
}
```

This program uses the helper module we have used before to load the ingredients table, which it does in the first two lines. We include the routine `calories-table` anyway for reference. As you probably remember, this was the code used in the previous chapter for the recipe that applied a series of transformations to a data set. Additionally, this routine uses `parse-measure`, also discussed in that chapter.

This is a divide-and-conquer algorithm, so we have to start with the biggest problem and solve smaller problems. That's what we do in the last lines, which set up the algorithm, establish the calorie count and the array of products (simply the keys of the `calories` table, which contain the name of the product), and call the recipes subroutine.

```
multi sub recipes( -1, $ ) { return [] };

multi sub recipes( $index,
                   $weight  where
                   %calories-table{@products[$index]}<Calories> > $weight ) {
    return recipes( $index - 1, $weight );
}
```

```
multi sub recipes( $index, $weight ) {
    my $lhs = proteins(recipes( $index - 1, $weight ));
    my @recipes = recipes( $index - 1,
                           $weight -  %calories-table{
                           @products[$index]}<Calories> );
    my $rhs = %calories-table{@products[$index]}<Protein> +  proteins(
    @recipes );
    if $rhs > $lhs {
        return @recipes.append: @products[$index];
    } else {
        return @recipes;
    }
}

my $max-calories = 1000;
my @products = %calories-table.keys;
my @ingredients = recipes( @products.elems -1 , $max-calories );
```

That subroutine is where all the fun is. We use Raku's multi for the different options we have.

- If index becomes negative, we're out of products. It just returns an empty array of ingredients. This is going to be the base case. Also, it does not really matter what weight is there, so we use the dummy variable $ to represent the weight.

- With a non-negative index, but when the product in that position in the array has more calories than we want, we skip one and go down one step, "eliminating" that product (simply skipping it). This will not occur in this case, except if we cut the calories to 400 and leave the chorizo out.

- The next multi is the real workhorse. We compare two things: the protein in the recipes without the current product, and the products that yield the optimal protein computed without the current product. That goes to the @recipes array. If the protein content in this product is better than without it, we pick the current product, appending it to the list. If it is not, we simply return the list of products without it.

You can play with the total number of calories to get different high-protein combinations. You will notice that every time you run it, you'll obtain a different set of ingredients. Something like this:

```
[Kale Tomato Olive Oil Kidney beans Lentils Chicken breast Rice] with 53.6g
protein
[Lentils Egg Tuna] with 43.9g protein
```

There are a couple of reasons for this. First, this divide-and-conquer method is a greedy algorithm: the order in which the products are sorted in the array will have an influence, since they will be dropped or added depending on the current calorie count when the recurrent algorithm reaches them. Second, this array is simply the list of keys in a hash table, so why is this random? The list of elements in a hash table are returned in random order, and it's also guaranteed to happen that way as a defense against denial-of-service attacks.

We need to run the algorithm several times to get the combination with the greatest calorie content. Chicken, lentils, and bean stew, anyone?

Recipe 4-3. Work with Matrices

Problem

Matrices are used the greatest for a variety of problems, from image processing to machine learning. Dealing with data structures whose dimensions is known in advance is quite convenient.

Solution

Raku has limited data support for two-dimensional matrices, but a few operators. Use `Math::Matrix`, an ecosystem module, to work with matrices.

How It Works

`Math::Matrix` is an ecosystem module, so you need to download it first. It is very well documented in the GitHub repository at `https://github.com/pierre-vigier/Perl6-Math-Matrix`. It enables you to work with matrices, which are simply two-dimensional arrays, or tables.

Matrix operations are great when you want to compute something on a series of quantities, and they can be used in our recipe-computing environment. For instance, we might have a table with the quantity of different ingredients in different recipes, and another table with the percentage of a dish that was actually consumed by several users. Say we want to compute the quantity of different ingredients that were consumed, so that we can, for instance, compute the amount of calories or protein.

The following table lists the amount, in grams, of three different ingredients—rice, chickpeas, and tomatoes—in three different recipes.

	Recipe 1	Recipe 2	Recipe 3
Rice	150	50	50
Chickpeas	50	150	50
Tomatoes	100	150	100

Now we have three different people who, because of being picky or simply being full, consume only a part of the three recipes.

	Person 1	Person 2	Person 3
Recipe 1	0.5	0.8	0.3
Recipe 2	0.9	1	1
Recipe 3	0.2	0.8	0.7

We need to know how many grams of every ingredient were consumed by each person. This program will compute that:

```
use Math::Matrix;
my $food-matrix = Math::Matrix.new( [[ 150, 50, 50 ],
                                     [ 50, 150, 50 ],
                                     [ 100, 150, 100 ]] );

my $person-recipes = Math::Matrix.new( [[ 0.5, 0.8, 0.3 ],
                                        [ 0.9, 1, 1 ],
                                        [ 0.2, 0.8, 0.7 ]] );
say $food-matrix dot $person-recipes;
```

This will print the following:

```
130   210   130
 170   230   200
 205   310   250
```

As with many problems in mathematics, once you have the correct representation, it's simply a matter of choosing the correct operator. In this case, the dot product (appropriately called dot) multiplies rows by the equivalent column and then adds the result. Good ol' Person 1 consumed 130 grams of rice, while Person 3 consumed 310 grams of chickpeas. That's almost 1,000 calories.

The module includes a good amount of operations, including decompositions and most matrix arithmetic, which you can use for anything in which this is essential, such as neural networks. And it uses the expected operators:

```
use Math::Matrix;
my $first = Math::Matrix.new( [[1,2],[3,4]] );
my $second = $first * 2;
say $second + $first;
```

The $second array is double the first; that is, every element is multiplied by two. Then we add the second to the first to yield the sum, in every case with the usual arithmetic operators. This expressiveness, and the ability to overload all kinds of operators with new operations (in this case matrices), are two of the things that make Raku useful and powerful.

Recipe 4-4. Compute the Mandelbrot Set

Problem

Just for fun, you need to compute the Mandelbrot set.

Solution

The Mandelbrot set is a set of numbers where the function doesn't change when the numbers are iterated (i.e. they remain bounded in absolute value). When you map the values after a number of iterations (what is usually called *escape time)* to colors, they produce visually amazing graphs. Essentially, you can work with complex numbers in Raku to program these sets. The Julia set and the Fatou set are two complimentary sets defined for specific functions, usually quadratic polynomials. They consist of complex plane elements for which the sequence value is bounded by a certain number.

How It Works

With Mandelbrot and Julia sets, it's about creating a recursively defined sequence and computing its value after a certain number of iterations. We'll work out the Mandelbrot set, and will leave the Julia set as an exercise.

This script will compute a section of the Mandelbrot set and print it to the console using filled squares:

```
use Array::Shaped::Console;

sub mandelbrot( Complex $c --> Seq ) {
    0, *²+$c ... *.abs > 2;
}

my $min-x = -40;
my $max-x = 40;
my $min-y = -60;
my $max-y = 20;
my $scale = 1/40;
my $limit = 100;
my @mandelbrot[$max-y - $min-y + 1; $max-x - $min-x + 1];
for $min-y..$max-y X $min-x..$max-x -> ( $re, $im ) {
    my $mandel-seq := mandelbrot( Complex.new( $re*$scale, $im*$scale) );
    @mandelbrot[$re-$min-y;$im-$min-x] = $mandel-seq[$limit].defined??
        ∞ !! $mandel-seq.elems;
}
say printed(@mandelbrot);
```

It looks a bit longish, but as a matter of fact, the gist of it is less than half a dozen lines. First, let's look at the Mandelbrot sequence itself:

```
0, *²+$c ... *.abs > 2;
```

To determine if a certain complex number $c belongs to the Mandelbrot set, we start a sequence with 0 and compute every subsequent number by squaring it and then adding $c. The number will belong to the Mandelbrot set if the values in the sequence do not go to infinity; that is, if the sequence goes on forever. We also know heuristically that if, at a certain point, the absolute value of the number in the sequence is bigger than 2, it will eventually go to infinity and thus does not belong to the Mandelbrot set. So this sequence will be an infinite (but lazy) sequence if $c belongs to the Mandelbrot set, and it will be finite if not.

We create a (coarse) grid with numbers. It's bound by -40,40 in the x axis and -60,20 in the y axis, which we have chosen so that the familiar picture of the Mandelbrot set really shows up. We use 100 as the limit: if within 100 iterations, it's not stopped, it's likely it will never stop (of course, we could be wrong, but that's what you need to do if you have a finite amount of resources and no way to prove a theorem about every single complex number). Also, we scale down that grid to have a better look at the set, and we use 1/40 as that scale. The grid will actually go from -1,1 in the x axis and - 0.5 to 1.5 in the y axis. That sequence is generated for every single number, and then we check what happens to element 100 (after the first 0) in the sequence. It exists, so it belongs to the Mandelbrot set. Let assign an ∞ to it, because it's going to go to infinity. If it does not, let's note the escape time, which will be what we represent.

We are storing this in a shaped array, which is a nifty feature of Raku. They are arrays that, instead of being one-dimensional (essentially vectors), are in different dimensions. Since we are computing elements of a grid and getting a value for every one of them, we store them in a two-dimensional array, with dimensions adjusted to the number of points we are going to have in every dimension. We use the semicolon ; to separate indices in every dimension: `@mandelbrot[$re-$min-y;$im-$min-x]`. The fact that it remembers its shape will be used later.

This is then handled to the printed routine, which belongs to the `Array::Shaped::Console` module. This routine uses symbols to represent values and automatically adjusts itself to the shape of the array and to the range of values available. It will eventually print something like this:

This image has the familiar, heart shape of the Mandelbrot set. The black squares, in this case, will be the elements that belong to it, and the white squares show those with a very low escape time, less than ten.

At any rate, this shows how easy it is to perform sequence calculations, even with complex numbers, using Raku. The key part of the computation is a sequence defined in a single line. The rest is mainly used for rendering it visually. Using more mathematically appropriate data structures, like shaped arrays, also makes life easier for programmers.

Recipe 4-5. Leverage the Infinite Precision of Integer Numbers

Problem

You need to check some property over the whole integer set, which implies working on an infinite set and working with numbers that might have infinite precision.

Solution

Just use normal Ints in Raku, which have arbitrary precision by default. You can also use infinite sequences or combinations of them, so you can apply any kind of operation to the infinite sequence and generate results only when needed.

How It Works

Let's start by computing contiguous prime numbers; these are prime numbers that are separated by two. They are also called *twin prime numbers,* and together they are called *twin prime pairs.* It's been proved that there is an infinite number of twin prime pairs, which is why we need infinite precision to compute them. It will obviously take a long time to work with them as we increase the number of digits. But since Raku can work with lazy sequences, we can compute contiguous numbers using this short script:

```
my Int @primes = (1,2,3…∞).grep: *.is-prime;

my $prev = 0;
my @contiguous = lazy gather {
    for @primes -> $prime {
```

```
        take [$prime, $prev] if ($prime - $prev) == 2;
        $prev=$prime;
    }
}
say @contiguous[300..310];
```

The essential part of this is the definition of a list of (potentially) all primes in the first line. That sequence will contain a generator for all possible primes and will compute them on demand. Which is what we do in the next loop. Again, the essential part of this is that we need to process lazy sequences lazily. The `gather` statement will pick up all data sent by `take` within the loop, but making it lazy will make the resulting data structure, `@contiguous`, lazy, and thus will not go over the (infinite) `for` loop before it stops. If we want to compute the 300th to 310th contiguous primes, it will not go to infinity and back, but will stop when the 310th pair of contiguous primes has been computed. It's [17791 17789], by the way. Also, this takes around two seconds on my laptop. It takes a good while to compute the 3000th, which is [300499 300497] and the 10000th, which is [1260991 1260989] (in this case, about five minutes). We could continue with any sequence, with no need to specify big integers or whatever, as long as we're ready to wait. But it's obvious that these numbers are in the ballpark of other integers used here and there, the only advantage being that there's no need to use some special data structure for them.

Let's try to work with *really* big numbers. We only need to start the sequence somewhere else. For instance, here:

```
my Int @primes = (2⁶⁴...∞).grep: *.is-prime;
```

In this case, the first prime is 18446744073709551629. If we want to know the first three pairs, the former program will print the following:

```
([18446744073709552423 18446744073709552421]
[18446744073709554151 18446744073709554149]
[18446744073709558603 18446744073709558601])
```

This happens in less than 1/20th of a second. There are, apparently, lots of contiguous prime numbers. These numbers do have lots of digits, showing the arbitrary precision we needed.

There are not so many *amicable* numbers, which are those pairs whose divisors (excluding itself and one), when added, yield the second number. In this case, it involves easily indexing the list of divisors of a number so that they can be summed and compared to other numbers. This was posted as a challenge in the *Perl Weekly Challenge,* and Laurent Rosenfeld came up with this solution (slightly transformed, because originally it only returned the first pair):

```
sub sum-divisors (Int $num) {
    my @divisors = grep { $num %% $_ }, 2..($num / 2).Int;
    return [+] 1, | @divisors;
}

for 2..Inf -> $i {
    my $sum_div = sum-divisors $i;
    if $sum_div > $i and $i == sum-divisors $sum_div {
        say "$i and $sum_div are amicable numbers";
    }
}
```

Again, it's using a `lazy` so that the whole set of integers can be processed; however, it needs to be stopped by using Control+C, because it will keep printing amicable numbers as soon as it finds them. Additionally, it's not storing the result of sum-divisors, so when `$sum_div` reaches the value of `$i` again, it's computed all over again. Let's make two small changes to take care of these issues:

```
use experimental :cached;
```

```
sub sum-divisors (Int $num) is cached {
    my @divisors = grep { $num %% $_ }, 2..($num / 2).Int;
    return [+] 1, | @divisors;
}

my @amicable = lazy gather {
    for 2..Inf -> $i {
        my $sum_div = sum-divisors $i;
        take [$i, $sum_div] if $sum_div > $i and $i == sum-divisors $sum_div;
    }
}

say @amicable[^3];
```

The (still experimental) cached feature stores the result of a routine with the is cached trait. With this, we will have the value of the divisors of a number if it has been seen before, and it saves quite a bit of time. Then we assign the result of the loop to a lazy sequence, so that we can compute the nth element on demand. We obtain the three classically known pairs of amicable numbers straight away, and in six seconds, we compute the first four pairs:

```
([220 284] [1184 1210] [2620 2924] [5020 5564])
```

Configuring and Executing Programs

So far we have been working with small scripts and modules that, in general, had everything they needed to get the job done. Most real programs, however, will need some information from the user to run properly, even if they work with default values. These will come in the shape of environment information, command-line flags, or configuration files in some standard format. In this chapter, we'll see how these work in Raku.

Recipe 5-1. Configure a Program Using JSON/ YAML/.ini Files

Problem

You need to run a program with a series of values that are not known at the time you design the program, or are simply different for different instances.

Solution

Nowadays, JSON is probably the most widely used format for configuration, as well as the serialization of data structures. You can use `JSON::Fast` (available from `https://modules.raku.org/dist/JSON::Fast:cpan:TIMOTIMO` and, as usual, using `zef`), a module in the ecosystem, to convert data stored in JSON format to the corresponding Raku data structure.

© J.J. Merelo 2020
J.J. Merelo, *Raku Recipes*, https://doi.org/10.1007/978-1-4842-6258-0_5

YAML, .ini, and other formats, such as TOML, are also relatively popular, and they can all be parsed by modules in the ecosystem. Choose the format you feel most comfortable with or the most popular one.

How It Works

Programs have many different ways to receive the values of variables such as filenames, port values, or any other string or number they might need. Using positional and named parameters on a MAIN sub is one way (and we will see how to do that next), but configuration files have the advantage of being legible, editable, and amenable to be put under source control files (or encrypted, if they contain sensitive information). At any rate, it makes sense to leave some values for the user to determine, and thus configuration files come in handy for that kind of thing.

Let's rewrite a program we used before, the one that computed the maximum amount of protein in a certain calorie count. We will use three configuration items: the file that holds the calorie count, the max calorie count, and the number of times we will repeat it to get the best of n. Since the result will depend on the order of the products in the product matrix, using several iterations will help us obtain a better value.

Here's the JSON configuration file:

```
{
    "calories" : 1000,
    "repetitions" : 3,
    "dir" : "."
}
```

We use unimaginative names for the variables and store them in a JSON hash table, with variables as key-value pairs. The program is as follows:

```
use Raku::Recipes;
use JSON::Fast;

my %conf = from-json(  slurp(@*ARGS[0] // "config.json" ) );
%calories-table = calories-table( %conf<dir> );
@products = %calories-table.keys;

my $max-calories = %conf<calories>;
```

```
my @results = gather for ^%conf<repetitions> {
    @products = @products.pick(*);
    my @ingredients = optimal-ingredients( @products.end , $max-calories );
    my $proteins = proteins( @ingredients );
    say @ingredients, " with $proteins g protein";
    take @ingredients => $proteins;
}
say "Best ", @results.Hash.maxpairs;
```

First, we renamed the routine used to maximize protein optimal-ingredients and placed it in the Raku::Recipes module, which contains other different subroutines we are reusing from former recipes. This routine will use the calories table in the same %calories-table variable; this and @products will be variables with module scope, but they get the value in this main program. That is only incidental to the main theme of this recipe, which is using the JSON configuration.

The main action, in that sense, is in the %conf variable. That variable will be a hash read from a file that will have either been received as the first argument in the command line (@*ARGS[0]) or will have the default value config.json in the self-same directory. The values of that hash are used to load the calories table (using the directory contained in %conf<dir>) to get the max calories allowed (in %conf<calories>) and the number of times we are going to shuffle the product array to get a new combination of products with optimal protein content.

The shuffle is done via @products = @products.pick(*). While pick will return a random element out of the array, using Whatever (*) will pick as many elements as there are in the array. Effectively, this will shuffle the array, and since optimal-ingredients uses that variable, we assign it back to the same variable.

Every repetition will generate a pair in the form *[array of ingredients], [protein content]*. We use gather and take to generate this result from the loop. This is conveniently arranged to use maxpairs, which will print the pair whose second element has the maximum value.

We run this recipe from the main directory of the example code repository like so:

```
raku -Ilib Chapter-5/max-proteins-with-conf.p6 Chapter-5/config.json
```

We will then obtain a result similar to this one:

```
[Chicken breast Kale Rice Chickpeas Kidney beans Cheese] with 77.7 g protein
```

```
[Potatoes Chorizo Beer Pasta Chicken breast] with 64.9 g protein
[Chicken breast Potatoes Cheese Chorizo Tomato Sardines] with 109.3 g protein
Best (Chicken breast Potatoes Cheese Chorizo Tomato Sardines => 109.3)
```

In order for maxpairs to work correctly, we need to turn it into a hash; the Best line shows a ingredients-protein pair that looks quite good, at 100 grams of protein. I wouldn't recommend mixing chorizo with sardines, though, so you might want to run it several times (or reconfigure it for another number of repetitions) so that you eventually get something palatable.

Configuration Using INI Files

The INI format, originally used in Windows but now found anywhere, is simpler and used in many cases when all you need are a few variable/value pairs. It's also divided into sections, whose names are surrounded by square braces:

```
[food]
calories = 500

[algorithm]
repetitions =  5

[meta]
dir = .
```

A reliable module for processing this is Config::INI, found at https://github.com/tadzik/perl6-Config-INI, and which you can install in the usual way. The previous program can be adapted to use it this way:

```
use Raku::Recipes;
use Config::INI;

my %conf = Config::INI::parse_file( @*ARGS[0].IO.e ?? @*ARGS[0] !!
"config.ini" );
say %conf;
%calories-table = calories-table( %conf<meta><dir> );
@products = %calories-table.keys;

my $max-calories = %conf<food><calories>;
```

```
my @results = gather for ^%conf<algorithm><repetitions> {
    @products = @products.pick(*);
    my @ingredients = optimal-ingredients( @products.elems -1 , $max-
    calories );
    my $proteins = proteins( @ingredients );
    say @ingredients, " with $proteins g protein";
    take @ingredients => $proteins;
}
say "Best ", @results.Hash.maxpairs;
```

This module reads the file directly with `Config::INI::parse_file`, and now the hash has a hierarchical organization of variables, with the first key being the section and the second the name of the variable itself. Other than that, the results are notably the same except for the change of repetitions and the number of calories, which we have reduced.

Configuration Using YAML Files

YAML has more recently become popular with its use in cloud configurations, but it has had a long life and thus has good support in many languages. This includes Raku, which has a library called YAMLish, frequently updated and with excellent support.

We'll try to tackle another problem, similar to the backpack problem, but simpler: we'll try to create a recipe with a certain number of calories using two ingredients. These ingredients must include one side and one main ingredient, and we can additionally impose restrictions like making them vegan or non-dairy. Before doing its job, the code will perform checks on the configuration and emit an error if it's not correct or if the restrictions are not met.

Here's an example of a configuration file in YAML:

```
---
main: Cod
side: Potatoes
calories: 500
```

The three dashes indicate the beginning of a *document* in YAML; the rest are key-value pairs. YAML admits the serialization of any kind of data structure, but for this problem, this will be more than enough. Specify a main and a side dish, as well as the amount of calories you want the dish to have. To simplify things, we'll just spread it evenly between side and dish.

We need to process this configuration file so that, if there's a problem, the user is informed of what we were expecting and what went wrong. This will also ensure that the error does not propagate further into the library and produce a more obscure error that the user can't interpret. We need to check anything that could possibly go wrong and produce an exception that can guide the user into fixing whatever was amiss.

Note   For this, we will use custom-defined exceptions, which will be covered more extensively in Chapter 8. For the time being, just take them at face value. Exceptions, and typed exceptions at that, can be designed into an application and conjured by giving them a parameter that will customize the exception to a specific situation.

This program will have to read the YAML file and then perform a series of checks, emitting exceptions (and ending the program) if there's something essential missing, or if there's simply something wrong. When everything is checked, it will then generate the recipe.

```
use YAMLish;
use Raku::Recipes::Roly;
use X::Raku::Recipes;

my $conf = slurp( @*ARGS[0] // "Chapter-5/recipe.yaml" );
my $recipes = Raku::Recipes::Roly.new;

my %conf = load-yaml( $conf );
%conf<calories> //= 500;
constant @conf-keys = <main side calories>;

die "There are unknown keys in the configuration file"
        if %conf.keys ⊖ @conf-keys ≠ ∅;

my @recipe;
for <main side> -> $part {
    without %conf{$part} { X::Raku::Recipes::MissingPart.new( :$part
).throw() };
    given %conf{$part} {
```

```
        when %conf{$part} ∉ $recipes.products {
            X::Raku::Recipes::ProductMissing.new( :product(%conf{$part})
            ).throw()
        }
        when not $recipes.check-type( %conf{$part}, $part.tc ) {
            X::Raku::Recipes::WrongType.new( :desired-type( $part
            )).throw() ;
        }
    }
    my %this-product = $recipes.calories-table{%conf{$part}};
    my $portion = %conf<calories>/( 2 * %this-product<Calories>);
    @recipe.push: $portion *  %this-product<parsed-measures>[0] ~ " " ~
        %this-product<parsed-measures>[1] ~ " of " ~  %conf{$part}.lc;
}

say "Use ", @recipe.join(" and ");
```

This program seems longer than it actually is, simply because all the checks that are being performed. This is essential, however, and even more so in a production environment, where the configuration must be just right.

The preface to the program includes the modules we've already talked about. X::Raku::Recipes is a file with all the exceptions defined and all of them will use that as their namespace.

After that, we read the configuration file (either from the command line or from a default value) and assign a reasonable default to the number of calories in case it's missing. We initialize (pun) the role, which also reads the calories table, and load the configuration into a Raku hash. That variable should have just the three keys, and every value there must be correct. From there, several checks are performed:

- Are there only the keys that we understand? If there's any other keys, the program will die and the user will be informed of that.

- Are the two parts of the dish included? If any of them is missing, a MissingPart exception will be thrown. In this case, we might want to include potatoes as a reasonable default. However, in Spain the default side is simply bread, so in absence of a reasonable default, let's throw an exception if it's missing. We'll get something like Object does not seem to be side if we use side: Cod.

- Do we know something about the ingredient mentioned? If it's missing from the table, throw a `ProductMissing` exception.

- Is that ingredient really that kind of dish? Are we requesting kiwi with potatoes, for instance? If they don't match, another exception should be thrown.

When all these checks have passed, it's simply a matter of dividing the measure the ingredient uses to measure calories by the number of calories it needs to fill (250 in this case). We elaborate that as a string, including lowercasing the ingredient, which is always uppercase. Eventually, this might print something like the following:

```
Use 236.111111 g of cod and 304.878049 g of potatoes
```

That's a good piece of cod and a medium-size potato. Seems reasonable.

Proper handling of the configuration should always go with precise handling of possible errors. We'll learn much more about this in Chapter 8.

Recipe 5-2. Configure a Command-Line Command with Flags and Arguments

Problem

You need to invoke a script with different values from the command line.

Solution

Use the `MAIN` subroutine to determine how the program is going to be invoked. Multiple instances can be defined, permitting more efficiency in the invocation. Besides, it's auto-documented, with a `-h` or `-?` generated automatically and an explanation of every one of the parameters and their values. `MAIN` is a normal subroutine, so it will also perform type checks for you and convert them from strings in the command line to the adequate format required by the program.

How It Works

At this point, we have a nice table of ingredients in a CSV file, and we might need some tool to consult it from the command line. For instance, how many vegan ingredients do we have? How many vegan side dishes? A command-line tool that used these as flags and gave us a list of ingredients would be really useful. We could use it to get a list that we could look up on the web to cook a recipe. We already have the ingredients on a CSV table in this form:

```
Ingredient;Unit;Calories;Dairy;Vegan;Main;Side;Protein;Dessert
Rice;100g;130;No;Yes;Yes;Yes;2.7;No
Chickpeas;100g;364;No;Yes;Yes;Yes;7;No
```

So there are five different characteristics we can filter by: Dairy, Vegan, Main, Side, and Dessert. That will make five flags in all for our command-line program. This small program will do the trick:

```
use Raku::Recipes::Classy;

sub MAIN( Bool :$Dairy, Bool :$Vegan, Bool :$Main, Bool :$Side, Bool
:$Dessert ) {
    my %ingredients = Raku::Recipes::Classy.new().calories-table;
    my @flags;
    for <Dairy Vegan Main Side Dessert> -> $f {
        @flags.push($f) with ::{"\$$f"};
    }
    my @filtered = %ingredients.keys.grep: -> $i {
        my @checks =  @flags.map: -> $k {
            %ingredients{$i}{$k} eq ::{"\$$k"}
        }
        so @checks.all;
    }
    say @filtered;
}
```

First, we use an object oriented version of our calories table (which now includes many more things) and load it into our program; we will include it in the %ingredients variable.

Let's look at how we use command-line flags. For every one we want to check, there will be a named variable in the signature of the specially-named MAIN sub. We will therefore have a variable for every one of the five filters we define, and we force them to be Bool. The presence of a flag will set the variable to True; we can also set the flag to False by using --/, as in --/Dairy. For instance, main ingredients that are not also side ingredients will be listed using the following:

```
raku Chapter-5/filter-ingredients.p6 --Main --/Side
```

It would be cumbersome to check every single variable in turn, so we use a nice Raku trick to access the value of a variable whose name is in a variable: ::{"\$$f"}. This builds the name of a variable, which will have the dollar (\$) and then its identifier, which is the value of the variable $f. If the variable exists, we add it to the array with the filters. This loop and declaration can in fact be shortened to this:

```
my @flags = <Dairy Vegan Main Side Dessert>.grep: { defined ::{"\$$_"} };
```

This effectively filters only those variables that are defined. We then filter again the list of ingredients by running a grep on its keys: the @checks variable will contain a list of the result of comparing the value for that ingredient to the value required. That will eventually be a list in the form [True False True]. But we need the ingredient to fulfill all conditions defined, so we create a junction out of that: @checks.all. Junctions are extremely useful for comparisons; with a single operator, we can perform an operation over all elements of a list (and possibly simultaneously using auto-threading), but in this case what we do is return that value converted to a single Bool value via so. This will be True only if all the elements in the list are true; @filtered will contain all elements for which all conditions are true. For instance, the result of the previous command will be as follows:

```
[Tomato Kale Potatoes]
```

These are only those sides that can't be main dishes at the same time. Others, like chickpeas, can be the main ingredient (chickpea stew or salad), or a garnish, so they wouldn't go on this list. Once it's clear what these commands are doing, we can also shorten them, eliminating any intermediate variables:

```
say %ingredients.keys.grep: -> $i {
    so all @flags.map:  { %ingredients{$i}{$_} eq ::{"\$$_"} };
}
```

Leaving the program, all in all, to fewer than 10 lines.

Note   This will also return a list instead of an array, but that detail is not so important.

As an added value, using MAIN automatically adds an -h flag, so that when you run this:

```
raku -Ilib Chapter-5/filter-ingredients.p6 -h
```

You get the following:

```
Usage:
  Chapter-5/filter-ingredients.p6 [--Dairy] [--Vegan] [--Main] [--Side]
[--Dessert]
```

What happens if you run it with no filter? It will return all ingredients. But it will still run the same code; it's designed in such a way that with no filter it will do that, but it will still have to run a good amount of code to achieve something that could be achieved very easily. To solve this, we can simply define multiple MAINs, using multi:

```
use Raku::Recipes::Classy;

multi sub MAIN() {
    say Raku::Recipes::Classy.new.products;
}

multi sub MAIN( Bool :$Dairy, Bool :$Vegan, Bool :$Main, Bool :$Side, Bool
:$Dessert ) {
    say Raku::Recipes::Classy.new.filter-ingredients( :$Dairy, :$Vegan,
    :$Main,   :$Side,   :$Dessert );
}
```

We also added filter-ingredients to the Raku::Recipes::Classy class, containing the same code as before. This new version uses the multiple schedule mechanism: Raku will simply call the method or sub whose signature matches the call. In the case of the MAIN sub, it will call one or the other depending on the flags that are used. No flags? It will call the first, which simply calls the method that returns the list of products or ingredients. Any flag? It will call the second. This is going to be marginally faster in this case, but conceptually it's going to show the intent more easily.

What happens if we want to use additional filters, for instance, by minimum quantity of proteins or max number of calories? Let's use this multiple schedule mechanism to add a new MAIN that will filter by minimum protein content. That's an integer number, so we add that to the new MAIN's signature:

```
# This is added to the previous example
multi sub MAIN(Bool :$Dairy, Bool :$Vegan, Bool :$Main,
          Bool :$Side, Bool :$Dessert,
          Int :$min-proteins) {
    my $rr =  Raku::Recipes::Classy.new;
    my @filtered = $rr.filter-ingredients( :$Dairy, :$Vegan,
    :$Main,  :$Side,  :$Dessert );
    my %ingredients = $rr.calories-table;
    say @filtered.grep: { %ingredients{$_}<Protein> > $min-proteins };
}
```

Actually, the only thing we added is a new statement that filters ingredients by the minimum amount of proteins; that's the last one before the closing brace. Using the already known grep, we take the filtered list of ingredients (which is in @filtered) and check that the amount of proteins is higher than the amount requested. This will eliminate from the original list, filtered by characteristics, those with less protein content and produce something like this:

```
raku -Ilib Chapter-5/filter-ingredients-proteins.p6 --min-proteins=5 --Vegan
(Chickpeas Lentils Kidney beans)
```

This result shows that chickpeas, lentils, and kidney beans are not only delicious, but also nutritious. At home, we eat dishes based on those three ingredients at least twice a week.

In the same way we used a configuration file to get the data for generating a recipe in this chapter, we can do this from the command line. The fact that we can add types to the arguments makes it much easier to catch errors in arguments before they get into the program, making it all much faster. Let's repeat the recipe on reading configuration files with YAML using the command line this time:

```
use Raku::Recipes::Roly;

my $recipes = Raku::Recipes::Roly.new;

subset Main of Str where {
    $_ ∈ $recipes.products && $recipes.check-type($_, "Main" )
};
subset Side of Str where {
    $_ ∈ $recipes.products && $recipes.check-type($_, "Side" )
};

sub MAIN( Int :$calories = 500,
          Main :$main!,
          Side :$side! ) {
    my @recipe;
    for <main side> -> $part {
        my $this-value = ::{"\$$part"};
        my %this-product = $recipes.calories-table{$this-value};
        my $portion = $calories/( 2 * %this-product<Calories>);
        @recipe.push: $portion *  %this-product<parsed-measures>[0] ~ " " ~
                %this-product<parsed-measures>[1] ~ " of " ~  $this-value.lc;
    }

    say "Use ", @recipe.join(" and ");
```

The part that performs the program, the last eight lines, is substantially the same. It's the setup that is different. We don't need to take care of exceptions, since Raku itself will do it for us, through several mechanisms:

- We create two subsets, Main and Side, that will only allow values that are of the right type and included in the set of products available in the product table. Anything other than those values will produce an invocation error.

- We make the two variables $main and $side mandatory. If they are not used, the program will die with the corresponding error.

- We don't produce an error if additional keys are added, but the usage string clarifies what's mandatory and what's optional:

Usage:
```
  Chapter-5/generate-recipe-cli.p6 --main=<Main> --side=<Side>
[--calories=<Int>]
```

In order to obtain the value of the variable whose name is in another variable, $part, we use the same trick as before, consulting the symbol table: ::{"\$$part"};.

If this runs with a main or side missing, it will produce the usage string. If the type is incorrect, like for instance here, it will produce the same kind of message:

```
 raku -Ilib Chapter-5/generate-recipe-cli.p6 -Ilib --main=Sardines --side=
"Green kiwi"
```

Note   You will have to use quotes if you want to pass as argument a product with whitespace in it.

This is not ideal, since it's not really clear why that argument didn't get through. You can however supplement the terse message with more documentation. If that proves inadequate for your use case, simply go to the recipe that uses the configuration file.

Recipe 5-3. Use Shell Environment Variables in a Program

Problem

In cloud environments, it's best practice for all information to be passed to the program using environment variables. They are also available all across the program, so they can be read when they are needed.

Solution

All environment variables can be read via the %*ENV default dynamic variable, with key as the variable name.

How It Works

Best practices tell you that some information should be kept inside environment variables. These are variables, defined from the shell, that the shell makes available to every program that's run. Depending on the shell we use (or the operating system), we will use something like this

```
export CALORIE_TABLE_FILE=../data/calories.csv
```

The lack of spaces around the = are important; also, conventionally, they use ALL CAPS for their names. In this case we will be telling the program we are running, or any program, for that matter, where that file will be placed. Every program will receive a copy of all environment variables and their values. Every language uses a different call or data structure to make them available. In the case of Raku, it's the %*ENV variable. The % sigil indicates it's an associative variable, the twigil * indicates that it's a dynamic variable. Dynamic variable values are similar to global variables, but instead of being defined with a global scope, they are defined with the scope of the caller. A dynamic variable in a routine can be set by the caller, or the caller will have a different value when it's changed inside a sub.

This concept is carried on to automatic variables that get a value when a program is instantiated, such as this one, except that changes in that variable will not be exported outside the program. They can only be used elsewhere in the program. Programs launched from programs using run will then get a copy of this (possibly modified) experiment.

We will use the content of the variable like so, in the Raku/Recipes/Roly.pm6 file:

```
method new( $dir = "." ) {
    my $calorie-table-file = %*ENV<CALORIE_TABLE_FILE> // "$dir/data/
    calories.csv";
    my %calories-table = csv(in => $calorie-table-file,
                             sep => ';',
                             headers => "auto",
                             key => "Ingredient" ).pairs
    ==> map( {
        $_.value<Ingredient>:delete;
        $_.value<parsed-measures> = parse-measure( $_.value<Unit> );
        $_ } );
```

```
    for %calories-table.values -> %ingredient {
        for %ingredient.keys -> $k {
            given  %ingredient{$k} {
                when "Yes" { %ingredient{$k} = True }
                when "No"  { %ingredient{$k} = False };
            }
        }
    };
    @products = %calories-table.keys;
    self.bless( :%calories-table, :@products );
}
```

This method creates the object and corresponds to a recipe in Chapters 3 and 4. The change is in first few lines: We check if that environment variable is defined, and if it is, set the name of the file we are going to read to it. If it's not defined, it uses the directory that has been defined when instantiating the variable. Effectively, this value overrides whatever value we used for the directory when creating an instance of Raku::Recipes::Roly.

One good thing is that you don't need to change any other files; it's only the internal implementation that changes. The scripts used in the previous recipes will still work in exactly the same way.

We will use this method often, mainly when deploying our applications to the cloud and when defining API keys, for instance. Or any time we want, really.

Recipe 5-4. Create a Docker Container for an Application to Distribute It Easily
Problem

You need a way to deploy your application easily in any cloud provider.

Solution

Create a self-contained Docker image that can be used anywhere Docker is installed, based on any of the published Raku images.

How It Works

Docker containers are the best way to deploy cloud applications, but they can also be used as convenience containers to deploy commands anywhere the Docker client and server is installed, which is almost everywhere nowadays.

Docker enables the creation of *images,* which are applications together with a filesystem that can be modified and used to store data or results, or simply thrown away. The best metaphor for these Docker images is the next version executables: you can download and run them directly, without worrying about installing anything, such as their dependencies or the language they're written in. So you can use them to *wrap* an application to use it anywhere.

We will use a Docker container to wrap the script we just created, the one that filters ingredients by type, and also minimum amount of protein. Let's suppose you need to get your command-line utility that creates a list of ingredients and filters by characteristics and proteins anywhere else. Normally that would be the cloud, but Docker containers can be used anywhere, and indeed they are.

There are many ways to create those images; you can simply start a container with the base image, install everything that's needed, and then *push* the image. You can also upload it to the Docker Hub to make it available to everyone.

But it's much better if you use a Dockerfile, which is a recipe that describes how to put everything into the container and includes what needs to be done to run it. Here's what you will use:

```
FROM jjmerelo/alpine-raku:latest
LABEL version="0.0.2" maintainer="JJ Merelo <jjmerelo@GMail.com>"

ADD META6.json Chapter-5/filter-ingredients-proteins.p6 ./
RUN mkdir lib && mkdir data
ADD lib/ lib
ADD data/calories.csv data

RUN apk update && apk upgrade && zef install . \
    && chmod +x filter-ingredients-proteins.p6
ENTRYPOINT ["./filter-ingredients-proteins.p6"]
```

It relies on a base image that already contains Raku, jjmerelo/alpine-perl6. You can use pretty much any one as long as it has raku and zef as an executable in the execution path. I maintain that image and upgrade it to the latest Raku version (2020.01

at the time of writing) as soon as it's produced. You can use Docker Hub to search for others if that's not convenient for any reason. This image is based on Alpine Linux, which is a minimalistic distro little known outside the Docker world, but quite popular there. The main intention of this image is to create an image that is compact and takes a short time to download.

Dockerfile commands are all in caps; the next one, LABEL, adds metadata to the image, which can be examined using Docker image or any other utility. It's not really needed, but it's convenient.

The rest is really very short. It creates directories so that files are found where they are expected. It copies the files. zef install . will install the Raku::Recipes modules so that they are available everywhere, and apk update and upgrade are Alpine orders used to upgrade the operating system, as it might have changed since the image was created.

The last command establishes an entry point: this is what is going to be run if the Docker image is invoked by itself, and this is where the flags will be added. We use the program we want to wrap, obviously, and put it in square braces to indicate the flags will be appended to it, before being run.

We have to build this image with buildah, a Red Hat utility that can build Docker images:

```
buildah bud -f Dockerfile -t jjmerelo/raku-recipes:latest
```

Or also this, if you use the standard Docker installation:

```
docker build -t jjmerelo/raku-recipes:latest .
```

Then, we can run it. Docker images can be run with several utilities, including, of course, the Docker client itself, used here. I favor podman, since it's an implementation of the OCI (Open Container Initiative) standard. It does not require a daemon running and is marginally faster:

```
podman run  -it --rm sh jjmerelo/raku-recipes:latest
```

It will print the whole list of ingredients, or just

```
podman run  -it --rm sh jjmerelo/raku-recipes:latest --Vegan
```

for only the vegan ingredients. This flag will be passed to the command defined by
ENTRYPOINT, and it will run the program in the same way it would be run directly from
the command line.

Using Docker images is an extremely convenient way to create module-specific test
containers, or to ship web services to the cloud. We will come back to that later.

Recipe 5-5. Use Advanced/Distributed Configuration with etcd

Problem

You need to get configuration values, or any other kind of relevant information, in a
cloud deployment.

Solution

Use etcd, which is one of many distributed key-value stores. It allows us to set the values
that are going to be used locally and retrieved in any cloud instance by querying the local
federated etcd daemon, which will be in contact with all the other daemons. This can be
done securely if needed. That way, any node can publish local values known only after
deployment such as IP, ports, or simply information they want distributed over all parts
and replicas of a distributed application.

How It Works

Using command-line options or environment variables is okay as long as you deploy
an application in a single node. If you want to deploy an application in one or several
nodes in the cloud, setting environment variables might be cumbersome, and using the
deployment script to do it also presents a series of problems, mainly that anything will be
set once and for all.

Using distributed configuration services, such as etcd, is an easy, efficient, and
secure way to distribute information across all instances of a deployment. In order to do
that, etcd needs to be installed in every node that is going to be deployed, with all these
nodes being conscious of each other. Explaining how to do this goes beyond the scope

of this book, but you can check out installation options at the website, etcd.io. Follow
the instructions there to install the etcd server and the command-line client, etcdctl,
which will be used in this recipe.

We are going to use etcdctl the same way we used environment variables before: to
set values we're interested in (such as filenames). We can do this using the following script:

```
my $can-haz-etcdctl = shell "etcdctl --version", :out;

my $output = $can-haz-etcdctl.out.slurp;
die "Can't find etcdctl" unless $output ~~ /"etcdctl version"/;

my $version = ($output ~~ / "API version: " (\d+) /);

my $setter = $version[0] ~~ /2/ ?? "set" !! "put";

sub MAIN( $key, $value ) {
    my $output = shell "etcdctl $setter $key $value", :out;
    my $set-value = $output.out.slurp.trim;
    if $value eq $set-value {
        say "💡 $key has been set to $value";
    } else {
        die "Couldn't set $key to $value";
    }
}
```

This script is mainly a wrapper around the etcdctl command line, but it has
the (small) added value that you don't need to remember the exact syntax. It will
fail if etcdctl is not installed, and it will complain if we don't use a key-value pair in
the command line, since we are using that in the signature of the MAIN sub. If we do
something like this:

```
raku etc-set.p6 hey
```

It will write out the following:

```
Usage:
  etc-set.p6 <key> <value>
```

The key functionality of this program is achieved through the use of shell,
something we have already seen in the chapter devoted to system interaction. This

program will run the command-line arguments as is, with no attempt to check or clean them, which means that they could possibly run other programs if they just include an && or a ;. This is a use case in which this is not a problem, since the resulting command line will be run with the same privileges as the user who is giving them a value. However, the user would be well advised to use the same method to run programs within an Internet-exposed backend.

Using the shell routine and capturing output allows us to do several things:

- Determine if etcdctl is working and available in the path.

- Since we capture the output of this command, we use it to check the API version. The value-setting command was changed from set to put when changing from version 2 to version 3. Version 2 is still available in some distribution repositories, so we need to take care of that.

- We use that again to capture the output of setting the key. etcdctl returns the value set if it's been done correctly, so we check that it has been set correctly. Since etcdctl returns the value with a carriage return, we trim it, that is, we eliminate all surrounding space so that we're left only with the value.

We can then run this script with this:

```
raku etc-set.p6 filename data/calories.csv
```

This will print the following if everything is okay (which it should be, as long as we have etcd correctly installed):

🔑 filename has been set to data/calories.csv

We need to then retrieve the value from our script:

```
my $can-haz-etcdctl = shell "etcdctl --version", :out;

my $output = $can-haz-etcdctl.out.slurp;
die "Can't find etcdctl" unless $output ~~ /"etcdctl version"/;

for @*ARGS -> $key {
    my $output = shell "etcdctl get $key", :out;
    my $value = $output.out.slurp.trim;
    say "🔑 $key -> $value";
}
```

After the (obligatory) check that we have a working copy of etcdctl, we launch etcdctl on every key we've set in the command line, capturing the output, and then print a line with the key-value pairs.

We can run it and obtain the result:

```
raku etc-get.p6 innie foo filename
⚲ foo -> bar
⚲ filename -> data/calories.csv
```

The shell command is quite powerful and flexible, and we can use it to interface with any program or API that can run from the command line, which most can. In many cases this will be a substitute for other more expressive APIs such as gRPC, whose support in Raku is not very complete right now. Alternatively, the NativeCall interface can be used to bind a shared library to Raku, or the REST API, if that's available. However, all these require more programming effort, so the CLI of these programs called from Raku will be more than enough in most cases.

CHAPTER 6

Automating System Tasks

Just to be on the same page, we will use a Docker image based on Debian to test the recipes in this chapter. In most cases, all Linux systems will work exactly the same, but if you are not already using one, you can use a Docker installation for your operating system and check the recipes from that image. The image can be downloaded using the following:

```
docker pull jjmerelo/raku-recipes:Chapter-6
```

You can run it with the following:

```
docker -it -rm --entrypoint bash jjmerelo/raku-recipes:Chapter-6
```

This will give you a bash prompt from which Raku (and other applications) will be available.

Recipe 6-1. Check Log for Certain Events
Problem

You need to check the system log, or any other kind of log, for certain events, such as repeated attempts to log in or errors of any kind.

Solution

You can set a watch on some system files and filter events you want to know about, and you have already seen how to do that in Chapter 2. You can also identify the last person who logged in using the Sys::Lastlog module in the ecosystem (we'll learn about that later in this chapter). We'll use a combination of Recipe 2-5 in Chapter 2, "Watch a File for Changes," and a set of regular expressions (maybe user-defined) to define which

© J.J. Merelo 2020
J.J. Merelo, *Raku Recipes*, https://doi.org/10.1007/978-1-4842-6258-0_6

events we're interested in and then log them or print them to the console. Alternatively, we can use `Syslog::Parse`, a module released by the author of this book, which converts the system log into a supply and includes a grammar for parsing syslog entries.

How It Works

Every entry in a Linux system log looks like this:

```
Feb 17 12:06:45 penny org.gtk.vfs.Daemon[5244]: ** (process:8299): WARNING
**: send_done_cb: No such interface 'org.gtk.vfs.Enumerator' on object at
path /org/gtk/vfs/client/enumerator/2 (g-dbus-error-quark, 19)
```

First, there's the date and time that something occurred. Next are the machine name, the process causing the entry, and the process number in square braces.

In some cases, there's additional information as well:

```
Feb 17 12:06:45 penny dbus[1450]: [system] Successfully activated service
'org.freedesktop.hostname1'
```

The name in square braces refers to the fact that it's a system informational message. The ** indicate that there's something relatively serious going on. The syslog format is normalized in RFC 5424, which includes a whole protocol to log remotely, so that it can be read and produced from any application.

A standard format is a nice format. We can process that. And then we can look for the stuff we're interested in. For instance, let's look only for warnings.

```
say "/var/log/syslog".IO.lines.grep: /"-WARNING **"/;
```

That's a lot to take in, however. Lots of lines, and all of them at the same time. This defeats the whole purpose of a warning, which is to, well, warn you that something fishy might be going on. Besides, these are actually warnings by gnome; warnings produced by other applications might just slip by. For instance, these are Docker warnings:

```
Feb 19 09:17:36 penny dockerd[2408]: time="2020-02-
19T09:17:36.865094510+01:00" level=warning msg="failed to rename /var/lib/
docker/tmp for background deletion: %!s(<nil>). Deleting synchronously"
```

They are in lowercase and in some cases they simply say `<warn>`. Let's try to take into account all those cases. This code will do that and will tell you who produced the message:

```
my @warnings = "/var/log/syslog".IO.lines.grep: /warn/;
for @warnings -> $w {
    my ($metadata, $message) = $w.split( ": ", 2 );
    say "→ ", $metadata.split(/\s+/)[*-1],
        " has produced this message\n\t$message\n\n";
}
```

It will produce lines like this one:

→ gnome-session[5475] has produced this message
        Window manager warning: Window 0x4800022 (win0) sets an MWM
        hint indicating it isn't resizable, but sets min size 1 x 1
        and max size 2147483647 x 2147483647; this doesn't make much
        sense.

At least we know who did it. Still, the rest of the information eludes us, although we could extract it using a regular expression. Or much better—we can use the grammar included with Syslog::Parse to make sense of it all.

```
use Syslog::Grammar;
use Syslog::Grammar::Actions;

"/var/log/syslog".IO.lines
    ==> map( { Syslog::Grammar.parse( $_,
                                    actions => Syslog::Grammar::Actions.
                                    new ).made; } )
    ==> grep( { $_<message> ~~ m:i/warn/ }  )
    ==> my @lines;

for @lines -> %w {
    say "⇒ %w<actor> has warned about\n\t%w<message>\n\tby $%w<hour>";
}
```

The grammar in Syslog::Parse *understands* the different components in the lines: there's metadata and there's a message (which might be empty) separated by a colon and whitespace. But that metadata has structure, things like dates or the application that produced it. We can use that application to apply specific filters to decipher the message or to filter it only by message content, not using the whole line.

Caution   There could be an application called `awarnia` that would trigger false positives in the warning filter.

While grammars parse, grammar actions convert the parsed content into something that's usable or take action when something happens. In this case, we used the default `Syslog::Grammar::Action`, which creates a hash that uses the information we're interested in as keys. For instance, it can produce a data structure such as this one:

```
{
  :actor("firefox.desktop"),
  :day(19),
  :hostname("penny"),
  :hour("12:29:14"),
  :message("... long message with warning ..."),
  :month("Feb"),
  :pid(Any),
  :user("∅")
}
```

While the parsing would only have produced a `Match` object with the raw strings obtained in the match, observe that, for instance, if no user is detected in the message, it shows an empty set. The script itself will produce a structured set of warnings, like this one:

```
⇒ firefox.desktop has warned about
      message repeated 2 times: [ [Child 11536, MediaDecoderStateMachine #1]
      WARNING: (some stuff)]
      by 12:29:14
```

Many other filters are possible and we can show preprocessed data in many different ways. We'll dive into this in the next recipe.

Recipe 6-2. Check Logs Interactively on the Console

Problem

You want to be warned about certain logs in the console and perhaps filter them as well.

Solution

Ecosystem modules such as Term::TablePrint allow you to statically check data tables on the console; you can generate data before calling it and add interactivity through asynchronous updating.

How It Works

In general, TUI (Terminal User Interface) is what we call an application interface that is oriented to the whole console, or at least set up to work with the console in all directions. Such an interface doesn't just print stuff to the console and disappear at the top.

Although command-line oriented interfaces are fast, get stored in the CLI history, and can be reedited and reused, sometimes you need to navigate a set of items and choose one based on context. For instance, say you need to check a particular log at the same time that you check all the logs in the system. And all that with a console-, not line-oriented user interface. Term::TablePrint to the rescue in the following script:

```
use Term::Choose :choose;
use Term::TablePrint;
use Libarchive::Filter;

my @files = dir( "/var/log", test => { "/var/log/$_".IO.f } );

while @files {
    my $file = choose( @files.map( *.Str ),
      :prompt("Choose file or 'q' to exit") );
    last unless $file;
    my $i;
    my $content;
    if $file ~~ /\.gz$/ {
            $content = archive-decode($file, filter=>'gzip');
    } else {
        $content = $file.IO;
    }
    my @lined-file= $content.lines.map: { [ ++$i, $_ ] }
    print-table([ ['⇒',$file], |@lined-file ]);
};
```

Again, this shows how Raku does lots of things without lots of instructions, but in this case it is due to the fact that we are using the aforementioned module as well as two others—Term::Choose (by the same author, Matthäus Kiem) and Libarchive::Filter.

The script is a loop that presents the contents of the /var/log directory (filtered to include only files, that is, excluding directories) and helps us choose a file by moving around with the cursor keys. We do that with the choose routine. See Figure 6-1. The while loop will be entered only if there's a file (there should be), and it will run until the user presses q to quit. When that happens, $file becomes null, and the last command, which exits the loop, is activated.

```
Choose file or 'q' to exit
/var/log/dpkg.log.6.gz                  /var/log/syslog.2.gz
/var/log/fontconfig.log                 /var/log/alternatives.log.10.gz
/var/log/apport.log.7.gz                /var/log/alternatives.log.12.gz
/var/log/alternatives.log.5.gz          /var/log/Xorg.1.log.old
/var/log/mail.log.4.gz                  /var/log/dmesg.4.gz
/var/log/dmesg.2.gz                     /var/log/wtmp
/var/log/pm-powersave.log.2.gz          /var/log/prime-offload.log
/var/log/dpkg.log.1                     /var/log/auth.log.2.gz
/var/log/dmesg.0                        /var/log/btmp
/var/log/mail.log.1                     /var/log/aptitude
/var/log/faillog                        /var/log/syslog.3.gz
/var/log/pm-powersave.log               /var/log/syslog.4.gz
/var/log/alternatives.log.11.gz         /var/log/dmesg
/var/log/alternatives.log.1             /var/log/alternatives.log.3.gz
/var/log/Xorg.2.log                     /var/log/mail.log.3.gz
/var/log/pm-powersave.log.1             /var/log/btmp.1
/var/log/kern.log                       /var/log/apport.log
/var/log/apport.log.5.gz                /var/log/boot.log
/var/log/alternatives.log.7.gz          /var/log/lastlog
/var/log/apport.log.2.gz                /var/log/gnustep-back-common.log
/var/log/dpkg.log.2.gz                  /var/log/mail.log
/var/log/pm-powersave.log.3.gz          /var/log/dpkg.log.8.gz
--- Page 1/3 ---
```

Figure 6-1. *Choosing a file among all the logs*

This routine returns a filename in the $file variable. In order to show the file line by line on the screen, we need to check if it's a compressed or simple file. The former type is passed through the archive decoding filter (from Libarchive::Filter) and then converted into a table with two columns—line number and line content. A header with an arrow and the name of the file are added to the top, as shown in Figure 6-2.

```
→ | /var/log/apport.log.7.gz
--|-------------------------------------------------------------------------
1 | ERROR: apport (pid 8547) Mon Feb 17 12:30:45 2020: Unhandled exception:
2 | Traceback (most recent call last):
3 |   File "/usr/share/apport/apport", line 524, in <module>
4 |     get_pid_info(pid)
5 |   File "/usr/share/apport/apport", line 89, in get_pid_info
6 |     cwd = os.open('cwd', os.O_RDONLY | os.O_PATH | os.O_DIRECTORY, dir_fd=pr
7 | BlockingIOError: [Errno 11] Resource temporarily unavailable: 'cwd'
8 | ERROR: apport (pid 8547) Mon Feb 17 12:30:45 2020: pid: 8547, uid: 0, gid: 0
9 | ERROR: apport (pid 8547) Mon Feb 17 12:30:45 2020: environment: environ({})
```

Figure 6-2. *Showing a compressed file in table form*

You can navigate line by line with the up and down arrows, including pagination, and quit with q when you're done. This is achieved simply with the print-table order (from Term::TablePrint); q is the default key to quit the current screen.

The gist of the script are three functions from three different modules, all present in the ecosystem. Combining them in different ways, you can create powerful system administration scripts with a simple, screen-oriented interface.

Recipe 6-3. Check Git Commits for Patterns and Metadata, or to Store Them

Problem

Source control is a synonym of Git, and sometimes you need to work with the logs to measure productivity, note the issues they work with, or simply chart work. Accessing the text log is easy, but you need to parse it to obtain workable data.

Solution

There are many modules in the ecosystem that work with Git. We'll check them out and use the one that's best for every task. For instance, Git::Log might be the best module to work with commits.

How It Works

You would like to know, for instance, your productivity in the book's repository of examples. How many commits have you made per day?

Git::Log can help you with that.

```
use Git::Log;

git-log()<>
    ==> map( { DateTime.new( $_<AuthorDate> ).Date } )
    ==> classify( { $_ } )
    ==> map( { $_.key ~ ", " ~ $_.value.elems } )
    ==> sort()
    ==> my @dates;

say @dates.join( "\n" );
```

This is a nice example of using the *feed* operator (which I prefer to call *rocket*, because it launches its result to the next stage of processing) to create a pipeline of operations that will, on the tail end, get what you want.

Let's look at the different stages:

1. git-log() makes the call that examines the Git log of the current directory, by default (which is why it should be called from the top directory in the repository, as in raku Chapter-6/commits-per-day.p6). This returns a scalar, which we de-containerize via <> to get to the array of hashes that's inside it. After this stage, we have an array of hashes, every one containing information on a single commit, including the date, which is the one we're interested in.

2. We map the array of hashes to the date by converting the time in UTC format to a DateTime object, and then get to the Date part of it. After that, we'll have an array of objects of the form 20xx-yy-zz.

3. We classify the array of objects into pairs by simply using their string form. The pairs will have the date as the key, and an array with copies of the same date as the value. We need to go further with this, because we're interested in the number of commits per day.

4. We map these pairs to a string that has the key (the date), separated by a comma from the value, which is the number of times that date appears in the log. It's disordered because hashes are guaranteed to be.

5. We sort the results so that earlier dates appear first. Then we send them to an array.

We can do whatever we want with this array, but we've chosen to print it as a single string, each element separated by a carriage return (\n). And that's it. We could use a slightly different variation of this technique to determine how many commits we have per author (not in this case, since there's a single author here), or even check productivity per month or by day of the week. Let's check that, for instance.

Note   It just piqued my curiosity.

We need to change a couple of things in the previous script to check productivity by day of the week:

```
my @dow = <Nope Mon Tue Wed Thu Fri Sat Sun>;

git-log()<>
    ==> map( { DateTime.new( $_<AuthorDate> ).day-of-week } )
    ==> classify( { $_ } )
    ==> sort()
    ==> map( { @dow[$_.key] ~ ", " ~ $_.value.elems } )
    ==> my @dates;

say @dates.join( "\n" );
```

Since the days of the week are numbered starting at 1, we insert a dummy element in the 0 index of the @dow array so that we don't have to perform an operation with it when using them. The position of sort and the last map has been inverted (it wouldn't have mattered if we had done the same in the previous example, anyway) so that we classify by the day's number and not alphabetically by its name (it wouldn't have mattered, either). Instead of using the key to generate the array directly, we use that as the index of the name of the week. Here is the result:

```
Mon, 15
Tue, 15
Wed, 20
Thu, 36
Fri, 15
Sat, 25
Sun, 39
```

There go my weekends...

Recipe 6-4. Clean Up Your Docker Image Store

Problem

When using Docker containers, you end up with many unfinished builds, images that you have used only once, and others that you simply don't need any more.

Solution

Use `Docker::API`, a module in the ecosystem, to perform this and other Docker-related tasks.

How It Works

First, you need to download this module from the ecosystem. Follow the instructions to install it, including the additional external library. Note that this recipe need not be run from within the Docker container.

Tip   Instructions for installing the module are included in `Chapter-6/README.md` in this book's repository. In every chapter directory, there's a chapter-specific `META6.json` that will let you install all the modules needed with `zef install -deps-only`.

If you've used Docker for some time, you will have lots of images lying around that you probably don't need. It's convenient to have a series of scripts that are run periodically (from a cron job, for instance) that do the clean up for you. You can obviously use Raku to clean up the Docker images.

Consider so-called *dangling* images, which are images or layers that are partial results of building an image and are not part of any image that has been tagged. That means that construction failed further down the line. You can still use those images, and in fact something might have been built on them. For instance, you might use them if you create a container calling such an image by ID.

Let's use this Raku script to get rid of any dangling images:

```
use Docker::API;

my Docker::API $docker-api .= new;

my @images = $docker-api.images( dangling => True )[];

for @images -> %i {
    say "Trying to delete %i<Id>";
    $docker-api.image-remove( name => %i<Id> );
    CATCH {
        default {
            if .message ~~ /"being used"/ {
                say "Image %i<Id> not deleted, since it's being used";
            }
        }
    }
}
```

As usual, it's a very short script that does the job wonderfully. It's essentially three lines of code, plus definitions, messages, and assignments.

The first two lines create a $docker-api object, which is the object-oriented interface to the Docker API. It can't do anything that the Docker command-line can't, but it's convenient for working with the images, getting information about them, or deleting them, which is what we will be doing.

We will only get the images that are *dangling*: `$docker-api.images( dangling =>` `True )[]`. All API commands can include a filter, which will make it return only those images that have a certain attribute. The `@images` array will have only those images, and all the attributes, especially the ID, which is the handle we'll use to delete them.

Inside the loop over these images, we issue the corresponding command to delete them by ID. However, sometimes that fails, and it does so with an exception. That's why we have the `CATCH` block: if the command fails, the module will capture the exception and print a helpful message, continuing with the next delete (instead of stopping the program with an error).

In my system, it printed something like this:

```
Trying to delete sha256:d20dfd5d508913ce0516b16f16f05cef5a9eac541372284db08
0f634d2e77b94
Image sha256:d20dfd5d508913ce0516b16f16f05cef5a9eac541372284db080f634d2e7
7b94 not deleted, since it's being used
Trying to delete sha256:47306096984d543f8c6fcfbedabbfb49debc9eb81fbd8605fe7
a1ca517a0d593
Image sha256:47306096984d543f8c6fcfbedabbfb49debc9eb81fbd8605fe7a1ca517a
0d593 not deleted, since it's being used
Trying to delete sha256:ab6c614ae59e2a640662179ad1e311f0c542f8404b9cb92935c
c2e4f31cc9eae
Trying to delete sha256:22c0389a61f83e2f1d9a4ad16b7d2f9790dfd0458defbc2b687
e8acfa75c590b
Trying to delete sha256:bf9a0c98b8a3dd48a313642dd014759dfe36625e0b2a2c0b35e
d3c8d095b6e6c
```

This shows that most of the dangling images were deleted; however, some of them couldn't be deleted, and we've been informed about that.

`Docker::API` is a nice piece of code, as a matter of fact, but since we also know how to interact with command-line programs, we could have worked with the command line directly. This API simplifies the interaction and gives a Raku-ish interface to Docker, so that we don't have to worry about the intricacies of the command-line syntax and its flags, and we can deal with errors from our program too.

Recipe 6-5. Process the Last Person Who Logged onto Your System

Problem

As the system administrator, you need to know who connected to the system last to prevent intrusions or check system usage.

Solution

Use Sys::Lastlog, a module in the ecosystem.

How It Works

As a system administrator of a Linux system, you can always issue the lastlog command, which will tell you the last time every user in the user table logged on. You might not have access to the console, however, or might want to have programmatic access so that it's logged, it raises alarms, or whatever.

Sys::Lastlog to the rescue. This an interface for UNIX-based systems (including OSX) that will help you work with logins.

First, you have to do something to make it work inside the Docker container, since users don't actually log in inside a container. Let's run it with the following:

```
docker run -itu root -v 'pwd':/home/raku --entrypoint sh jjmerelo/raku-
recipes:Chapter6
```

That way, you can run with superuser privileges (that's the u root part of -itu root). You need to create a password for a user so that you can then log in using it. For instance:

```
passwd rakurecipes
```

(The user defined within that container is raku, and you might not want to have a password for that one. Alternatively, you might use some other throwaway user like uucp or www-data.) You can give it any password you want and repeat it. You can then log in from the command line:

```
login rakurecipes
```

and then do anything or log out, it does not matter.

You won't need to do this if you're using a UNIX system like Ubuntu, but you might need to do something similar if you're using Cygwin or the Windows Linux subsystem.

Let's try, for instance, to obtain a list of the users who logged in and the times they did so. This script will do that:

```
use Sys::Lastlog;
say .user.username, ", ", .entry.timestamp
    for Sys::Lastlog.new().list.grep: *.entry.time > 0;
```

It's actually a single line of code, but let's examine first the loop. Sys::Lastlog is an object-oriented interface, so we need to create an object to work with it. Once we have the object, we obtain a list of the last logins in the system via the .list method. Most of those elements will be users who have never logged in (system users like daemon or backup, for instance), so we need to filter only those that have done so at least once. By using grep, we get only those elements of the list whose last login time is greater than 0. *.entry will be an object of type Sys::Lastlog::Entry, which represents every element of the lastlog file. One of those elements is the time, which will be 0 if that user has never logged in.

Inside the loop, we use the implicit variable $_ implicitly; .user. username is equivalent to $_.user.username and $_.user will be an object of type Sys::Lastlog::UserEntry, which will contain information about the user the entry is about, gleaned from the system user table. .entry.timestamp will print the last login time in standard format. In our container, we might see something like this:

```
rakurecipes, 2020-02-15T17:19:12Z
While in my own system,
jmerelo, 2019-05-20T21:43:46Z
```

In general, it's a good idea to look in the Raku ecosystem for scripts that will do the usual system administration tasks. If such a script does not exist, you can always create your own. You'll see how to do that in the next chapter.

## CHAPTER 7

Modules

Programming involves creating layers of abstraction, and programming languages provide ways of creating interlocking and stackable layers of classes and functions, so that the programmer can think in higher-level constructs and get the job done as fast as possible. These module applications can be implemented in many different ways in Raku. Once they are implemented, we encourage you to release your modules to the ever-growing (in size and awesomeness) Raku ecosystem, so that others can benefit from what you have done.

Recipe 7-1. Design Classes, Roles, and Modules in Raku

Problem

You need to package a set of functionalities into a class or role so that they can be easily used in other programs.

Solution

Raku includes a very extensive object model that includes classes and roles, which are data and function sets that you can combine into other roles or classes.

How It Works

Raku offers many different ways to do this kind of packaging. Besides the ready-made classes, packages, and roles, there is a meta-object protocol that gives you the capability to create new kinds of packaging functionality.

109

© J.J. Merelo 2020
J.J. Merelo, *Raku Recipes*, https://doi.org/10.1007/978-1-4842-6258-0_7

Let's start with the simple things: modules. For instance, in previous chapters, you used Raku::Recipes, a module that includes a set of routines previously used in other recipes. Here's how it looks (the actual routine code has been suppressed for brevity):

```
use Text::CSV;
# Utility functions for the Raku Recipes book
unit module Raku::Recipes;
our %calories-table is export;
our @products is export;
# Parses measure to return an array with components
sub parse-measure ( $description ) is export {...}
# Returns the table of calories in the CSV file
sub calories-table( $dir = "." ) is export {...}
multi sub optimal-ingredients( -1, $ )  is export  { return [] };

multi sub optimal-ingredients( $index,
                               $weight  where  %calories-table{
                               @products[$index]}<Calories> > $weight )  is
                               export  {...}

multi sub optimal-ingredients( $index, $weight )  is export  {...}

multi proteins( [] ) is export { 0 }

multi proteins( @items )  is export  {...}
```

The name of the module is declared (almost) on the top—unit module Raku::Recipes—right after the very first line, which declares the module you'll be using. The use keyword imports all exported functions from an installed module into the current scope. This is precisely what the is export declarations state: these methods, and the two variables, are exportable. In the case of methods, they actually are *exportable* only in the context of the object that's used to invoke them. They do so using traits, which are properties that are attached to objects (such as routines) at compile time. In this case, the statement affirms that the export property is going to be attached to the routines we want to export.

That means that they will show up where they have been imported, as if they had been declared in the same scope. In the case of the two exported variables, they are declared with our, stating that they can be accessed from where they are imported. This is done by using, if needed, their fully qualified name, such as @Raku::Recipes::products.

The our keyword indicates that they can be exportable, but are used as locally scoped variables if they are not. In this case, all routines and variables are exported. If we want to keep something *private,* we simply don't add that trait to the object and declare it with my.

Note   Actually, use does two things: it makes accessible all objects with package scope (that is, those declared with our) and imports them into the current namespace, making them accessible without having to use their fully qualified name. We would still have been able to access the two variables that are declared our under their FQN—Raku::Recipes::<%calories-table>—for instance, even if they had not been exported.

The unit keyword is used to simplify the declaration of a module (or class); it simply says that the declaration comes right after that, and whatever is going to be contained in the package (which can be a module, a role, or a class) will come next. If unit is not used, we have to wrap the module code and declarations in curly braces, just like this:

```
module Raku::Recipes {
 # Code and declarations would go here...
}
```

That keyword simply saves us a bit of typing and cleans up the code by avoiding the braces (and indentation).

The way the name of the module is organized is via namespaces; in this case, declaration of this module automatically declares a Raku namespace (it will be used to store the names of all modules and variables in that namespace). Importing the module also declares a namespace with the name of the module. It's also customary to store packages in files whose filename has the last name in the package (the one behind the last double colon) and is stored in a directory hierarchy that reflects the rest of the namespace, and everything below a lib top directory. In this case, the file would be called lib/Raku/Recipes.pm6 (since late 2019, lib/Raku/Recipes.rakumod can also be used).

The main problem with this package is that we had a couple of package-wide variables that had to be initialized from outside and were also package-scoped and used from routines. It's a way of doing it, but there are many ways to do it, so later we repackaged the same functionality in a class, which we called

Rakudo::Recipes::Classy. There's the definition of methods and attributes, where, as in the last case, code occupying more than one line has been replaced with ellipsis (you can consult it on this book's code repository):

```
use Text::CSV;
use Raku::Recipes;
# Utility functions for the Raku Recipes book
unit class Raku::Recipes::Classy;
has %.calories-table;
has @.products;
method new( $dir = "." ) {...}
multi method optimal-ingredients( -1, $ )  is export  { return [] };
multi method optimal-ingredients( $index,
                                  $weight  where  %!calories-table{
                                  @!products[$index]}<Calories> >
                                  $weight )   {...}
multi method optimal-ingredients( $index, $weight )  {...}
multi method proteins( [] ) { 0 }
multi method proteins( @items )   {...}
method products () { return @!products };
method calories-table() { return %!calories-table };
method filter-ingredients( Bool :$Dairy, Bool :$Vegan, Bool :$Main, Bool
:$Side, Bool :$Dessert ) {...}
```

The functionality offered by this class is the same, except that, since one function was already defined in Raku::Recipes and didn't use the object attributes, we just import it from Raku::Recipes. We also need to add a couple of utility methods, products and calories-table, which will return the value of those attributes for that instance.

The package is defined in the same way as we did with modules instead of classes: we use unit to create a scope. Routines are now methods, and package-scoped variables are object attributes now. However, we need a way to instantiate them. In Raku, any method can return objects of a particular class. There is a default new constructor that takes attributes as named parameters. In this case, we need to instantiate objects from a directory location and will not know these values in advance. We then declare our own object builder, which will perform the same function.

We can then create objects of this class as we have done before:

```
say Raku::Recipes::Classy.new.products;
```

This will create an object on the fly, reading the data file from the default location or from what is defined in the environment variable and printing it.

This class can be extended by subclassing it, and Raku allows objects of new classes to inherit interface as well as attributes. But modern design favors composition over inheritance. That means creating new classes of objects by combining several ready-made ones. Raku can also do that using roles. Roles are *composable classes*; they have attributes and methods that can be thrown together to create a class. Roles define interfaces if they use *stubbed* methods (methods with no implementation, which force reimplementation when they are composed), but also provide functionality that makes sense autonomously. Stubbed methods can be combined with more code or roles to create a full-blown class.

For instance, we can create a role that includes the ingredients in a recipe. For the time being, ingredients are going to be an array of undetermined objects. The only functionality we need, besides counting the number of ingredients, is a gist method that prints the ingredients as a bulleted list, separated by newlines:

```
#| Role that describes generic recipe ingredients
unit role Raku::Recipes::Ingredients;

has @.ingredients;
method how-many { return @!ingredients.elems }
method gist {
        return @!ingredients.map( "* " ~ * ~ "\n").join;
}
```

This role can be used for several things. For instance, it could be used to create a shopping list (that would add functionality for checking which items have been purchases), but we will use it to create a recipe that includes a recipe name and description.

```
use Raku::Recipes::Ingredients;

#| A class with a fragment of a recipe: description + ingredients
unit class Raku::Recipes::Recipe does Raku::Recipes::Ingredients;
```

```
has Str $.title;
has Str $.description;

method gist {
    return "#$!title\n\n$!description\n\n## Ingredients\n "
        ~ self.Raku::Recipes::Ingredients::gist;
}
```

The attributes and methods of Raku::Recipes::Ingredients are incorporated into this class. An instance of the class will have the how-many method and it will have the gist method if needed. However, we need to print a recipe in some other way, in a mock-Markdown (mockdown?) fashion. The attributes declared in the class are used directly, and we could also do the same with @!ingredients, which is, by its own right, an attribute. However, why would we want to throw away a perfectly good gist method, declared in the role? We incorporate it in this method, calling it explicitly by its fully qualified name, which includes the name of the role where it was declared.

In general, roles shouldn't be instantiable. However, as a matter of fact, Raku allows you to instantiate them (in a mechanism called *punning*) and even subclass them:

```
role A { has $.foo = "Foo" };
role B is A { has $.bar = "Bar" };
say A.new; # OUTPUT: A.new(foo => "Foo")
say B.new; # OUTPUT: B.new(bar => "Bar", foo => "Foo")
role C does B { has $.baz = "Baz"};
say C.new; # OUTPUT: C.new(baz => "Baz", bar => "Bar", foo => "Foo")
```

So while classes can't be composed, roles can be subclassed, instantiated (in a procedure called *punning*), and composed, so in many cases it's better to create your application around roles instead of classes.

We'll do precisely that—let's refactor the Classy class so that a good part of the functionality is spun off to a role, which we will call Raku::Recipes::Roly. It's included here:

```
# Utility functions for the Raku Recipes book
unit role Raku::Recipes::Roly;

has %.calories-table;
has @.products;
```

```
method new( $dir = "." ) {...}
method products () { return @!products };
method calories-table() { return %!calories-table };
```

And now our *old* Raku::Recipes::Classy class will look like this:

```
unit class Raku::Recipes::Classy does Raku::Recipes::Roly;
# "method new" and attributes used to be here...
multi method optimal-ingredients( -1, $ )  is export  { return [] };
# Everything below is the same, except for the products and calories-table
methods....
```

The new Raku::Recipes::Classy does, that is, includes or is composed of Raku::Recipes::Roly. This is actually a plug-in replacement for the old method: nothing else needs to be modified, and we will be able to use that class exactly as before, except we now have an additional role that we can use as a standalone object or combine it into other classes if we so want.

Recipe 7-2. Document Your Module

Problem

You need to explain the usage of your module, so that anyone wanting to include it in their programs knows what to do. You also want to make it searchable and include a few illustrative examples for how to use it.

Solution

Comments in Raku are *smart*, which means they are compiled alongside the rest of the program. Some format marks within otherwise normal comments (which use the hash mark, #) will be interpreted to add documentation to the method or data around it. Additionally, Raku uses its own markup language, called Pod6, which can add structured text together with the code or can be used in an independent file.

How It Works

Documenting your work is important and essential if you are going to release your module to the world or simply intend to come back to it later. Modules need to be documented in general, so that clients understand what they do. Every one of the methods and functions also need to be documented, so that their behavior is clearly explained.

Raku code can be commented via hash marks. A comment like this would extend to the end of the line and not generate any kind of code or change in behavior:

```
# this would be a comment
```

We have also already seen that MAIN routines automatically generate documentation that is printed when the command line is invoked with -h. Additionally, we will document the role created previously in the way shown next, using a special syntax to indicate to Raku that a comment is intended to be printed when asking information about a routine or variable.

```
#| Utility functions for the Raku Recipes book
unit class Raku::Recipes::Classy does Raku::Recipes::Roly;
#| Compute optimal ingredients, knapsack style
multi method optimal-ingredients( -1, $ )  is export  { return [] };
# ...
#| Adds up the amount of protein for the items in the argument.
multi method proteins( @items )   { ... }
# ...
#| Filters ingredients by type
method filter-ingredients( Bool :$Dairy,
                           Bool :$Vegan, Bool :$Main, Bool :$Side, Bool
                           :$Dessert ) {...}
```

Again, this code is part of the code in the book repository, and just the relevant parts are shown here. The basic idea, however, is the concept of *active* comments. These comments, which use the pipe symbol (|) right after the hash mark, are called *declarator blocks,* and they are related directly to the method, package, or routine that is declared right after them. The first one will be attached to the class, the rest to the corresponding routines below them. They are *active* because they can be accessed as part of the metadata, using the WHY method:

```
use Raku::Recipes::Classy;
say Raku::Recipes::Classy.WHY;
say Raku::Recipes::Classy.^lookup('filter-ingredients').WHY;
```

This will print the following:

```
Utility functions for the Raku Recipes book
Filters ingredients by type
```

Every line will be the result of one of the instructions. Let's look at this code more carefully. The first thing you will notice are the all caps used in the WHY method. This is not whimsical; it corresponds to a naming convention that uses all caps for the HOW function.

Okay, maybe it's a bit whimsical, including the convention of using HOW and WHY. But what can you expect from a language with a rainbow butterfly as its mascot?

HOW methods answer questions about the meta-object itself, not the data that is held in it. It stands for Higher Order Working, or maybe it's simply a retronym so that its name fits the WHAT and WHYs that are included in this HOW. And HOW is a generic name for the functionality or the meta-object protocol (MOP). In Raku, not only can you create type objects with a certain behavior (such as composability) by using this MOP, but you can also look under the hood of existing objects, including type objects, and see what they are, what they do, or, as in this case, what their documentation is.

WHY accesses the documentation of the Raku::Recipes::Classy type object, and it does so by calling a method on the type object itself.

This also serves as an introduction to the next statement, which is calling the WHY, but using a different way. Let's see first why we need this; it boils down to the fact that there's no other way to get to the method object in a class. Routines can be easily accessed, since simply preceding them with & will give you access to the higher order workings of HOW. For instance, you can access the HOW of a module and a routine declared in it easily. We use these declarator blocks for the Raku::Recipes module:

```
#| Utility functions for the Raku Recipes book
unit module Raku::Recipes;
# ...

#| Parses measure to return an array with components
sub parse-measure ( $description ) is export { ... }
```

117

This can be accessed with the following:

```
use Raku::Recipes;
say Raku::Recipes.WHY;
say &parse-measure.HOW;
say &parse-measure.WHY;
```

This will print the following:

```
Utility functions for the Raku Recipes book
Perl6::Metamodel::ClassHOW.new
Parses measure to return an array with components
```

Using the ampersand in front of a routine name describes the container itself, and using it, you can either access its HOW (although, as shown, it holds only private variables) or its WHY, the metadata with the routine documentation. This object, however, allows a bit of introspection into its contents. You can find out, for instance, what kind of object it is:

```
say &parse-measure.HOW.name(&parse-measure);
say &parse-measure.^name;
```

These two sentences print exactly the same—"Sub". In fact, it's the same code. The second version has that funny caret in front of the method name and eliminates the reiteration of the object name. It's simply syntactic sugar for the first part. In short, a caret in front of a method name calls the HOW method by that name using as an argument the object to its left.

This is kind of a roundabout introduction to the next sentence in our first example:

```
say Raku::Recipes::Classy.^lookup('filter-ingredients').WHY;
```

You already understand that syntax. We are calling the lookup method of the HOW class with the name of the class, and the name of a method we want to look up. We need to do this because there's no easy syntax to refer to the name of a method in a class, or for that matter, to an object. First, there's the ambiguity: If we slap & in front, what do we really mean? With this somewhat verbose syntax, we obtain a reference to the method object for that specific class, on which we can then call WHY or anything else:

This additional code:

```
say Raku::Recipes::Classy.^lookup('filter-ingredients').^name;
say Raku::Recipes::Classy.new.^lookup('filter-ingredients').HOW;
```

Will return the following:

```
Method
Perl6::Metamodel::ClassHOW.new
```

What we have is a `Method`, and the `HOW` it works with is the `metamodel` for classes, the same as the last example.

Note   You might wonder why subs and methods share the same HOW, which is the one for classes, `ClassHOW`. This is because subs and methods are classes, simply put. There's a finite amount of HOWs in the Raku core, but that's outside the point of this chapter.

You might have noticed (and if you haven't, the reviewer for this chapter probably has) that we have made no reference to the declarator blocks of `multi` modules. It's because we needed some information on how the HOW works to get to it. But we have that information now, so let's dive in. What happens if we look up the name of a `multi`-method?

```
say Raku::Recipes::Classy.new.^lookup('optimal-ingredients').raku;
```

This returns:

```
proto method optimal-ingredients (::T : |) {*}
```

This is the prototype for all three methods that we declared under that name. `lookup` will only return the first method under the name it's been called with. We haven't actually declared this method; trying to access its WHY will return an empty string. How can we add documentation online for it? Just document the `proto`:

```
#| Uses the knapsack algorithms to compute the ingredients that maximize
protein content.
proto method optimal-ingredients (Int,$) {*}
```

And then use the same mechanism as with any other method to print it:

```
say Raku::Recipes::Classy.new.^lookup('optimal-ingredients').WHY;
```

This will print the content of the previous block.

What happens with the rest of the delimiter blocks in the different `multi`s? Can we erase them? Should we? No, because *documentation is good*. And also, keep reading.

Using the delimiter blocks from a program is not the only way to check out documentation. You wouldn't go to all that trouble if you had to go to additional trouble to actually check what's in there. Documentation is important, and it's an integral part of the code, which is why it can be shown directly from the command line:

```
raku --doc=Text lib/Raku/Recipes.pm6
```

This will show the following:

```
module Raku::Recipes
Utility functions for the Raku Recipes book

sub parse-measure(
        $description,
)
Parses measure to return an array with components
```

Let's break this down a bit. We are calling Raku from the command line by using-doc=Text as an argument and the name of the module whose documentation we need to print. This flag, `--doc`, is a clever one: it checks for the existence of a module called Pod::To::*XXX*, where *XXX* is the argument passed to it, in this case Text. It then uses a specific function to pass the module through. That function extracts all the *active* documentation and prints it in the way shown: documented unit and documentation in the next line. In this module, the module itself is documented, as well as the `parse-measure` sub. The name as well as the *signature* (how it's called) is shown, followed by the text of the declarator block. That's a fast and dependency-free way to document code and show the documentation.

But the fact that we call Raku indicates that we are actually compiling the text, only instead of running it, we're rendering it through the indicated filter. Compiling is compiling, and if you need to render to text something with an external, dependent module, you will have to write something like this:

```
raku --doc=Text -Ilib lib/Raku/Recipes/Classy.pm6
```

The additional flag, `-Ilib`, will tell Raku where to look for the modules Raku::Recipes::Classy uses, namely the directory `lib`. The nice thing about Pod::To::Text is that it does not care about the intricacies of getting the declarator block for `multi`s: It will render every single instance of the `multi` together with its signature.

Documentation need not be reduced to a single line, especially not a single *long* line, which will make it difficult for most editors to handle. There's ways to include several lines, even several pieces of documentation per method. We'll try that in the Raku::Recipes::Roly class:

```
# ... (some more code above and below suppressed for brevity) ...
#|[
Creates a new calorie table, reading it from the directory indicated,
the current directory by default. The file will be in a subdirectory data,
and will be called calories.csv
]
method new( $dir = "." ) { ... }
#| Basic getter for products
method products () { return @!products };
#= → Returns an array with the existing products.
```

For the first comment, we use multiline comments. These can use any type of braces as long as they are paired. In this case, we use square braces, but curly braces or parentheses can also be used, as long as they are paired. In the second case, we used the syntax for *footer* comments; these are attached to the routine they follow in the same way #| leads it. When rendering the documentation for this block, they will follow one another, this way:

```
method new(
        $dir = ".",
)
```

This creates a new calories table, reading it from the indicated directory, which is the current directory by default. The file will be in a subdirectory data, and will be called calories.csv:

```
method products()
Basic getter for products
→ Returns an array with the existing products.
```

But we can do it better, by adding whole blocks of formatted documentation to the module. What we have seen so far is a per-sub method and package documentation, but we can't document class attributes or multis. We need a way to document the whole module. The solution is POD6, which is a language, or actually what the Raku world calls a *slang* or a *braid*. It's a mini-language within a bigger one (Raku) used to write documentation. We'll add this to the top of Raku::Recipes::Roly that uses it.

```
=begin pod

=head1 NAME

Raku::Recipes::Roly - Example of a Role, which includes also utility
functions for Raku Recipes book (by Apress)
=head1 SYNOPSIS

=begin code
use Raku::Recipes::Roly;

my $rrr = Raku::Recipes::Roly.new; # "Puns" role with the default data dir

say $rrr.calories-table; # Prints the loaded calorie table
say $rrr.products;       # Prints the products that form the set of
ingredients
=end code

=head1 DESCRIPTION
```

This is a simple data-loading role that can be combined into classes that will deal with tables of ingredients, every one with tabular data.

```
=head1 CAVEATS

The file needs to be called C<calories.csv> and be placed in a C<data/>
subdirectory.

=end pod

#| Basic file-loading role
unit role Raku::Recipes::Roly:ver<0.0.2>;
```

While we were at that, we've also changed that line above, which now includes a version. Raku allows versioning of distributions (which include several packages) and packages (such as this role). That makes it easy to have several versions of the module living at the same time, but from our point of view, it's simply metadata that helps us (and the users) know which version of the functionality we're dealing with.

The Pod6 header is on top of that, and it starts with =begin pod and ends with =end pod.

Note   When you start to use more advanced syntax such as this, you definitely have to use the Comma IDE. So far, normal syntax is relatively well covered by Raku modes (or, as some are still called, Perl 6 modes) in normal editors. But when you start to mix these slangs, it's better to use the specific IDE for this.

POD6 blocks (which might have changed its name by the time you read this, since it's still tinged with the number 6) use that syntax to mark the beginning and end. There might be several POD blocks in a document; in this case there's only one.

Within a pod block, =begin and =end will still mark the limits of different types of blocks. For instance, the block of code we use to illustrate several examples.

Other markup will use = when it covers a whole line: =head1 for headers, for instance. Additionally, word- or sentence-level markup will use a letter and angular braces, such as the code markup we've added in C<calories.csv>.

Note   The full syntax can be consulted in books such as *Perl 6 Quick Syntax Reference*, and of course the documentation at https://docs.raku.org.

In this POD block, we added the usual sections that describe a package: name, SYNOPSIS on how it's going to be used, DESCRIPTION, and so on. Instead of adding per-method sections, we reuse the *smart comments* we had added before.

Note   The fact that these sections are written in all caps shows the Perl legacy, where the original documentation markup, called POD, used that convention.

You can again use raku -doc=Text on the module; it will now render in text the POD blocks, followed by the definition blocks attached to all the different role elements.

With this, you have covered all the documentation needed in your packages. Always use documentation in all your packages and test that everything is documented. And talking about tests, we'll see how to test modules in the next recipe.

Recipe 7-3. Test Your Module
Problem

You need to check that the code of a module, class, or role works as expected.

Solution

Raku includes an assertion module, called `Test`, which can be used to write assertions about results of functions, as well as additional functions to plan and manage tests. Scripts that use this module can be run directly or processed using the distribution manager, `zef`.

How It Works

The `Test` module, which is included with Raku, features a series of functions with the same structure: They get one or more arguments and test expected output against obtained output. The last argument is a message that describes the test itself and helps the developer understand what failed and where. Here's the test for `Raku::Recipes::Roly`.

```
use Test; # -*- mode: perl6 -*-

use Raku::Recipes::Roly;

my $rr = Raku::Recipes::Roly.new( "." );

my @products = $rr.products;
my %calories-table = $rr.calories-table;

subtest {
    is( %calories-table{@products[0]}<Dairy>, True|False, "Values
    processed" );
    cmp-ok( @products.elems, ">", 1, "Many elements in the table" );
}, "Products";
```

```
subtest {
    ok( %calories-table<Rice>, "Rice is there" );
    is( %calories-table<Rice><parsed-measures>[1], "g", "Measure for rice
    is OK" );
}, "Calories table";

done-testing;
```

Additionally and while we're writing the module, we could create a test that would only check if it can be loaded correctly, that is, if it's syntactically correct:

```
use-ok("Raku::Recipes::Roly");
```

We will skip that and go directly to check the functions of the role. It has three of them—new, `calories-table`, and `products`.

All tests include a setup phase; during it, we create the objects we are going to test or need for testing. In this case, we instantiate (via punning) an object of that role, and then instantiate two variables which are the result of calling the two other methods we will be testing. All three methods are then called, but is the result correct?

We divide the four tests in two different subtests: one for products, the other for `calorie-table`. Subtests fail if one of the tests within them fails; this is just a convenient way of expressing that a block of functionality is not complete until all the tests in that block are green. Subtests use a block of code and a message describing the block.

We use three different assertions. The ok assertion is the simplest: if the object tested is truish, it will pass; it will fail if it's falseish or undefined. There's an equivalent, but contrary, test, called `nok`. The next one, `is`, uses the eq operator to compare the expected with result. The other one used, `cmp-ok`, is also a comparison, but it takes three arguments, the middle one being the operator we will be using for comparison, which we will pass as a string.

All tests can be run with `zef test.` (the last one being the current directory); `zef` is smart and it loads all modules found in the `lib/` path in order to test all the tests under the `t/` directory. We can also run this in an independent way, but we will need to specify the path where the tested module resides:

```
raku -Ilib t/01-recipes-role.t
```

Test scripts conventionally take the `.t` extension, and they reside in the `t/` directory. This will print the following for the previous code (and the role defined at the beginning of the chapter):

```
    ok 1 - Values processed
    ok 2 - Many elements in the table
    1..2
ok 1 - Products
    ok 1 - Rice is there
    ok 2 - Measure for rice is OK
    1..2
ok 2 - Calories table
1..2
```

Indicating that the two subtests are correct, as is every test within them.

As indicated, documentation is important, so we would need at least to test, for every class, that there's a POD block describing what it does. However, documentation is not exported in any variable. If we want to check POD blocks, we have to export them explicitly. Let's do that for the `Raku::Recipes::Roly` class this way:

```
our $pod is export = $=pod[0];
```

This is a module or package-scoped variable, declared immediately before the declaration of the role.

Note   Roles can't have `our`-scoped variables. In the case of a class, we could include it inside the class, as a class variable with class scope, and use it without scoping via its fully qualified name.

Once we import the role, that variable is inserted into our namespace, so this would test the existence of this documentation:

```
subtest "There's documentation for the module", {
    ok $pod, "There's documentation";
};
```

In the same fashion, we can test the presence of declarator blocks, in this case for `Raku::Recipes::Classy`:

```
subtest "Test declarator blocks", {
    ok Raku::Recipes::Classy.WHY, "Class described";
    ok Raku::Recipes::Classy.new.^lookup('filter-ingredients').WHY,
    "Declarator blocks retrieved";
}
```

We access the declarator blocks in the way described in the previous recipe about documentation. That way we make sure that descriptions are maintained through implementation drifts. Besides existence, we could also check that certain words are in there, using other assertions, but the basic mechanism for testing documentation is there. Documentation is understood as code, and untested code is broken. Ergo, untested documentation is also broken. Let's then test it all across our distributions.

Recipe 7-4. Release Your Module as an Open Source Module

Problem

You solved an original problem, or a known problem in a new way, and want to distribute your solution with an open source license, so that it is readily available to everyone, including your own applications in different environments.

Solution

The Raku ecosystem has two ways of publishing modules to make them available for download via `zef`—one is called CPAN, and it stores versioned `tar` files of your distribution; the other is called `p6c` and it downloads code directly from GitHub, GitLab, or BitBucket repositories. We will focus on this second one.

Besides deciding on where to release, there's additional metadata we need to include, which is included in the `META6.json` file we have already seen. We'll provide a checklist of all the fields that need to be there in order to publish a distribution.

How It Works

The first thing you need to decide is the license you are going to use for the module. Open source is, in general, free, so you need to choose a license that clarifies what the users are allowed to do with the code. All licenses have the provision that the original author is going to be acknowledged, but some are more restrictive than others regarding what users can do with the code.

Traditionally, the Perl world that includes Raku has used the so-called Artistic License; version 2.0 was created for Raku. You'll need to go a bit into legalese to understand the finer print of the differences between this one and, say, the MIT license. Suffice it to say that it's a rather permissive license, and that your authorship is going to be respected no matter what.

You probably chose a license when you created the repo, so you can stick with that one. Changing it will only involve changing the extensive text of the license in a file called LICENSE; a note about the license should be conveniently included in the POD blocks of every module. You'll need to put it as metadata in the META6.json file as well.

This is the example file that's used for the distribution described in this chapter:

```
{
    "authors" : [
    "JJ Merelo"
    ],
    "auth": "github:JJ",
    "description" : "Raku Recipes, modules and examples",
    "license" : "Artistic-2.0",
    "name" : "Raku::Recipes",
    "perl" : "6.d",
    "provides" : {
        "Raku::Recipes": "lib/Raku/Recipes.pm6",
        "Raku::Recipes::Classy": "lib/Raku/Recipes/Classy.pm6",
        "Raku::Recipes::Roly": "lib/Raku/Recipes/Roly.pm6"
    },
    "tags" : [
    "book","Apress", "Raku", "examples", "recipes", "cooking"
    ],
```

```
"depends" : [ "Text::Markdown",
                "Text::CSV" ],
"source-url" : "https://github.com/JJ/raku-recipes-apress",
"version" : "0.0.2"
}
```

Not all of them are required, but most of them are convenient when released and read by the `modules.raku.org` site. It lists all available modules (around 3,000 at the time of writing this):

- `authors`: An array of all the people who have participated in the development of the module; you can use real names or screen names.

- The `auth` field is slightly different: You list the screen name, that is, the name used in the repository or the name used in CPAN. This will make the module description link the profile of the person (or collective) who developed it. Distributions are referred to by name *and* author; you can fork or simply start from scratch distributions with the same name if they happen to do exactly the same thing. `Zef` will be able to tell them apart, and you will be able to use them locally using the corresponding syntax.

- The `description` field is a short description of what the module does. Try to optimize this description so it's easy to search.

- The `license` field will include a standardized name of the license you are using. The standard that is being followed is called SPDX or Software Package Data Exchange Standard, described in `https://spdx.dev`. This de facto standard provides a series of strings to describe all available open source licenses; `Artistic-2.0` would be the SPDX name for the license we've talked about here.

- The `name` field will have the name of the distribution that includes all modules. In this case, `Raku::Recipes` (which is also the name of the module). If there's only one module, the name of the module will go here; if there are several, it's convenient that there's at least a module with the same name as the distribution. This name will be the *namespace* you will be using for your classes; other, different-level classes (higher or lower) will use that namespace. In this case, we have `Raku::Recipes::Classy` and `Raku::Recipes::Roly`. This is conventionally preferred to making them siblings, as in `Raku::Recipes-Classy`, for instance, but you have absolute freedom to name and place your modules wherever you want within your folder hierarchy. In the same fashion, it's not convenient to have different namespaces within a single distribution. If one of the classes naturally seems to need another namespace, it's probably reasonable to create a different distribution with it. The only exception are the exceptions. Exceptions for `Raku::Recipes` would be using the namespace `X::Raku::Recipes` (but more on this later, when we deal with exceptions in the upcoming chapters).

- The (probably becoming obsolete soon) `perl` or `raku` key describes the minimum version that the distribution will work with. For the time being, only 6.c (first production version) and 6.d (current version as of 2020) are available. Future versions will use a different letter; also, this field will take only major versions. Monthly releases will have to be dealt with at a different level. Since the name change in October 2019, `raku` is the preferred key.

- The `provides` key needs a hash that uses the name of the modules included in the distribution as a key, and as values where they can be found in the filesystem using relative paths. Conventionally, there will be a more or less direct mapping from names to folders, if the convention for filenames and directory layout has been followed. The fact that this hash is provided indicates that there is more than one way to do it, but still.

- `Tags` is a free-form array to make the distribution easier to find. Use as many tags as you want.

- The next key, `depends`, is an array with upstream dependencies. These distributions will need to be installed for the current one to run; these are the ones we are using in our module.

- The `source-url` indicates the URL of the website where this distribution can be found. This will be the URL or URI used to download it, so make sure it can be found there. It can be an URL with a tarfile instead of the GitHub repo URL; that way, you can publish several versions of the distribution simultaneously.

- The `version` expressed in the next key is quite important. `Zef` will consider versions when deciding about installing a distribution. If the version available on the ecosystem (or CPAN) is higher than the one installed locally, it will be downloaded and installed. Otherwise, it will refuse to install, even if the code has evolved without this specific metadata changing. This is why these versions should be changed every time there's a change of any nature, from adding or obsoleting functionality to fixing bugs. This is true even if an internal refactoring has happened without any outward API change. This version string is, again, free form, but most follow the semantic versioning convention: the first number will be the *major*, the second the *minor*, and the third the *patchlevel*. Increase them to reflect changes of different natures.

The `META6.json` file is the mandatory step to get your module released. Tests, as shown in this chapter, are mandatory too. You should test all the features of your module, including the documentation if needed. If the standard `Test` module is not enough, you can try to use other modules that will test from output to connections, through the documentation itself (without needing to resort to exporting the $=pod variable).

Additionally, consider these suggestions, although they are not mandatory:

- The `README.md` file should contain some documentation, including installation instructions (in addition to using `zef`, if needed; for instance, additional dependencies) and anything else you want to add.

- It's convenient to add a `CONTRIBUTING.md` file that helps others report on bugs and patches and create a pull request correctly.

- Set up some automatic testing when pushes and pull requests are done. This will save you the trouble of checking every contribution by hand (or finding errors after you've released). There are many ways to do this, from GitHub Actions through GitLab pipelines to Travis or CircleCI. If you want to test everything in Windows, AppVeyorCI provides good facilities to do so. Your code is going to be used in multiple operating systems, so you should test it across all platforms.

Once that is done, you need to tell the world that this distribution is ready to be downloaded. Let's leave aside for the time being the CPAN option and focus on the other. Since the source code will be downloaded directly from the repository, no additional packaging is needed.

Note   You can, and should, use Git tag to tag the last commit in that release with the same version as the one in the `META6.json` file. That way, ecosystem releases and GitHub (or other) releases will go hand in hand.

Two steps, however, are necessary:

1. Pick up the URL of the `META6.json` file by clicking on it in GitHub or GitLab and then clicking on the Raw button. This will show the content of the file onscreen. Go to the address bar and copy it to the clipboard. This URL will look like this: `https://raw.githubusercontent.com/JJ/p6-math-constants/master/META6.json`.

2. Go to `https://github.com/Raku/ecosystem` and edit the file called `META.list`, on its home directory. Add that line wherever you think it should go. The last line is as good an option as any. This will create a fork of the repository, from which you will then create a pull request, writing something like `Add My::Distro to the ecosystem`. It does not really matter, but making it descriptive will help maintainers (like myself) assess that you know what you're doing. The `META6.json` file will undergo some tests; if it fails for some reason (some JSON syntax error, or a non-compliant SPDX description of your license), you'll need to go back to the repo you're submitting and fix it. Then you'll need to change the file again in the pull request to relaunch the tests. Simply adding whitespace will take care of that.

Normally, it'll be ready to accept the request quickly, but it will take up to a couple of hours for zef to catch up. When it's done, anyone will be able to write zef install Your::Published::Module and use it in their own programs.

Recipe 7-5. Use Multiple Dispatch To Speed Up Applications
Problem

Depending on the type of arguments a routine gets, or even its value, it might be convenient to use different code. Doing so can prevent slow ifs, allow for type-safe code dispatch, and make optimization of the resulting application easier.

Solution

Use multiple dispatch via multi in your class/role methods or module routines.

How It Works

Multiple dispatch is a mechanism by which languages run different code depending on how that code is called. In Raku, different routine calling conventions are called *signatures* and you can declare different versions of the same function that will be invoked depending on the signature.

Let's suppose we want to compute the calories in a certain quantity of food. We can have a string in the form "100g rice", or separate the quantity and product, as in "100g" and "rice", or have three separate pieces of information. We can process that in a single subroutine, this way:

```
sub gimme-calories( $first, $second?, $third?) {
    my ($product, $unit, $how-much);
    if $third {
        ($how-much, $unit, $product) = ($first, $second, $third);
    } elsif $second {
        ($how-much, $unit, $product) = (|parse-measure( $first ), $second);
    } else {
```

```
        my @parts = $first.split: /\s+/;
        ($how-much, $unit, $product) = (|parse-measure( @parts[0] ),
        @parts[1])
    }

    if %calories-table{$product}<parsed-measures>[1] eq $unit {
        return %calories-table{$product}<Calories> * $how-much
                / %calories-table{$product}<parsed-measures>[0];
    } else {
        fail;
    }
}
```

The second and third positionals are optional, indicated by a ? suffix (as in $second?), and we use them as guards to check the information we're given. What we do is to try to extract the same information from all three possibilities. We use variable destructuring to assign three variables to three others at the same time. In order to *flatten* an array into another, we use the *slip* operator, |. At the end of the if, we have the values in three different variables, from which we compute calories. There are decisions in the middle that take some time.

The many ifs and elses make this code a bit convoluted, and the signature of the method is not too informative, with non-informative names that can take different types. There's no type checking of values. It works, but we can do better. Let's try to use multis:

```
multi sub how-many-calories( Str $description ){
    return samewith( | $description.split(/\s+/))
}

multi sub how-many-calories( Str $quantities, Str $product ) {
    my ($how-much, $unit ) = parse-measure( $quantities );
    return samewith( $how-much, $unit, $product )
}

multi sub how-many-calories( Int $how-much, Str $unit, Str $product ) {
    if %calories-table{$product}<parsed-measures>[1] eq $unit {
        return %calories-table{$product}<Calories> * $how-much
                / %calories-table{$product}<parsed-measures>[0];
    } else {
```

```
        die "Die $how-much $unit $product";
    }
}
```

There's one multi for every combination. These are actually type safe, and they use a kind of cascade, calling each other to the lowest part of the cascade, the one that has a signature, an Int, and two strings. Among other things, we can use default values and use stricter constraints here, but it's the multiple dispatch that's interesting. We use the same with function. It calls the multi with the same name, but the signature we give it makes it faster than calling it by its name, since it only needs to check the rest of the functions with the same signature.

The code path is clear: every signature corresponds to an entry point, and they're chosen in an straightforward way. From a software design point of view, this one's a winner. But in the speed department, how fast is it?

Let's use this little benchmark to check out the speed:

```
my @measures = 1000.rand.Int xx 10000;
my @food = <Rice Tuna Lentils>;
my @final = @measures.map( {$_ ~ "g "}) X~ @food;

my $start = now;

for @final {
    my $calories = how-many-calories($_) ;
}
say now - $start;

start = now;
for @final {
    my $calories = gimme-calories($_);
}
say now - $start;

$start = now;
for @measures X @food {
    my $calories = how-many-calories( @_[0].Int, "g", @_[1]) ;
}
say now - $start;
```

```
$start = now;
for @measures X @food {
    my $calories = gimme-calories( @_[0].Int, "g", @_[1] );
}
say now - $start;
```

It calls either the single-string form or the split one, and does so 30,000 times. This returns, on my system, something like this:

```
3.0829807
3.13236452
0.9351156
1.1699724
```

So the string form is around one percent faster than the `multi`. That's not anything to write home about, but the three-element form is around 20 percent faster. All in all, the difference in speed will obviously depend on the actual combination of calls your code makes, but if you mix in the better design with the difference in speed, using `multis` is clearly a good idea.

However, `multi` design need not be always faster in and by itself. For instance, we need to parse the quantity and unit we are using to compute the number of calories for every one of our ingredients. These are expressed in two (or three) different ways: one of them has the quantity in front, others are simply descriptions, like "unit". We were using this code to parse it:

```
sub parse-measure ( $description ) is export {
    $description ~~ / $<unit>=(<:N>*) \s* $<measure>=(\S+) /;
    my $unit = +$<unit>??+$<unit>!!1;
    return ($unit,~$<measure>);
}
```

The regular expression becomes a bit complicated, because it has to take into account all the different cases. We also have to find out where there's a quantity (which we assign to the $<unit> variable) in front or not and assign a default value in that case. But there are clearly two different options, and we can speed processing up dealing with them in different `multi` routines. Like this:

```
multi sub unit-measure ( $description where /^<:N>/ ) is export {
    $description ~~ / $<unit>=(<:N>+) \s* $<measure>=(\S+) /;
    return ( +$<unit>, ~$<measure> );
}

multi sub unit-measure ( $description where /^<alpha>/ ) is export {
    $description ~~ / $<measure>=(\S+) /;
    return ( 1, ~$<measure> );
}
```

We need to declare them as `multi` to clarify that they are two versions of the same routine, different in the way they are invoked. In this case, by the content of the variable they are invoked with. `Multi`s need to differ in the signature, and the signatures should be disjoints. If they are not, the first one that covers the arguments it's been called with will be triggered.

In this case, they are mutually exclusive: Either the string starts with a number or it starts with a letter. But when it's a number we know how it works: there will be at least a number-like character, and then whitespace (or not), followed by a word. This will cover `"100g"` and `"⅓ liter"`. On the other hand, if it starts with a letter, it will simply be a word, so the regex is greatly simplified and we just assign it to a variable, which we then stringify by prepending `~`. Also, defaults are easier to create and describe, and we avoid the `if`s, which is exactly what we were looking for.

Whenever your code follows the antipattern of checking for type or values of the arguments, and then calling different blocks of code using them, that's calling for multiple dispatch, which creates cleaner code by shortening the amount of lines in every routine.

Although a priori it should, does that really speed things up? Let's use this script to find out:

```
use Raku::Recipes;

my @measures = 1000.rand xx 10000;

my @units = <g l liter tablespoon>;

my @strings = @measures X~ @units;
my @things = <Unit Clove Pinch>.pick xx 10000;

@strings.append: @things;
```

```
my $time = now;

for @strings {
    my $result = parse-measure( $_ );
}

say Duration.new(now - $time);

$time = now;

for @strings {
    my $result = unit-measure( $_ );
}

say Duration.new(now - $time);
```

After generating a series of strings of the two available types, they are examined using the two routines available. On my system, the non-multi version takes around one second, and the multi version takes around three seconds, give or take.

What gives? Well, the fact is that the multi is using two regular expressions, while the non-multi is using a single one. Although a priori dispatching itself would be faster, you should always make sure that what you're dispatching on actually makes it faster. So some refactoring is needed.

This is a lesson about always doing what we did in the previous recipe: testing. There's still the advantage of better architecture and cleaner code, but, wow, three times as slow can be a big deal. As a matter of fact, they don't work exactly the same, because parse-measure does not take into account that units can be Unicode numbers. We can also refactor the multis so that they use a single regular expression this way:

```
multi sub unit-measure ( $description
                         where  /$<unit>=(<:N>+) \s* $<measure>=(\S+) /) is
                         export {
    my $value = +val( ~$<unit>  ) // unival( ~$<unit> );
    return ( $value, ~$<measure> );
}

multi sub unit-measure ( $description ) is export {
    return ( 1, $description.trim );
}
```

But this will only decrease the difference a tiny bit, with the `multis` taking around 2.5 seconds and the non-`multi` in the ballpark of 1.1 second.

Clearly, this is not a difference you will want in a critical part of your software; speed is essential in many places. However, instead of using signatures to differentiate `multis`, we're using constraints in this example. By themselves, constrains add some overhead, but there might be additional overhead involved.

The bottom line is, always test. Architectural decisions are not always matched by speed increases, so depending on how critical a specific code path is, you might want to go for single-schedule instead of multiple-schedule.

CHAPTER 8

Dealing with Errors

Errors get a bad rep just because they make it look like something is wrong, and it's your fault. It shouldn't be that way. Errors are normally misunderstandings between the application and whoever is interacting with it—the programmer or the final user. It's then our responsibility to determine what the misunderstanding is, and up to a point, figure out what the application was expecting. Designing *errors* (we will call them errors, for the sake of brevity, when we mean misunderstandings) and the messages they deliver is a big part of getting an application or module just right. In this chapter, we focus precisely on this.

Recipe 8-1. Design an Exception Hierarchy
Problem

A defensive approach to code design requires graceful and type-safe handling of exceptions. Every piece of code must be accompanied by its own set of exceptions, as the ones provided by the system are not enough to fully explain why the unexpected event happened.

Solution

Together with the class hierarchy you designed, Raku applications conventionally add an X:: set of classes and deliver precise and meaningful messages. These error classes subclass the Exception class, but they can be customized, at least by message. Use them along conventional exceptions in your module or library.

© J.J. Merelo 2020
J.J. Merelo, *Raku Recipes*, https://doi.org/10.1007/978-1-4842-6258-0_8

How It Works

We already used a set of exceptions in Chapter 6 to describe things that could go wrong with the configuration file. We didn't show the code, however, so here it is:

```
use Raku::Recipes::Roly;

class X::Raku::Recipes::WrongType:api<1> is Exception {
    has $.desired-type is required;
    has $.product;
    has $.actual-types;

    submethod BUILD(:$!desired-type,
                    :$!product = "Object") {
        my $rrr = Raku::Recipes::Roly.new();
        if $!product ne "Object" {
            $!actual-types = $rrr.calories-table{$!product}<types>
        }
    }

    multi method message( X::Raku::Recipes::WrongType $x where $x.product eq
            "Object": ) {
        return "The product if not of the required type $!desired-type";
    }

    multi method message() {
                    return "$!product is not of the required type
                    «$!desired-type», only
types $!actual-types";
    }
}

class X::Raku::Recipes::WrongUnit:api<1> is Exception {
    has $!desired-unit is required;
    has $!unit;
```

```
submethod BUILD(:$!desired-unit,
                :$!unit) {}
method message() {
    return "$!unit does not match the unit type, should be $!desired-
    unit";
}
}
```

These two exceptions are in the same file: X/Raku/Recipes.pm6. They differ in the kind of message they convey, and they have been named so that they convey that message clearly. WrongType clearly says this is not the kind of thing the code was expecting and WrongUnit indicates that the unit of measure was not correct. All that happens in the context of a recipe, so it's clear what we're talking about. If we throw an exception, for instance the first one, using the default value, which is Object, as follows:

```
The product is not of the required type Main  in block <unit> at
/home/jmerelo/progs/perl6/raku-recipes-apress/t/00-exceptions.t line 9
```

Then the message indicates where the exception was thrown. <unit> indicates that it was a block declared on line 9 of the test file. We might have no more information about the desired object in that context, which is why we use a default value.

However, we use multiple schedules to throw different messages depending on what we have. If we know the product, we can find out which types the product has. In that case, the exception will look something like this:

```
Apple is not of the required type «Main», only types Dessert Vegan
```

These types are obtained from the Raku::Recipes::Roly object that we create during the exception BUILD phase and are also available as attributes of the object.

There's an interesting aspect to the multiple dispatch we are using: it's done depending on the value of the object itself. One of the interesting things about Raku signatures is that you can use the invocant as part of that signature, which, among other things, allows you to constrain the value and dispatch according to it.

Other than that, the two exceptions have the same kind of structure: they subclass Exception, the Raku-provided base class for this kind of thing. You can just go along with it and provide nothing else, letting the type of the exception sink in by force of its name. You also could override the message method to provide a specific message. And you could provide attributes that will allow some kind of personalization of the message.

Okay, it's the wrong type, but what would be the right type? For WrongType, $!desired-type will provide that information, and it will also indicate the type of the provided product. In general, any type of exception should be clear about the context and provide a way out for the programmer as well as the user, who might need to inform the development team what's wrong or try to overcome the error with a different input or sequence of actions.

We also note which product is missing and which part is required. In every case, those attributes are required so that the objects can't be instantiated unless the information is provided. In all three cases, the BUILD submethod provides a way to bind the argument provided in new to the attribute. In Chapter 5, we learned how to use them:

```
# Check out the whole program in Chapter 5
when %conf{$part} ∉ $recipes.products {
    X::Raku::Recipes::ProductMissing.new( :product(%conf{$part}) ).throw()
}
```

However, we can do better than this. In most cases, we are dealing with something that is missing. We only have to specify the type of thing that's missing and the name of the thing that's missing. We can spin off a hierarchy to deal with this or a composable one. Let's do that next. First, the role:

```
role X::Raku::Recipes::Missing:api<1> is Exception {
    has $!part is required;
    has $!name is required;

    submethod BUILD( :$!part, :$!name ) {}

    method message() {
        return "the $!part $!name seems to be missing. Please provide it";
    }

      method gist(X::Raku::Recipes::Missing:D: ) {
        self.message()
      }
}
```

First, note that we are specifying the api attribute when declaring the class. Raku allows for class and module versioning (and also authoring). This piece of metadata can mainly be used to issue a warning when you're trying to use a class that has been superseded. An error that states `"This class does not have the correct API version"` is much more informative than `"Class not found"`. Since we have refactored this module, we have given it an API number to clarify that we will be working with this API version. No API version is equivalent to API version 0, also.

All these exceptions are user-facing, not really addressed to other programmers. That is why we have overloaded `gist`; the main effect of this is to avoid printing information about the line where the exception was thrown. The `gist` method is the one called when you call `say` on an object, so it's the one called when the exception is thrown and printed.

Whenever you want to reuse attributes, it's better to use roles instead of classes. That is, composing as opposed to subclassing (or inheriting), since class attributes in Raku are private. Subclasses will not have access to the class attributes unless you declare them public, and you might not want to do that. Composed attributes, however, are still private, and you can still access them. These attributes will both be mandatory. And when there are no more specific classes, we can just throw this role as an exception by punning it. However, the classes above can be reformulated by composing this role like this:

```
class X::Raku::Recipes::Missing::Part does X::Raku::Recipes::Missing {
    submethod BUILD( :$!part="part of meal", :$!name) {}
}

class X::Raku::Recipes::Missing::File does X::Raku::Recipes::Missing {
    submethod BUILD($!part = "file", :$!name){}
}

class X::Raku::Recipes::Missing::Product does X::Raku::Recipes::Missing {
    submethod BUILD($!part = "product", :$!name){}
}
```

Creating an expressive base role really simplifies the creation of the rest of the hierarchy. New classes will compose the base class, but all they'll have to do is assign a default value to an attribute, in this case `$!part`. The `message()` method will be reused from the base role, and we will be able to use them directly in our programs.

Previously, we were using only exceptions in applications. Since we added a new exception that complains about missing files, we can rewrite a part of our `Raku::Recipes::Roly` role to include it.

```
method new( $dir = "." ) {
    my $calorie-table-file = %*ENV<CALORIE_TABLE_FILE>
        // "$dir/data/calories.csv";
    X::Raku::Recipes::Missing::File.new(:name($calorie-table-file)).throw
            unless $calorie-table-file.IO.e;
# Rest remains the same as in the previous chapters
}
```

Previously, the next statement would just fail if it couldn't find the file. Now we check that it exists, and if it does not, it will throw an exception saying that it's not been able to find it.

Adding an exception class hierarchy adds value to your application: it allows the programmer to zero in immediately on exceptions and selectively catch and deal with them. It allows them to ignore non-critical exceptions (or simply issue a warning) and provide meaningful messages, in the context of the application, for those that cannot be ignored, especially whenever the default message is not understandable in the context. We'll see how to do that next.

Recipe 8-2. Deliver Meaningful Error Messages to the User

Problem

Developers using your code should be able to understand what has happened if something fails or does not work as expected, due to the descriptive exception or error that's thrown.

Solution

Provide a comprehensive exception hierarchy, use backtraces of code to further help the users, and clearly express in the messages what you were expecting in your code and what you got instead.

How It Works

If unchecked, an exception will blow up your program. And it will do so in a context that might not be entirely clear to the user, because it need not have any information about where the issue is. However, exceptions carry a lot of information and you can leverage them to provide as much information as possible to the final user—the person who is running the program or the client of our class who's had her program bail out in front of her. We will see in the next section how to catch these errors. This recipe will be rather pragmatic and will provide a series of ingredients that will make the exceptions you provide take a bit of bad reputation off the shoulders of the misnamed errors.

Even if you have not designed a class hierarchy, you can use one of the exceptions in the standard library. There are literally hundreds of them, but they are designed mainly to cover exceptions that occur during code interpretation and execution. There are a few that you can use for your own code: X::TypeCheck (https://docs.raku.org/type/X::TypeCheck) and X::Obsolete (https://docs.raku.org/type/X::Obsolete). You might also find X::NYI, as in "not yet implemented," to be useful.

For instance, for this chapter we created a new version of the X::Raku::Recipes clases, including a new version of X::Raku::Recipes::WrongType. We can reformulate its code in this way:

```
class X::Raku::Recipes::WrongType:api<0> {

    submethod BUILD() {
        X::Obsolete.new(old => "X::Raku::Recipes::WrongType:api<0>",
                    replacement => "X::Raku::Recipes::WrongType:api<1> in
Raku::Recipes",

                    when => "using Raku::Recipes"
                    ).throw;
    }
}
```

When you try to use it, it will print the following:

```
Unsupported use of X::Raku::Recipes::WrongType:api<0>; using Raku::Recipes
please use X::Raku::Recipes::WrongType:api<1> in
Raku::Recipes
  in submethod BUILD at /home/jmerelo/progs/perl6/raku-recipes-apress/
  lib/X/Raku/Chapter5/Recipes.pm6 (X::Raku::Chapter5::Recipes) line 6
  in block <unit> at /home/jmerelo/progs/perl6/raku-recipes-apress/t/00-
  exceptions-chapter-5.t line 4
```

This message is rather informative. It puts the skinny at the front. Use the new version, with API 1, instead of this old version. Then it shows what is called the *backtrace*, that is, where everything happened. The bottom is at line 6 of the X::Raku::Chapter5::Recipes file, and we called that from line 4 of the test script. The backtrace is actually an object that you can use from the Exception base class; it contains a list of *frames*, which are objects that show the part of the stack frame the exception bubbled through. The default way of rendering an exception, done through the gist method, is to list these frames from bottom to top

We have seen how to override this behavior by eliminating the backframe completely. You can also do the exact opposite: print it more beautifully so that the information stands out. We will do that next:

```
use Raku::Recipes;
use Colorizable;

class X::Raku::Recipes::Obsolete is Exception {
    has $!old-stuff is required;
    has $!new-stuff is required;

    submethod BUILD( :$!old-stuff, :$!new-stuff){}

    method message() {
        return "You seem to be using $!old-stuff, which is deprecated.
        Please switch to $!new-stuff";
    }

    multi method gist(X::Raku::Recipes::Obsolete:D: ) {
        my @nice-bts = self.backtrace.list.grep( ! *.is-setting() );
        @nice-bts.shift;
```

```
my $output =  ("Hey! " but Colorizable).colorize: :mo(bold);
$output ~= ( self.message but Colorizable).colorize:
:mo(underline);
$output ~= "\nThis happened on ⇒\n";
for @nice-bts -> $bt {
    $output ~= (("\t» Line " ~ $bt.line()) but Colorizable).
    colorize:
            blue;
    my $subname = ($bt.subname eq "<unit>")??  "an anonymous
    routine"!!
                                $bt.subname;
    $output ~= " in " ~ ($subname but Colorizable).colorize: cyan;
}
return $output;
}

}
```

We have created our own, pimped up, version of the Obsolete exception, and we have done so by rewriting the gist method. Remember that this method is called when you want to say an object, and when an Exception is thrown, it's said aloud (unless it's caught, which we will do next). As a mnemonic, it's "the exception in a gist" (but it's defined for every object). Anyway, this new exception subclasses exception, which means it automatically gets a backtrace. There are some uninteresting parts in the exception and we get rid of them. We do so by eliminating those that are *settings*, which means basically that if there's a part of it that occurs inside system libraries, we don't want to know about that. In this case, we eliminate the part of the backtrace that happens inside the exception itself, since we are using throw from the base class.

We are using shift to eliminate the first frame. In this particular case, it's not really interesting, because what we are interested in is where you were trying to use the obsolete class. And those are the only things left.

For those, we use Colorizable, a module published in March 2020 by Luis Uceta, which is a nice way of creating colored messages. In order to colorize a string, first you have to mix in the Colorizable role, like so: ("Hey! " but Colorizable). Once that is done, you can call Colorize on the string and then give it modes (like bold or underline) and colors (which we will use later). So we print a friendly message, and then a line for every backtrace, explaining that this is where it happened. We also turn <unit> into "an anonymous routine." This is where we called it for this example. In a program, it would show the name of the routine and the line in the file where it happened. Figure 8-1 shows an example of what will be printed.

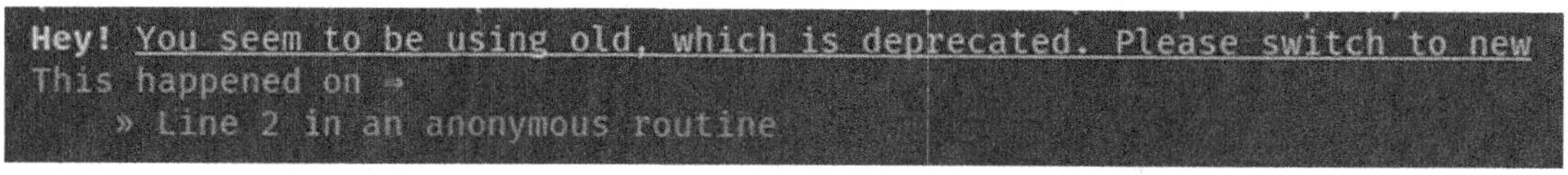

Figure 8-1. *Friendly error message that explains the backtrace and the message*

The loop lines are more verbose than they seem, but essentially what they are doing is extracting the bits of information, like $bt.line and $bt.subname, to print them in that particular way.

The main takeaway of this section, anyway, is not really technical. Designing error messages is hard, but it's your window to the public. Well-designed messages will save you on technical support in the shape of issues in your project. A well-designed exception, with only the information that will allow the user to determine what happened, where it happened, and, if possible, where to fix it, is a piece of defensive programming that will save you a lot of trouble in the future. So strive to create and deliver the best exception messages possible.

Recipe 8-3. Catch and Deal with Errors in Your Program

Problem

Errors can't simply go unchecked. You should capture them and provide a way out if possible, or simply go ahead with them.

Solution

Raku uses block-scoped `catch` statements to capture errors. Use them, along with Raku control structures, to provide solutions to exceptions that often depend on the type of exception thrown.

How It Works

Exceptions would not be as useful if there was no way to overcome them. The terminology talks about *throwing* or *raising* exceptions, so it's only fair that dealing with them is called *catching* them. Since we have class-y exceptions, the blocks that catch them will have to deal with every class in a different way.

Let's try to put this to use in a seemingly simple, but underlyingly complex, script. It generates a recipe by assigning some amount of food to the main disk and to a side dish and returns how many calories the meal has. The main and side dishes will be entered at the command line. But what if there's an error? Let's deal with it this way:

```
use Raku::Recipes::Calorie-Computer;
use X::Raku::Recipes;
use X::Raku::Recipes::Missing;

my $rrr = Raku::Recipes::Calorie-Computer.new();
my $main = @*ARGS[0] // "Chickpeas";
my $side = @*ARGS[1] // "Rice";
my $calories = $rrr.calories-for( main => $main => 200,
                                  side => $side => 250 );
say "Calories for a main dish of $main and side of $side are $calories";
CATCH {
    default {
        given .message {
            when /Main/ || /$main/ { $main = "Chickpeas" }
            when /Side/ || /$side/ { $side = "Rice" }
        }
        $calories = $rrr.calories-for( main => $main => 200,
            side => $side => 250 );
        .resume;

    }
}
```

The first thing you need to take into account is that this code extensively uses methods from Raku::Recipes::Calorie-Computer, a class that mixes in the Roly role and includes methods to compute calories from the list of ingredients. The exceptions are defined in the two modules that are used; the main method used is calories-for.

This method will take two named arguments—`main` and `side`—and everyone of them will be a `Pair` whose key is the name of the ingredient and whose value is the amount we're going to use of it, in whatever metric it's using. We set 200 grams for the main dish and 250 grams for the side, which is pretty much what I do when I cook.

The complexity of this function is not evident in this script. It will raise exceptions if the products mentioned do not exist (say you want a main dish of fishtails with a side of rice) or if you use as a main or side something that is not a main or a side, respectively (I want apple with tuna on the side). We can do several things with this (including dealing with them *before* calling that method), but why should we? It takes care of all possible exceptions already. All we need to do is to *catch* exceptions in order to deal with them.

That is why we use a `try-catch` combo, or so to say, a main serving of `try` with a `catch` on the side. The `try` blocks contain any exception that happens within them and create a scope to catch exceptions. Exceptions will probably leave some variable in a bad state, so the `CATCH` blocks, which are blocks labeled with the `CATCH` keyword in front (all caps, remember), analyze what went wrong and go about fixing it, if that's even possible. These `CATCH` blocks are outside the normal flow, and they will catch any exception happening in the same scope. This is why we set them at the end.

If some part is missing, we'll substitute it with a sensible default. Chickpeas with rice, anyone? (They're delicious with a hint of tomato, garlic, maybe a bit of onion, and of course olive oil.) The `CATCH` block is similar to a given block: it puts the exception as a topical variable, and then we can use `when`/`default` to deal with it. This last keyword is a catch-all: it will fire when everything else fails. In this case, it's the only one and it exemplifies how we would create a block of this type in the most generic case.

We need to know if a main or a side dish produced the error, to provide defaults for one or the other. The message (which will be either a `X::Raku::Recipes::WrongType` or a `X::Raku::Recipes::Missing::Product`) will contain the name of the product or the part. Why will it be that way? Because we, as promised in the previous recipe, produce meaningful errors. We will parse the error to determine how to fix it. We'll add something that hints to the value that produced the error and explain how to process it and recover from it if possible.

Once the variables have been assigned, we know that both `$main` and `$side` have a valid value (provided or default). So we again compute the calories, this time without a hitch, and call `.resume` to resume execution at the point the exception was thrown. This will produce something like the following:

```
Calories for a main dish of Tuna and side of Rice are 585
```

Hmm, tuna and rice. I wanted the side dish to be sawdust, but I'll settle for that.

We can do better, however. What if there's another unknown error? It will be contained within the try block, but since the CATCH block will not deal with it, it will have no value for $calories and nothing reasonable will be printed. Besides, you might want to provide different defaults for different kinds of errors. Or just throw up your hands in a gesture like "I can't do this."

Here it is, including only the main part of the code:

```
{
    $calories = $rrr.calories-for( main => $main => 200,
                                   side => $side => 250 );
    CATCH {
        when X::Raku::Recipes::Missing::Product {
            given .message {
                when /$main/ { $main = "Pasta" }
                when /$side/ { $side = "Potatoes" }
            }
            $calories = $rrr.calories-for( main => $main => 200,
                    side => $side => 250 );
        }
        when X::Raku::Recipes::WrongType {
            given .desired-type {
                when "Main" { $main = "Chickpeas" }
                when "Side" { $side = "Rice" }
                    }
            $calories = $rrr.calories-for( main => $main => 200,
                    side => $side => 250 );
        }
    }
}
```

Different defaults will be used if the problem is with the product (we will use pasta as the main and potatoes as the side), or with the type of the product (main or side). The CATCH block acts as a given block, and the topical variable is the exception. The when clauses will smart-match the exception, and will keep it in the topic variable. We will recharge the topic variable in the given clause as we've done before. If the exception is a different one, we don't know what to do it with, so it's probably better to just propagate it to the user, who will see the program stop (and hopefully take action).

Matching the exceptions, in the case of WrongType, is done using the desired-type attribute. Using this instead of the message is more specific, since you need to know the specific attributes of the type, but less brittle in the sense that message content might change more often than attributes (or APIs). Anyway, there are always many ways to do it.

However, the repetition of the code to compute the amount of calories is not smart. Let's try to reformulate this all over again to avoid this repetition. Showing only the CATCH block here:

```
CATCH {
    when X::Raku::Recipes::Missing::Product {
        given .message {
            when /$main/ { $main = "Pasta" }
            when /$side/ { $side = "Potatoes" }
        }
        proceed;
    }
    when X::Raku::Recipes::WrongType {
        given .message {
            when /Main/ { $main = "Chickpeas" }
            when /Side/ { $side = "Rice" }
        }
        proceed;
    }
    when none(X::Raku::Recipes::Missing::Product,
            X::Raku::Recipes::WrongType) {
        die "There's something wrong with ingredients, I can't generate
that";
    }
    default {
        $calories = $rrr.calories-for( main => $main => 200,
                side => $side => 250 );
    }

}
```

The main change here is the use of proceed, which is the way given says "Don't leave yet, there's more." The when clauses in given might match several times; proceed is a way of saying "Okay, I'm good, but there might be other clauses that match too." It's not going to be like that in this case: it's a `Missing::Product`, a `WrongType`, or none of them. We take care of that in the third clause, which will again make the script die. But the gist of it is in the default clause: it will always match, and it will always be run *after* the matches, computing the calories once we have values for the `$main` and `$side` variables. That prevents the dreaded repetition of code, and the program flow is much more clear.

At the end of the day, this shows how a good design of an error hierarchy, together with informative messages, makes it easier for you to design solid programs that are ready for almost everything users will throw at them.

Recipe 8-4. Debug Your Application in Comma IDE

Problem

Your program fails, and it's difficult to determine what's going on.

Solution

Comma IDE has an integrated debugger that you can use to set breakpoints and examine variable values.

How It Works

Comma is an integrated development environment, with everything that's needed to see what's going on in your modules and applications. I have used the Community version routinely in this book, to see what was going on or investigate when something failed.

You learned in Chapter 1 how to select a script to run, so now you will use that same selection to debug a program. This can be the one you used there, one of the programs in this chapter, or whichever you want. You can get into debug mode by clicking on the little bug next to the Play icon, as shown in Figure 8-2.

Figure 8-2. *The Debug icon (a little bug) is next to the Run icon in Comma IDE*

However, by default it starts a background debugger that will allow you to stop it and check breakpoints. If it finishes too fast, you will not be able to check it all. You need to insert a breakpoint, by clicking between the line number and the text of the line where you want to stop. See Figure 8-3.

Figure 8-3. *Inserting a breakpoint in line 16; just click in that general column between the numbers and the window*

The breakpoints will be shown as a purple line, along with a red disk. The program will now stop when it gets to the breakpoint, changing the color of the line to blue (in the theme I'm using; it will be another light color in other themes). Once the program is paused, you can access the rest of the goodies by clicking on the Debugger tab in the bottom panel (this is the default layout, it might be somewhere else on your screen). You will see something like Figure 8-4.

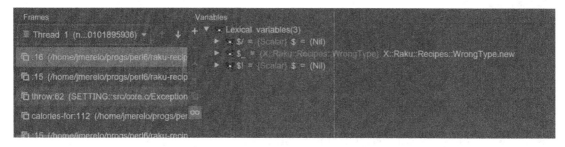

Figure 8-4. *Debug panel showing variable values on the right*

There are three lexical variables in this block, but the interesting one is the topical variable: $_, which shows that it contains an exception of type X::Raku::Recipes::WrongType. We can click the Play symbol, and it will display the values of the attributes. Showing that $!product is Apple (that was wrong) and $!desired-type is Side. Apple is a dessert (although apple sauce makes a nice side dish), which is why the exception was raised.

You can click the rest of the call frames, which will correspond to what was called before, and see, for instance, how calories-for was called and the values it received.

But we're happy that this value is what we were looking for, and we can resume execution. We can go step by step, or click any line and run until that line is reached. We will click the "default" block to see what's happened there. Or you can step over by clicking F8. You probably don't want to "step in" since things will get hairy pretty fast there. When you get into Rakudo's own code, you might use "step in" if you want to get into a block.

If you want to set fixed breakpoints, do so and click the icon at the left side, kind of a sideways "eject" button (a reference that you will probably not get if you're under ten years old). That will resume and run until the next breakpoint. We can navigate until the frame contains all the lexical variables, $main and $side, along with many others, as shown in Figure 8-5.

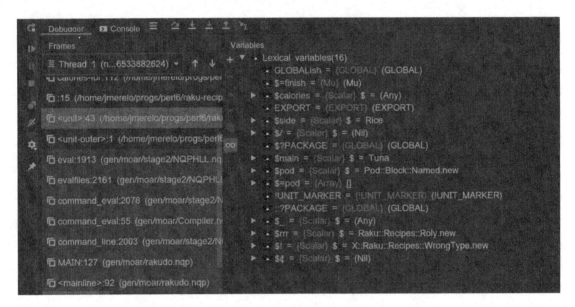

Figure 8-5. *Examining "global" variables*

That frame, tagged <unit>, shows all the "global" variables we have, or actually global in the outer-most scope. We can see some mentioned in other chapters, such as $=pod and $pod, which we created for convenience, as well as $main, $side, and $rrr. By staying in that frame and stepping "over," you will run precisely that line and nothing else.

When something is not just the way you want it, this debugger will help you point-and-click your way into the inner workings of your program. It beats "say $this" and "say @that" here and there, right?

Recipe 8-5. Debug Grammars by Making Them Fail Graciously with Pretty Errors

Problem

When a grammar fails, it's difficult to drill down to where the parsing actually failed.

Solution

Use `Grammar::Tracer` to determine what the grammar was doing and where it was stopping.

How It Works

Grammars either fail without a single hint of what's happened, or you need to use `Grammar::Tracer` and find out quite verbosely that some rule that needed to be triggered was not. Fortunately, we can install `Grammar::ErrorReporting`, which will not only report errors, but will also allow you to deal with them programmatically.

Grammars are the most powerful thing you don't know you need, and one of the most outstanding features of Raku, shared with no other language for the time being. Grammars are a programmatic way to express the structure in a group of texts and they give you a way to extract the parts of the structure you're interested in easily. As routines are to classes, methods are to grammars. A grammar is a hierarchical collection of regular expressions that call each other to build a complex data structure that faithfully expresses the structure of the text you want to analyze.

Note   We devote a whole chapter to grammars, later in this book.

We will create a simple grammar to analyze the list of ingredients in a recipe that is written in markdown. We can start with this:

```
unit grammar Raku::Recipes::Grammar::Ingredients;

token TOP       { <row> }
token row       { "*" | "-" | "✓" \h+ <ingredient> }
token ingredient        { <quantity> \h* <unit>? }
```

```
token quantity { <:N>+ }
token unit     { "g" | "tbsp" | "clove" | "tbsps" | "cloves" }
```

The structure is similar to that of a class. We unit it, same as for classes, to avoid indentation. Grammars are composed of rules, tokens, or regexes. Tokens and rules are regexes with a small difference: tokens *ratchet*, that is, they don't backtrack. Rules are tokens in which whitespace is significant. That means, by default, that tokens and regexes can use whitespace as a decoration and for clarity. Ratcheting makes tokens faster for grammars, which is why they are used by default. You can, of course, still use rules or regexes if you want.

Grammars have a TOP token; in this case it simply delegates to the next token, row. A row has a dingbat (which, via |, is one of three options), plus the description of an ingredient, which includes a quantity and a unit. We will just use that before we include ingredients behind the quantity, because we're already stuck. When trying to parse * 2 tbsps, which should be totally AOK, it matches the * and then stops.

Grammar::Tracer to the rescue. We insert it at the top of the grammar file. Without any other change, it will print the result shown in Figure 8-6 to the console.

Figure 8-6. *Grammar::Tracer in action*

The match is okay, but it stops at the first match for no reason. That's not good. But it indicates that, somehow, the first * in the token does meet the grammar. Hmm.

We go back to the documentation. It's always good to go there, because you might not remember correctly how regular expressions work. And | happens to be "longest alternation." Hmm, not what we were looking for. The grammar matches * or – or "✓" \h+ <ingredient>, so it's just happy with the first option and then exits. We need to use || instead: Alternation. Besides, || has a higher priority than whitespace, so we need to group those three things, without capturing, because we're not really interested in the dingbat. So use this code:

```
token row     { ["*" || "-" || "✓"] \h+ <ingredient> }
```

This does it. If we keep `Grammar::Tracer`, we will see the result in Figure 8-7.

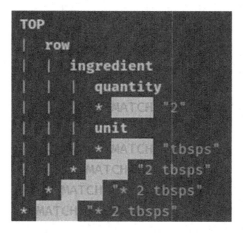

Figure 8-7. *Matching the whole sentence*

Figure 8-7 shows that it gets to the first rule, tries to match the ingredient, which is composed of a quantity (and 2 is matched there) and a unit (tbsps, tablespoons). It then backtracks to indicate it's matched the token that's higher in the hierarchy, and we're good with the result. This program will produce "`We need to use 2 tbsps of whatever`":

```
use Raku::Recipes::Grammar::Ingredients;

my $row = Raku::Recipes::Grammar::Ingredients.parse("* 2 tbsps");
say "We need to use $row<row><ingredient><quantity>
$row<row><ingredient><unit> of whatever"
```

The resulting match follows the same structure as the one printed by `Grammar::Tracer`; it's a set of nested hashes, with the top hash using the name of the top token as a key, and down from there, to the rest of the tokens. Every level will have as many keys as tokens are mentioned in it.

Still, things can go wrong. Let's try to parse *2 `tbsps`, while leaving `Grammar::Tracer`. See Figure 8-8.

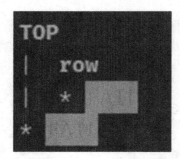

Figure 8-8. *Failing parsing now*

Figure 8-8 shows that it's failed and it's done so in the very first token. Well, that helps, but not really. Let's try to find out what really happened. Debugging will not help us here, because it will only show the value of the Match variable, $/, which will be empty because, well, the match failed. Ditto for "say $this or $that." But you have a powerful tool in your tool chest: *refactoring*.

As a matter of fact, that rule where it fails has three different parts. We might not be interested in all of them, but for the time being we need to know where it failed, so let's break it down:

```
token row       {  <dingbat> <whitespace> <ingredient> }
token dingbat    {  ["*" || "-" || "✓"]  }
token whitespace { \h+ }
```

A row is now three different tokens; the Tracer will help us know exactly where it failed. See Figure 8-9.

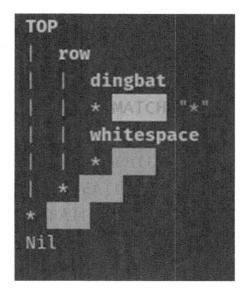

Figure 8-9. *Showing failure*

A-ha! So it was that sneaky whitespace (or absence thereof) that failed! Let's fix that and it will work. The following code:

```
use Raku::Recipes::Grammar::ErrorReporting;
```

```
my $measure = Raku::Recipes::Grammar::ErrorReporting.parse("* 2 tbsp");
say ~$measure<row><ingredient><quantity>, " of ",
        ~$measure<row><ingredient><unit>;
```

Will produce this:

```
2 of tbsp
```

We're still not interested in the whitespace, though, and, for that matter, in the dingbat either. The resulting match will include them. By using a dot in front of the rule name, we will use it, but not store it:

```
token row      { <.dingbat> <.whitespace> <ingredient> }
```

That will produce the self-same result, but with less noise.

Please bear in mind that not everything marked with FAIL will eventually produce a failure to match; the grammar might be exploring one of the branches of an alternative fail there, but then succeed in other branch and eventually return a match. But with all this, we see that Raku not only provides powerful grammars, but also powerful tools in the ecosystem that help you work with and debug them when something does not work the way it should. That, and a little programming craft, will help you create great text parsing and analyzing tools, but we'll get to that later in the book.

CHAPTER 9

Client-Side Web and APIs

The web is the infinite source of information, and it's right there for you to tap. Lots of services can be used straight away, in other cases you have to do some massaging, and in yet other cases you need to be properly authorized. In all these cases, Raku is there to help you.

Recipe 9-1. Query a GeoIP Database

Problem

You have a bunch of Internet addresses in your log file, and you need to know where they come from to check out which countries are interested in your content.

Solution

Use GeoIP2, a module in the Raku ecosystem, to query a MaxMind database, a database that includes information about geolocation of groups of IPs.

How It Works

You've got in your hands a whole set of files with logs from your recipe web server, and you'd like to know where all those IPs are from. That way, you can create more content about regional cuisine. Or maybe you just want to know out of sheer curiosity. Proprietary solutions will give you that information, but it goes along with some loss of privacy for your users, so it's better to develop your own.

Fortunately, there's a company, called MaxMind, that produces a series of databases. These databases are in an open format and you can use them to query about IPs. You can access them through the GeoIP2 downloadable module.

© J.J. Merelo 2020
J.J. Merelo, *Raku Recipes*, https://doi.org/10.1007/978-1-4842-6258-0_9

These databases, however, are proprietary. There are several ways to get one of them:

- Your company might be extremely interested in one, and it will buy one for you.

- There are open source tools written in several languages, like Perl, which can produce data in that format, and they are open source. See https://github.com/maxmind/MaxMind-DB-Writer-perl. You might want to create your own, limited, database, using for instance IPs within your company's VPN (if it's a multinational one).

- Finally, you can download GeoLite databases for free. These have limited precision, but we're only interested in the country and continent, so this will do.

We will create a simple script that checks the IP of the machine you're using to connect to the Internet and tells you which country and continent you are from.

```
use GeoIP2;

my $ip = qx{curl -s ifconfig.me};
my $geo = GeoIP2.new( path => 'Chapter-9/GeoLite2-Country.mmdb' );
my $location = $geo.locate( ip => $ip );

say "The IP is in $location<country><names><en>, $location<continent><names
><en>";
```

Since locally we will only know the local IP (or IPs) your system is connected to, which will typically be a local IP issued by your router, we use the ifconfig.me Internet service via curl to obtain our own IP. We need to have curl installed and accessible, and the -s will make it return the IP without printing anything else to the screen (s = silent). The qx quoting construct is yet another way of running external programs, similar to what we did in Chapters 1 and 2 with shell and run.

We then initialize the database object with the path to the database file (that previously I had registered to download; you can do the same by registering at https:// dev.maxmind.com/geoip/geoip2/geolite2/). We call the locate method to obtain the location, which will be returned in a data structure that includes the names of countries and continents in several formats, as well as some geocoding information. We'll just access the name (stored in the <names> key) of the country and continent in English (stored in a key that represents the language code, <en>). This will print the following for me:

```
The IP is in Spain, Europe
```

Right on!

If what you want is to parse the log, you need to process this log using any of the text-processing recipes you've seen so far.

Recipe 9-2. Download and Extract Information from a Website

Problem

You need to get some information that is included on a website.

Solution

Download the page using an external CLI tool or using one of the available libraries, such as HTTP::UserAgent, Cro:HTTP, or LWP::Simple. As their names imply, LWP::Simple is simpler, HTTP::UserAgent gives you a bit more flexibility to create specific headers, and Cro::HTTP is the best designed and maintained. You will probably will not need all the functionality of Cro::HTTP. Once the content is downloaded, use regular expressions to capture the information you're interested in or, if that's not easy or possible, capture the information in an HTML document object model parser such as DOM::Tiny.

How It Works

There's a lot of information on the web. If only there was a way to get it and process it...

But there is! From the beginning of time, *scraping* has been a way to gather information and data that is semi-structured and published on the web. However, scraping is still an arcane art, with many different degrees of freedom: from how the information is structured, to more esoteric challenges like throttling (making request responses slower when there are repeated requests from an IP) or terms of service (you can be banned from a site if you download information from it, even if you're not actually publishing that information anywhere else).

167

There are also technical challenges. Essentially, when you are scraping, you will need to download the page written in HTML and then parse that HTML for the information you need. In many cases (for instance, if that information has a clear prefix, or is structured in a certain way), parsing is straightforward. In some others, you will need to parse the whole page to the DOM and then look for a particular leaf of the tree that hangs from a certain branch.

Note   In yet others, you might get lucky and obtain the information from a data div or from a user-accessible JSON file.

That's the case also for recipes. There's a myriad of sites that publish recipes daily, or where recipes are laid out, often in a format that has a certain structure.

Note   Unfortunately, a *microformat* called hRecipes for including recipes in HTML is no longer fashionable, and I doubt it's ever been.

For a myriad of reasons, however, it's probably better if we stick to open license sites like Wikipedia. Wikibooks includes a whole lot of recipes at https://en.wikibooks. org/wiki/Category:Recipes, which pretty much follow the same format. This script will download one of them and extract the ingredients.

```
use HTTP::UserAgent;

my $URL = @*ARGS[0] // "https://en.wikibooks.org/wiki/Cookbook:Apple_
Pie_I";
my $recipr = HTTP::UserAgent.new;
my $response = $recipr.get($URL);

die $response.status-line unless $response.is-success;
my $ingredients = ( $response.content.split(/"<h2>"/))[1];
my @ingredients = ($ingredients ~~ m:g/"\/Cookbook:"(\w+)/);
say @ingredients.map( ~*[0] ).unique;
```

You will need to download the HTTP::UserAgent module before using it; it's a frequently updated module in the ecosystem.

Note   As with other modules in this fast-moving ecosystem, there might be some quirk in installation with the version of Raku you're using. If you don't want to live on the edge, use the Rakudo Star distribution, which includes many other useful modules.

The script will take the URL for a recipe or use the one for the apple pie, because what's better than apple pie, right? It will instantiate a version of the HTTP user agent, and will fetch the URL in the next sentence. If there's an error, it will bail out with a message.

Note   For the sake of getting to the point, we'll be skipping checks and graceful handling of errors. For instance, we're not checking the URL so that it effectively has the right pattern. That's left to the reader. Tip: A simple regex will do.

If everything is okay, we can proceed to extract the information. We know that there's going to be an H2 section called Ingredients; that's the first H2 segment indeed. So rightfully we split using the simple `<h2>` and take the second one, index 1 in the array.

Note   That's one good thing about Wikipedia: clean markup. It would probably be a bit more difficult to split sections if they were marked with some other bit of markup and CSS classes.

Within that section, we realize that for every ingredient there's a link to a section that describes different recipes that use that ingredient. They all follow the same pattern: `https://en.wikibooks.org/wiki/Cookbook:`+ingredient(and it will always be a set of word-like characters). Thus, the pattern we use: `m:g/"\/Cookbook:"(\w+)/`; `:g` will match all of them, and the parentheses will capture just the word, so we get a set of `Match` objects in an array. We need to extract the precise string that's been matched: `.map( ~*[0] )` will get the first match in a `Match` and will stringify it. We extract the unique elements out of this array, just in case any of them are repeated. This will print something like this:

```
(Flour Margarine Lard Salt Water Apple Lemon_Juice Butter Sugar Cornstarch
Cinnamon Nutmeg Milk)
```

Note   Yes, there seems to be a section devoted to recipes with water. Hmm, yummy! "This soup is delicious! What was your secret ingredient?" "Water"

Please note that the ingredients that consist of two separate words, like Lemon Juice, use an underscore to separate them; underscore is also matched with \w, so no problem here.

This was moderately successful, but we still need to be a bit crafty to get to the information we want, by extracting it from an URL that has a certain shape.

Tip   Scraping is an arcane art and you need to be crafty all the time. You can also learn the art and craft of scraping from *Website Scraping with Python* and *Practical Web Scraping for Data Science*, two excellent books published by Apress. Although the language is different, the techniques and methodology is not that different.

Let's try to use the DOM. While this will, in general, get you pieces of data with much more precision, it should be taken into account that modern DOMs are, in general, dynamic, so you can't get them from the source (you would need a *headless* browser of which, for the time being, there are none for Raku). Additionally, you need the DOM structure to be static, and many sites change that routinely. Let's stick to this same Wikibooks source, which is cleaner and scrapable in that aspect.

```
use WWW;
use DOM::Tiny;

my $URL = @*ARGS[0] // "https://en.wikibooks.org/wiki/Cookbook:Apple_Pie_I";
my $content = get($URL);

die "That $URL didn't work" unless $content;

my @all-lis = DOM::Tiny.parse( $content.split(/"<h2>"/)[1]).find('li').map:
~*;

my @my-lis = @all-lis.grep( /title..Cookbook ":"/)
        .map( { DOM::Tiny.parse( $_ ) } );

say @my-lis.map( "→ " ~ *.all-text).unique.join("\n");
```

We've switched to a different library with HTTP commands, the simply and aptly named WWW, which gives us a simple `get` command to download from the web (it can also parse JSON on the fly). `DOM::Tiny` will provide the DOM-parsing abilities.

Although HTML is a document structure description language, there's not really a great way to provide a top-down structure for it. For instance, division in sections does not show in the structure (it could, by using the section tag; however, it's not used here). That is why, to extract the ingredient section, we still have to do the same tag-based splitting we did in the previous version. That way, we make sure that what we parse really contains what we're interested in. The HTML for this page is quite clean, meaning that there're no semantic class attributes anywhere to be seen. If the ul tag that contains our list items had a `class='ingredients'` tag, it would have been way easier. Be that as it may, from looking at the source we see that every ingredient is in an `<li>` tag, so `find("li")` will get all of them in a Raku `Seq` (that is, a sequence of items over which you can iterate). Learn all about sequences at `https://docs.raku.org/type/Seq` or from Chapter 5 of *Perl 6 Quick Syntax Reference.* We need to do additional checking, so we render them back to HTML by stringifying them via `~*`.

What we need to do is the next `grep`: if there's no link to an ingredient page, it's not an ingredient. On the apple pie page, they are all this way, but we'll stay on the safe side and actually check this. There could be some additional instructions about, I don't know, using some special pan or pre-heating the oven (you *always* need to pre-heat the oven). We parse them again, simply because it's the simplest way to get rid of the markup and get all the text, which we do next using `.all-text`, another `DOM::Tiny` method.

The result will be as follows:

→ 8 oz (225 g) plain flour
→ 4 oz (110 g) margarine
→ 2 oz (55 g) lard
→ pinch of salt
→ 2 tablespoons cold water
→ 1 lb (500 g) apples, sliced
→ 2 tbsp lemon juice
→ 1 oz (28 g) salted butter
→ 2½ c sugar, and additional for sprinkling
→ ¼ c flour
→ 2½ tbsp cornstarch
→ cinnamon

→ `nutmeg`
→ `1 oz (28 g) milk`
→ `sugar`

Again, we use `unique` because cinnamon is repeated (and maybe a bit overrated), since it's used in two parts of the pie. That way, we get all ingredients together, and we can subject them to additional processing (using a grammar, for instance, which we'll get to later).

You will scrape if there's absolutely no way out of it. If you get to use an API, things will be much easier. We'll get to that next.

Recipe 9-3. Use a Web API to Get Information from a Site

Problem

You need to download information from a site that makes data available via a REST API.

Solution

Use a web client in Raku, such as `WWW` or `Cro::HTTP`, or a specific module for the API if it exists in the ecosystem.

How It Works

Recipes and food, in general, are thriving areas on the web.

Note   Even more so during the Coronavirus pandemic, when a big part of the world was confined at home and had more time to spare.

There's a constellation of websites that can be consulted daily, but that has also created a whole industry of services that provide content for those sites, as well as added value that goes from composing recipes to checking all kinds of information about ingredients. There's Yummly, which provides a pay-per-use API, and many others. We'll settle for Edamam. It does provide a free tier, limited to five petitions/minute, if you sign up as a developer. So please do so for this recipe at https://developer.edamam.com/ edamam-recipe-api and get an app ID and an API key.

```
use Cro::HTTP::Client;
use URI::Encode;

my $appID = %*ENV{'EDAMAM_APP_ID'};
my $api-key = %*ENV{'EDAMAM_API_KEY'};
my $api-req = "\&app_id=$appID\&app_key=$api-key";
my $ingredient = @*ARGS[0] // "water";

my $cro = Cro::HTTP::Client.new(base-uri => "https://api.edamam.com/" );
my $response = await $cro.get( "search?q="
                                        ~ uri_encode($ingredient) ~ $api-req);
my %data = await $response.body;

say %data<hits>.map( *<recipe><label> ).join: "\n";
```

Cro is an amazing piece of work, a framework for distributed applications that includes all kinds of goodies for different protocols, including of course this HTTP client we are using here. Unlike the clients we have been using before, it's asynchronous. We've worked with asynchrony before, but in this case it's entirely appropriate. You don't really know when the response to a request is going to arrive, and keeping the rest of the program hanged up waiting for it will result in low performance. In cases where you'll be doing a single request and processing it serially, it's probably okay (as we have done in the previous recipes) to just fire the request and wait for the result; as a matter of fact, this is what we do here. But later.

The first block of statements will set up the necessary variables, taking as usual the query string from the command line if it exists. You'll need to define environment variables by copying and pasting them from the Edamam account. It won't work if these don't have valid values. Since all requests will use these two values in precisely that order, we set up the $api-req variable to reuse it later.

Cro::HTTP::Client sets up a client with a base URL. It will reuse connections if the version of the protocol allows it, which is also a difference with respect to the other two modules we've used before. Production and features-wise, Cro is way ahead of other modules in the same niche.

Since it's asynchronous, a request will return a promise. We *await* on that promise to get to the response. But the response itself is a promise too: it's a *connection* and we'll need to await on it again to get the body of the response. That explains the two awaits in sequence. The API uses `GET` to access the search function, and it uses `q` as a parameter for the query string. We build an URL, which is convenient in this case (and an alternative to giving the method a hash), since the API asks explicitly for the authentication parameters in that order (and you can't be sure how the keys of a hash will be ordered otherwise).

`Cro::HTTP::Client` will even decode the body of the response for you and give you a Raku data structure. By default, Edamam API will return ten *hits*, and up to a 100 for the free tier. We'll settle for the first page; as a matter of fact, this particular query string returns several thousand hits. "hits" is one of the keys the resulting data structure returns. But we're just interested in the recipes that are returned. The data structure will be a hash, and it will store the hits as an array under the `hits` key. Among other things, every hit will have a `recipe` key, and that recipe will have a `label` key, which will be its description. So the last statement runs a map over these hits and extracts the names of these recipes. It will go like this:

```
Summer water
Pineapple Coconut Water
Water Toast
Water Kefir from 'Mastering Fermentation'
Grapefruit Sparkling Water
Coconut-Water Gelatin
Cucumber-Orange Water Recipe
Tomato Water Pasta
Rose Water Marshmallows recipes
Rose Water Syrup
```

Hmm, summer water. Can't wait to cook that. Will I be able to buy dehydrated water at my local supermarket?

In general, most APIs will use REST, and you will be able to deal with it using `Cro::HTTP::Client`. Authentication will be done in different ways, in most cases adding them as metadata to the request. The essence of dealing with APIs is there. Get your arguments together, build the request (including header metadata if you need it), and fire it, decoding the response.

In some limited cases, you will have a Raku module custom-made for a particular API: API::Discord will handle that conversational system, there's Twitter for that social network, GlotIO for Glot.io, and even a thin wrapper for Wikidata, called Wikidata::API, that was published by yours truly.

Wikidata is the less beaten track of Wikipedia devoted to, well, data. It stores data and relationships between items of data. It includes what ingredient was used to make which recipe. As the rest of the WikiRealm, it's crowd-sourced, so your mileage might vary. The good thing is that it has an API that needs no authentication, based on a query language called SPARQL. This query, for instance, would return all recipes that include garlic:

```
SELECT ?recipe ?recipeLabel
WHERE
{
  ?recipe wdt:P31?/wdt:P279* wd:Q219239;
          wdt:P527 wd:Q21546392.
  SERVICE wikibase:label { bd:serviceParam wikibase:language "en", "fr". }
}
ORDER BY UCASE(STR(?recipeLabel))
```

The prefix wdt is used for relationships, and wd is for data. The two fixed pieces of data we have are Q219239 which is, well, recipe (check it out in its URI https://www.wikidata.org/wiki/Q219239 or by simply searching for "recipe" on www.wikidata.org). The two relationships are an instance of or a subclass of. A recipe for carbonara sauce is an instance of a recipe. P527 means "is composed of," and Q21546392 is garlic. Check out the Q prefix for entities and P for relations between them. So essentially we are saying "Give me all things that seem to be a recipe *and* include garlic." Spoiler: There are only two at the time of writing this. We'll need this script to get to them:

```
use Wikidata::API;

my $query = "Chapter-9/ingredients.sparql".IO.slurp;

my $recipes-with-garlic= query($query);

say "Recipes with garlic:\n",
        $recipes-with-garlic<results><bindings>
            .map: { utf8y( $_<recipeLabel><value>) };
```

```
sub utf8y ( $str ) {
    Buf.new( $str.ords ).decode("utf8")
}
```

There's not much to it, really. Read the SPARQL query, launch a query, show the results. The results are in a relatively complex data structure, but the only part that's interesting is the `recipeLabel` key that, as you have seen before, was created by the query. The rest is boilerplate (`results` will be the key storing the results, and `bindings` will show the different variables bound to results, including `recipeLabel`).

We had to create a little subroutine, `utf8y`, to deal with the results, since the JSON modules used cannot. That routine breaks down a string into its characters, reconstructs it, and returns it encoded in `utf8`. That will print the following:

```
Recipes with garlic:
(Anchoïade ratatouille)
```

That first word is the one that caused the existence of that routine. Those are the two only recipes that seem to use garlic. They had to be French, of course.

If you know SQL or another query language, SPARQL is not too difficult to learn, and it can really help you with lots of mundane things. In this article for the Raku Advent Calendar, Santa used it to check if what the boys and girls were asking for in their letters wasactuallyanobject`https://perl6advent.wordpress.com/2017/12/03/letterops-with-perl6/`.

In general, APIs will help you enrich your applications, and working with them is easy with Raku.

Recipe 9-4. Check IPs and Addresses by Querying Internet Services

Problem

You have an IP and you need to check if it's on or if a service is available.

Solution

You can use Net::IP to manipulate addresses or Net::IP::Parse to check them, as well as IP::Random to generate random IP addresses. Sys::IP will give you local IP addresses. You can also use whois to map domains to names. In many cases, there will be a Raku module available to check a certain service, in others you'll have to create your own querying service for APIs using one of the recipes discussed in this chapter.

How It Works

Working with IP addresses involves querying system services, as well as using protocols such as TCP for making calls and examining what's returned. For instance, very often we need to check if a service is running, and if it's not, do something like log a failure event or take other measures like send an email. In general, doing system calls, and doing them in a system-independent way, is not easy.

Services generally are mapped to "ports," which are addresses within the system that usually have a agreed-upon number. These numbers are published and you usually ensure that if you need to run something, you avoid them and create your own.

Anyway, putting this together means that if you want to check if certain services are running on your system, you'll need to check if there's anything in that port responding to a certain protocol, which is usually TCP. You can do that with this simple script

```
use Sys::IP;
use Services::PortMapping;
use CheckSocket;

my $this-ip = Sys::IP.new.get_default_ip();

for <www-http ssh> -> $service {
    if check-socket(%TCPPorts{$service},$this-ip) {
        say "Your service $service is running in port %TCPPorts{$service}";
    } else {
        say "Apparently, your service $service is not running";
    }
}
```

The script is simple because there are three modules that hide all the complexity from you. Sys::IP finds the IP or IPs that the local system has, the ones that can be used to check (of course, there's always 127.0.0.1). Services::PortMapping exports four hashes that map standard service names to ports and the reverse. And finally, CheckSocket checks if there's a TCP service running in a port in a certain address.

So we do that in sequence: first we find local IPs via get-default_ip, and then we check two common services, ssh and http (whose standard name, according to the "Service name and Transport Protocol Port Number Registry," is http, www, or www-http), by running check-socket over them. Different messages will be printed if they are running or not. In my case, it will print the following:

```
Your service www-http is running in port 80
Your service ssh is running in port 22
```

Which is how I discovered I had Apache httpd installed and running all along.

Raku is a general purpose language and it is as adequate for system-level tasks as the next one. It's true that there are not as many modules in the ecosystem as in other languages that have taken that niche like Perl or Python, but there's extensive support in the Net:: namespace of the ecosystem for protocols like DNS or BGP. Other protocols, like ICMP, are unfortunately missing. However, the Raku ecosystem is growing by several modules every week, so that might not be true by the time you read this.

CHAPTER 10

Text Processing

Scripting languages are great for whipping up scripts that work with text, extract
information, render it in some format, or manipulate it in other useful ways. In this
chapter, we see how to extract information, identify differences between files, and render
static pages to HTML. We will see many basic Raku techniques, as well as be introduced
to useful modules in the ecosystem.

Recipe 10-1. Scrape Markdown Documents
Problem

You need to extract information from a markdown document, extracting only the
headers, for instance, or certain information you can identify by position or content.

Solution

Regular expressions are a powerful domain-specific way to extract information from
semi-structured text, such as markdown text, which is always an option. You can use the
Text::Markdown module in the ecosystem if the information is in the structure.

How It Works

Scraping is the process of extracting information from text with some kind of markup,
be it on the web or on documents with a known format, such as PDFs or word
processing documents. Scraping is used to process legacy documents, create APIs out of
information on the web, or prepare data for opening to the public.

We use markdown in the recipes in this book. One of the things that you need to
extract, in any recipe, are its ingredients. Let's say you need to determine the ingredients

© J.J. Merelo 2020
J.J. Merelo, *Raku Recipes*, https://doi.org/10.1007/978-1-4842-6258-0_10

of a certain recipe so that you can add them to your shopping list or compute the amount of calories in them (as we did in Chapter 2).

For example, this could be the markdown for a recipe to make carrot wraps:

```
# Carrot wraps

A healthy way to start a meal, or to munch between them.

## Ingredients
* 200g carrots
* 200g cottage cheese or cheese spread
* 4 wheat tortillas

## Preparation

    1.    Cut the carrots in long sticks or slices
    2.    Spread cheese over tortillas, cut them in half
    3.    Put carrot sticks on tortillas, wrap them around
    4.    Add fresh parsley, mint or coriander to taste.
```

The title and sections are clearly indicated. The first is the level 1 header (indicated with #), and then we have ingredients as a level 2 header, and then the preparation as another level 2 header. We're interested, as before, only in the ingredients and their measures. Since these markup languages only mark paragraphs, not sets of them, nothing *wraps around* ingredients. We'll have to find another strategy to obtain them. Note, however, that they are the only list items in the structure of the document. Preparation uses numbered items. So that might be a good way to extract them. We do that here:

```
use Text::Markdown;

sub MAIN( $filename = "recipes/appetizers/carrot-wraps.md") {
    my $md = parse-markdown-from-file($filename);
    my @ingredients = $md.document.items
            .grep( Text::Markdown::List )
            .grep( !*.numbered );
    for @ingredients[0].items -> $i {
        say "Ingredient → {(~$i).trim}";
    };
}
```

Note   The markdown file mentioned here will be included, along with the rest of the code, in the GitHub repository for this book.

We will use a module in the ecosystem, `Text::Markdown`. It's not perfect, but for simple documents such as this one, it does its job fairly well. `Text::Markdown::Discount` is another alternative, which uses a C library to do the parsing. Both modules also generate markdown from data structures if needed.

Anyway, `parse-markdown-from-file` creates a data structure from the file directly; this data structure will be a `Text::Markdown::Document` object with a series of items. `Text::Markdown` has different types for every possible markup; they are called `Text::Markdown::Whatever`. For instance, a text paragraph will be `Text::Markdown::Paragraph`, and, effectively, `Text::Markdown::List` will be a list. However, there is no specific type for numbered or regular lists; that's differentiated by an attribute in the object.

What we need to do is extract the items in the document object, which will be an array, filter all the lists (there will be a regular list for ingredients and a numbered one for instructions), and then take only those that are numbered.

There will be a single one, and that will be the first element in the array. Again, the items in the list data structure will contain all the different list items, which we effectively list in the loop. We need to do some additional processing, though. Every item will be a `Text::Markdown` data structure that we need to stringify; even so, the text will include carriage returns and possibly other whitespace, which we trim. Eventually, the result will be this:

```
Ingredient → 250g carrots
Ingredient → 200g cottage cheese or cheese spread
Ingredient → 4 wheat tortillas
```

These ingredients can be processed further by extracting the measures and the actual ingredients used. That will be left for later, when we deal with mini-languages.

Note, however, the importance of always giving a fixed structure to documents that will be destined to be processed automatically. In this case, the distinguishing feature has been the type of list. If we had used also a numbered list, we would have needed additional processing; for instance, splitting the document by section (as we did in the previous chapter, when we were processing web pages) and then extracting the items in the second section. However, in that case, we didn't have any kind of control over how the information was presented. In the case of markdown documents, we usually do. Some simple guidelines will be enough to make text with a little structure as regular as any kind of (serialized) data structure.

Note   You need to be structured in the text itself. For instance, the second item has an "or" that would make it difficult to process automatically. When we process ingredients that way, we will need a way to express those alternatives in a principled, yet not awkward, way.

Recipe 10-2. Generate a Set of Static Web Pages
Problem

You need to generate a few pages for a static website that's going to be published cheaply (and safely).

Solution

Use a static site generator that will generate HTML pages from markdown documents, or roll out your own using templates and a script. The simplest way of doing this is to generate HTML from the markdown documents you already have. Markit, for instance, will parse markdown and convert it to HTML.

Besides these systems, there are three others—Uzu, Pekyll, and BreakDancer. The latter is probably outdated, and Uzu has been updated most recently. But instead of any of them, Markit is probably good enough to generate a set of pages from its markdown source, which is what we're looking for.

Additionally, we can use a templating system, such as `Template::Classic`, to fill boilerplate with values from a program. This is what we will use here.

How It Works

The first thing we could think of was to use a tool that uses the source in the markdown directly and generates a static site in HTML. The closest thing to that is Pekyll, but I can't really advise you to use it since its documentation is not up to date (or complete) and it's not been updated in three years. It's probably perfectly fine, however, since Raku is a (mostly) stable language. But let's just try another path.

Uzu has been updated lately, and it's been used frequently. However, it uses HTML instead of markdown source for site generation. This means that we need to take one step back and figure out a way to generate HTML directly.

Markit is the solution. As a matter of fact, if all you want is a plain vanilla markdown-to-HTML processor, this one is quite good and will do a good, if stark, job. We will use it to generate HTML files for all our recipes (these aren't really pages, since they do not have the full HTML head/body structure, although they're serviceable).

```
use Raku::Recipes;
use Markit;

my $md = Markdown.new;

for recipes() -> $recipe {
    my $html-path-name = ~$recipe;
    $html-path-name ~~ s/\.md/\.html/;
    $html-path-name ~~ s/recipes/build/;
    my $html-path = IO::Path.new($html-path-name);
    my $html-dir = $html-path.dirname.IO;
    $html-dir.mkdir unless $html-dir.d;
    spurt $html-path-name,  $md.markdown( $recipe.slurp );
}
```

We will be using a `recipes` routine from `Raku::Recipes`, which corresponds to the counting files recipe we created in the first chapter. We have incorporated it into our Raku Recipes utility module. It will return a list with the paths of all the files in the `recipes` folder by default (or another absolute or relative path where markdown recipes might be stored). That loop will run over these files. It generates the path of the HTML file in two steps: it changes the extension and then changes the directory from the original (which included `recipes`) to the final one, `build`. We then need to create the directory if it does not exist, because otherwise the creation of the file will fail. We create a `IO::Path` object, check that it exists, and unless it does, we `mkdir` that directory.

The `spurt` routine will directly write the result of generating HTML from the markdown to the file, in a single step. This will be the content of the `carrot-wraps.html` file, for instance:

```
<h1>Carrot wraps</h1>
<p>A healthy way to start a meal, or to munch between them.</p>
<h2>Ingredients</h2>
<ul>
<li>250g carrots</li>
<li>200g cottage cheese or cheese spread</li>
<li>4 wheat tortillas</li>
</ul>
<h2>Preparation</h2>
<ol>
<li>Cut the carrots in long sticks or slices</li>
<li>Spread cheese over tortillas, cut them in half</li>
<li>Put carrot sticks on tortillas, wrap them around</li>
<li>Add fresh parsley, mint or coriander to taste.</li>
</ol>
```

However, an HTML file does not mean a site, not even a single page, so we need to wrap the whole document structure around the fragment that we generated. In order to do that, we should avoid just lobbing around HTML strings that are difficult to edit for the website designer. The best option is to use a template, and we will choose `Template::Classic`, recently published by Chloe Kekoa. It's very simple, with a single function, `template`, that creates a routine that renders values of variables into the template. It is also an excellent piece of code if you want to learn to do things the Raku way (or at least one of the Raku ways), making excellent use of many exclusive Raku features, including grammars.

Obviously, templates are gonna template, so we need to create the basic skeleton of the page this way:

```
<!DOCTYPE html>
<html lang="en">
<head>
    <meta charset="UTF-8">
    <title>Test page</title>
<link rel='stylesheet' id='style-css'  href='raku-recipes.css' type='text/
css'
```

```
        media='all' />
</head>
<body>
<!-- This is a Template::Classic template -->

<% take $content %>

</body>
</html>
```

The key part of this template is in here: `<% take $content %>`. In
`Template::Classic`, `<% %>` runs Raku code, and it will return whatever is in the variable
`$content` and include it precisely in that part of the HTML file. We will need to use that
variable to generate the file. We do so in this program:

```
use Markit;
use Template::Classic;

my $template-file = "resources/templates/recipe.html".IO.e
              ??"resources/templates/recipe.html".IO.slurp
              !!%?RESOURCES<templates/recipe.html>.slurp;

my $md = Markdown.new;
my &generate-page := template :($content), $template-file;

for recipes() -> $recipe {
    my $html-fragment = recipe($md,$recipe);
    my @page = generate-page( $html-fragment );
    spurt-with-dir($recipe, @page.eager.join );
}
```

The generate-page routine is exactly as in the previous recipe. It will generate the
HTML fragment from markdown; spurt-with-dir will, as was done in the previous
recipe, write to a file and create the directory if it exists. They've been eliminated for
brevity. The remainder goes directly to the point.

First we obtain the template from the filesystem. This template will be, as most of
the resources used by a module are, in the resources/ directory. Conventionally all
the contents of this directory are declared in META6.json and subsequently installed to
an immutable place. You don't need to find out where that place is: The %*RESOURCES

dynamic hash will have an entry for every resource. We don't know in advance if we're using this template from the same directory or once we've installed the `Raku::Recipes` module, so the first statement takes care of that.

Same as we did before, we generate a markdown renderer object, but now we additionally create a *templater* function. We do that using `template`, the only routine exported by `Template::Classic`. It takes as an argument a signature and a template and returns a function that applies the template to its arguments. We use binding `:=` instead of assignment; this is how the module documentation tells us to do it, and it makes sense, since binding creates a kind of alias. What we are doing is simply saying that that function will point to the result of calling `template`, instead of to a copy. That might give it a small speed edge as well.

This is, then, a higher order function. A function that returns a function, takes a template, and returns a function that applies that template. This is what we call a *templater*. The templater is a function that will apply that template to the variables submitted to it, embedding their values where it's been defined.

This is a kind of pattern we usually find in functional languages such as Haskell and Scala. But Raku is also a functional language, and functions are first-class objects (same as types or grammars). We can use them wherever we can use any other type of data. This is one of the reasons why we chose this module for the recipe; even if it's quite recent, it really highlights the capabilities and features of Raku. Think about how this would have been done in an object oriented way: we would have created a template object, which would have included the template as an attribute, and then we would have called a method of that object to apply the template (and possibly changed the state of the object in the process). The method would have to use a generic signature (say, a hash) to receive the variables. This is functional programming at its full extension: the created *templater* is a stateless function—it takes variables that are type-checked and returns the filled-out content.

Note   There are, however, many ways to do it. If you're happy with objects, or with a purely procedural interface, Raku will also provide you with the tools to use it.

A *signature* is simply a combination of arguments a routine uses. It's a way to declare what kind of arguments it takes, and can be used to type check not only the arguments when calling the function, but also the function itself, whose type includes signature *and* return types. The signature mechanism works in most modern languages. Raku, besides, includes signatures as first-class objects. In case you want to say, hey, create this function that I want to be called in this precise way, you can use signature literals such as this one: ($content).

Note   The signature mechanism in Raku is quite extensive, including runtime checks, sub-signatures, named and positional parameters, slurpies… You can find all about it in the *Perl 6 Quick Syntax Reference* book, by the same author.

The baseline is that we're going to call the *templater* as a function. With this signature, we tell this signature how we're going to call it, using which parameters, its type, in which order , and so on.

As we did in the previous recipe, we generate the HTML fragment, apply this templater to it, and generate a Seq. The content of $html-fragment will become $content in the template, and the result will be returned. It returns a sequence with every element being a fragment of the result, which you can deal with separately, or even create a supply out of them. Using a Seq makes it more flexible, but in this case we're just interested in the whole thing. Since it's a lazy sequence, we make it eager so that all its components are vivified, and then we simply join it into a single string. That string is then written to the filesystem, keeping the original path.

The result (once you get the CSS file in the right place) will look like Figure 10-1.

Carrot wraps

A healthy way to start a meal, or to munch between them.

Q Ingredients

- 250g carrots
- 200g cottage cheese or cheese spread
- 4 wheat tortillas

Figure 10-1. *Rendered recipe via templater*

Still, we can do a bit better. For instance, the title is generic and the same for every page. It would be much better if we could use the title of the recipe there. Also, it would be nice to have an index page with links to every page. Right now we don't really have that. But we can leverage `Template::Classic`, as well as the first recipe in this chapter, to achieve that effect. There are two kinds of templating solutions: code-less and the other kind, with code. Code-less solutions like Mustache create their own adaptation of the template language so that certain data structures can be processed in an implicit way. For instance, you can create a way to express how to render an array or a hash. `Template::Classic`, on the other hand, allows you to include all kinds of Raku code. We will use that for the index template, as follows:

```
<!DOCTYPE html>
<html lang="en">
<head>
    <meta charset="UTF-8">
    <title>Raku Recipes: index</title>
<link rel='stylesheet' id='style-css'  href='raku-recipes.css' type='text/css'
    media='all' />
</head>
<body>
<!-- This is a Template::Classic template -->
<h1>Recipes: index</h1>

<ul>
    <% for %links.kv -> $file, $title { %>
    <li><a href="<%= $file %>"><%= $title %></a></li>
    <% } %>
</ul>

</body>
</html>
```

The main difference here is the for loop in the body of the HTML document. The `<% %>` includes Raku statements, the `<%= %>` fragments just include the value of the variable. So here, we're taking a hash that has file paths as keys and titles as values, and creating a list item out of every one. But that template must be used from the program itself, like this:

```
use Raku::Recipes;
use Markit;
use Template::Classic;
use Text::Markdown;

my $md = Markdown.new;
my &generate-page := template :($title,$content),
                         template-file( "templates/recipe-with-title.html" );

my %links;
for recipes() -> $recipe {
    my $this-md = parse-markdown-from-file($recipe.path);
    my $html-fragment = recipe($md,$recipe);
    my $title = $this-md.document.items[0].text;
    note "Can't find title for $recipe" unless $title;
    my @page = generate-page( $title, $html-fragment );
    my $path = spurt-with-dir($recipe, @page.eager.join );
    $path .= subst( "build/", '' )
    %links{$path} = $title;
}

my &generate-index:= template :( %links ),
                         template-file( "templates/recipes-index.html" );

spurt("build/index.html", generate-index( %links ).eager.join);
```

In this program, routines have been again eliminated for clarity. The first lines of the previous script have been converted to the template-file routine that finds where the file is stored and loads it.

This program is remarkably similar to the first version. The first change is that the page template now includes the title of the recipe, which we extract using Text::Markdown: my $title = $this-md.document.items[0].text.

Note   Surprisingly, we can't use Markit despite being a markdown parser, since it does not offer an interface for actually obtaining the parsed version of the document. We're thus parsing the .md document twice.

You will also observe that `spurt-with-dir` now returns the name of the path used for the HTML file. We will need that to create the link hash. With `subst`, we eliminate the prefix for the used `build` directory and store it in the hash.

The index generation statement consists of a couple of sentences: one builds the templater for this template (the same as you saw previously), and the other saves it to the standard location, `build/index.html`. The result will look as shown in Figure 10-2.

Recipes: index

- <u>Rice pudding</u>

- <u>Carrot wraps</u>

- <u>Buckwheat pudding</u>

- <u>Guacustard</u>

- <u>Tuna risotto</u>

- <u>Chilentils</u>

- <u>Tuna risotto</u>

Figure 10-2. *Recipe web index*

The rest of the pages will be generated as Figure 10-2 shows, except they will have their name in the title tag of the HTML file.

Using these simple templates and a small Raku script, static site generation is fast and quite flexible, since you can customize the script (and the script part of the templates) to create exactly what you like. If you need something that is much more complete, like generating a blog in which every new file regenerates different files, from index to RSS feeds, probably what you need is Uzu. Uzu is highly programmable, configurable, and also quite fast. However, just two templates and a script will go a long way for a simple website composed of a set of web pages and an index.

Recipe 10-3. Create a Dictionary and Do Fast Searches Over It

Problem

There's a set of words and their definitions, and you need to do fast searches by word or content.

Solution

Use Data::StaticTable, an in-memory database with fast indexing capabilities.

How It Works

Hashes are great when you know the key, and you need to access the corresponding value. However, doing inverse searches, that is, finding the key that corresponds to a value, is not so easy, especially when you need to extend the search over several columns. Of course, databases are great for that, but they're no faster than doing it in memory if at all possible and you still need extra tooling besides your script. Using something similar to a database, but in memory, is just what we are looking for.

In the same way we need to arrange data in a particular way to put it into a database, we need to arrange data to enter it into the static table. We'll do that next:

```perl
#!/usr/bin/env perl6

use Data::StaticTable;
use Raku::Recipes::Texts;

my %recipes = Raku::Recipes::Texts.new().recipes;

my @recipes-table;
for %recipes.kv -> $title, %content {
    @recipes-table.append: [ $title,
                             %content<description>,
                             %content<ingredients>.join ];
}
```

```
my $recipes = Data::StaticTable.new(
        <Name Description Ingredients>,
        ( @recipes-table)
        );

my $recipe-query =  Data::StaticTable::Query.new($recipes); # Query object

$recipe-query.add-index( "Ingredients" );

my Data::StaticTable::Position @rice = $recipe-query.grep(rx/rice/,
'Ingredients'):n;
say $recipes.take( @rice ).display;
```

The first thing to observe is that we're using a new module: Raku::Recipes::Texts. This module uses the routines we used in the previous recipes to create a single object: a hash that contains (for the time being, part of) the text of the recipes—title, description, and ingredients. The hash will use the recipe title as a key, and for every recipe ,the value will contain two additional keys: Description and Ingredients.

Note   As we start to use other parts of the recipe, we will enrich this module. For the time being, it just contains the new method and an accessor to the attribute recipes, which contains the scraped data.

We get the text scraped from the markdown recipes in the %recipes hash, and we run a loop over it, extracting in every iteration the title (which is the key used in the hash) and the value (another hash). Since Data::StaticTable takes an array, with every iteration, we add a row with the three columns: recipe name, description, and ingredients.

Data::StaticTable needs the name of the columns and the data. We create $recipes with that. It will contain our data and will be used for searching. But we need an additional Query object to do that. The Data::StaticTable::Query object takes a Data::StaticTable object. Additionally, you can add an index, which will make searches faster, according to the documentation.

Data::StaticTable queries use the known method grep; instead of taking just an expression, they take both an expression and the column you want to search. We want to search the recipes for those containing rice, which is what we do in this query:

```
my Data::StaticTable::Position @rice =
      $recipe-query.grep(rx/rice/, 'Ingredients'):n;
```

It returns an object of type `Data::StaticTable::Position`. These are like indices, except they may contain additional information. We can use them as if they were positioned to obtain the table rows that contain that term. We use the `display` method so that the result is similar to database queries:

```
Name    Description  Ingredients
..........   ..............................   ...........................
["Tuna risotto"]   ["A relatively simple version of this rich, creamy dish
of Italian origin."]   ["500g tuna\n\n 250g rice\n\n ½ onion\n\n 250g
cheese (parmegiano reggiano or granapadano, or manchego)\n\n 1 tbsp extra
virgin olive oil\n\n 4 cloves garlic\n\n"]
```

(This might look better on a bigger screen.)

You might observe there's a `:n` behind the result of the query. Colon-prefixed literals are called *adverbs*; they are equivalent to flags set to `True` (or `False` if the colon is followed by an exclamation mark, aka bang). The `grep` method defined for static table queries takes several named arguments, one of which is `:$n` In that case, it will return the row numbers instead of the content, or some other format. But you might have noticed I'm talking about named arguments, not adverbs. That's because named arguments in subroutines and methods can also be applied as adverbs. That invocation is equivalent to the following:

```
my Data::StaticTable::Position @rice =
      $recipe-query.grep(rx/rice/, 'Ingredients', :n );
```

   or

```
my Data::StaticTable::Position @rice =
      $recipe-query.grep(rx/rice/, 'Ingredients', n => True);
```

The way `:n` is used here is relatively unusual, but totally allowed in Raku. Remember, there is always more than one way to do it.

Recipe 10-4. Compute Differences in Plain Text Documents

Problem

You need to determine if there's been any changes between two versions of a document, and determine what those changes are.

Solution

If the documents are versions of the same document in a Git (or other source control) repository, you can directly use Git to compute this difference, if you know the commits where the two versions reside. If they are not, different modules in the ecosystem will give you this difference: `Algorithm::Diff` is the most veteran, `File::Compare` is more full-featured, and `Text::Diff::Sift4` the newest and probably the fastest.

How It Works

Suppose you need to check new versions of incoming recipes and determine how they differ exactly, so that you can create a single page that presents both versions when clicking. You are comparing text files and you need to know which lines are different.

We will create a new version of a recipe we used earlier, a tuna risotto. The new version will use canned tuna and margarine instead of olive oil. Let's test it for the sake of testing these capabilities of Raku.

Let's try first `File::Compare`:

```
constant $prefix = "recipes/main/rice/";
say "Different"
    if files_are_different( "$prefix/tuna-risotto.md",
                                     "$prefix/tuna-risotto-low-cost.md");
```

This one will only tell us if the files are different, so it might be okay if we want a quick check, or if we are using non-text files. It does not serve our purposes here, however. Let's try `Text::Diff::Sift4` with this script:

```
constant $prefix = "recipes/main/rice/";
say sift4( "$prefix/tuna-risotto.md".IO.slurp,
             "$prefix/tuna-risotto-low-cost.md".IO.slurp, 100, 400);
```

This module has a single function, and it's programmed to be fast. However, this just returns 43 as the number of different characters in both "strings" (which is while we slurp the whole file to check). Again, it might serve as a quick check not only that there is a difference, but also how big the difference is. We are looking for something more specific here.

Let's try the next suggested module, `Algorithm::Diff`:

```
use Algorithm::Diff;
constant $prefix = "recipes/main/rice/";
for sdiff( "$prefix/tuna-risotto.md".IO.lines,
             "$prefix/tuna-risotto-low-cost.md".IO.lines).rotor(3)
     -> ($mode, $deleted, $added )
 {
     say qq:to/EO/ unless $mode eq 'u';
# $mode
     ← $deleted
     → $added
EO

};
```

This does just what we want. The output will be something like this:

```
# c
     ← * 500g tuna
     → * 500g canned tuna

# c
     ← * 250g cheese (parmegiano reggiano or granapadano, or manchego)
     → * 250g whatever cheese is in your fridge

# c
     ← * Extra virgin olive oil
     → * 2 tablespoons olive oil
```

```
# +
    ←
→ * 1 tablespoon butter or margarine.
```

c indicates "change" and a +"indicates a new line. The API of this module is straightforward enough: sdiff compares the lines of the two files (which is why we read the files and extract them) and outputs the changes. We need to group them in sets of three (thus the .rotor(3)) to make sense of it all. The first is the type of change, and the second and third are the lines in the first and second file. We use a signature to destructure every iteration in the array, with three elements produced by rotor in the three variables we use inside the loop: $mode, $deleted, and added.

We use the heredoc format (which you saw in Chapter 3) to present this in a nice format. The unless statement filters out lines that have been marked with u, for "unchanged," in order to show only changes.

It's also quick enough, and it might be suitable for big files. So this solves the problem.

CHAPTER 11

Microservices

The world of websites gave way to the world of web services, and this eventually spawned the world of microservices, which are small reactive applications, with a REST API, that respond to HTTP commands using JSON or some other serialization language. Since the introduction of the `Cro` microframework, most needs related to microservices are covered. In this chapter, we will see how to use this microframework in several, different, ways.

Recipe 11-1. Create a Microservice

Problem

You need to create a microservice that acts as an API to a service you are offering.

Solution

Create a layer over your business logic using `Cro`, Raku's premier microservices framework. It works concurrently, and it can be easily programmed using Raku idioms.

How It Works

Application architecture nowadays is a complex mesh of different microservices that are tied together by a service bus and deployed to the cloud. This complexity makes it much easier to create backends that can service many different frontends efficiently. They do this by creating small services—so small in fact that they are *micro*—that can be designed, implemented, deployed, and tested independently of the rest of the application, as long as the interfaces are respected. This makes the whole application much more reliable and keeps service time uniform by independently scaling the microservices that compose it. This also makes applications more efficient in the use of cloud resources, which are typically pay-per-use.

197

© J.J. Merelo 2020
J.J. Merelo, *Raku Recipes*, https://doi.org/10.1007/978-1-4842-6258-0_11

Anyway, the whole point of a microservice is to offer an alternative, language independent, API that can be consumed from different frontends, so it's usually designed around an existing class or module. It's always important, from an architectural point of view, to separate the business logic from the API, so that they can be developed and tested independently.

This API is built around HTTP verbs—GET, POST, PUT, and DELETE—and status codes, with 200 meaning "Everything is OK" and 4xx returned when there's some kind of client-side error. The API is then created around *routes*, which are functionally equivalent to *objects* or modules. These routes work with URIs, with the lifecycle of an object reusing the same URI.

In this case, we are going to create a microservice for our ingredients database. We'll use the /Ingredient route, and the URI will add the (capitalized) name of the ingredient to this fragment. Our first microservice will return the information we have about an ingredient.

```
use Cro::HTTP::Server;
use Cro::HTTP::Router;
use Raku::Recipes::Roly;

my $rrr = Raku::Recipes::Roly.new();

my $recipes = route {
    get -> "Ingredient", Str $ingredient {
        content 'application/json', $rrr.calories-table{$ingredient};
    }
}

my Cro::Service $μservice = Cro::HTTP::Server.new(
        :host('localhost'), :port(31415), application => $recipes
);

$μservice.start;

react whenever signal(SIGINT) {
    $μservice.stop;
    exit;
}
```

We use two `Cro` modules, `Cro::HTTP::Server` and `Cro::HTTP::Router`. The first one contains the multithreaded server, and the other is used to create the routes. `Cro` is a modular framework, and it has different downloadable modules for different capabilities. These modules can be installed by issuing `zef install Cro::HTTP`.

Tip Remember that all this code is in the book's repo, and that every chapter has its own `META6.json`, mainly so you can install all the specific modules just by writing `zef install –deps-only .` once you are inside the directory.

The `route` command is used to create all the routes our application will have; first the command (`get` in this case), and then a Raku block for which we provide positional arguments whose sequence creates the route. In this case, the two arguments are `Ingredient` and then the variable that is going to be used for the ingredient name, `$ingredient`. Together, they will form the URI that will be used to retrieve the ingredient data. For instance, one URI could be `/Ingredient/Rice` or `/Ingredient/Olive+Oil`. Since the URI needs to be MIME encoded, the space will be converted into a +. The browser will do that for you anyway, if you decide to use the browser to test this.

Note It's OK to "test the waters," so to say, but not the proper way to test a microservice. You need a proper integration test, which is what we will see in the next-to-last recipe in this chapter.

The same module also provides the content order, taking two arguments: MIME type and the actual content. This order is *smart* in the sense that it will be able to transform the data structure into something adequate for the MIME type, as long as it knows how. In this case, it's simply JSON, so it knows how to do it. We return the hash that describes every ingredient, with a result like the one shown in Figure 11-1, seen from the browser.

```
{
    Unit: "1 tablespoon",
    Vegan: true,
    Dessert: false,
    Protein: "0",
    Side: false,
    Main: false,
  ▼ parsed-measures: [
        1,
        "tablespoon"
    ],
    Calories: "119",
    Dairy: false
}
```

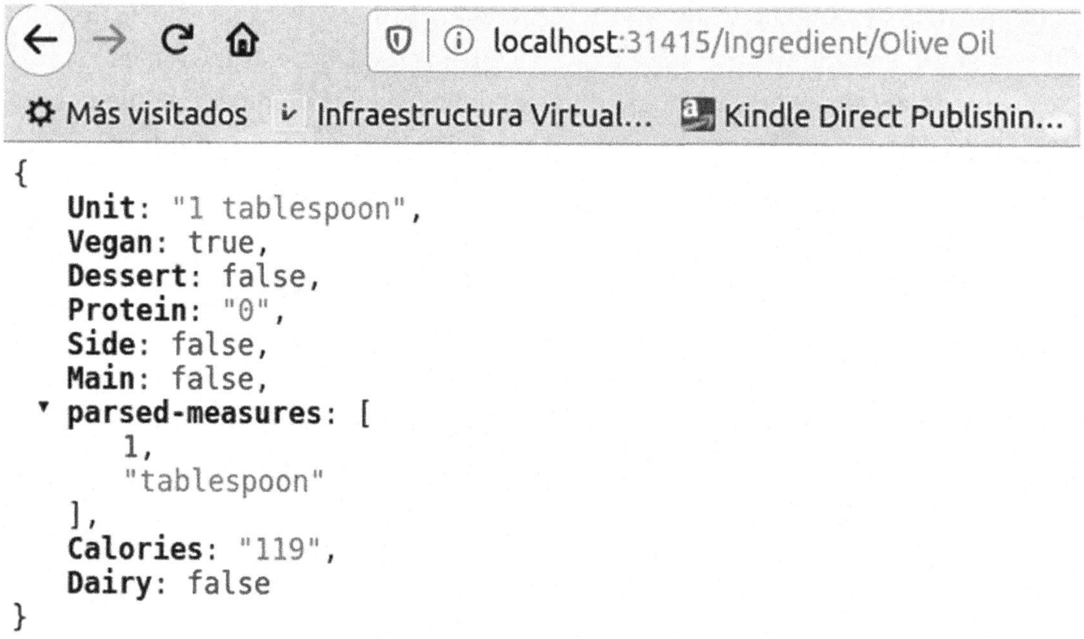

Figure 11-1. *Accessing a microservice from the browser*

This part defines the route, but we need to define the microservice, setting the
address it's going to use (which will determine the interface it will be listening), the port
it's going to use (I love the pi port, 31415), and the name of the application that's going to
be served. We obviously call this variable $μservice, using the Greek letter *mu*.

Last, we need to start the microservice and set up a way to actually stop it. It will be
running until the process receives the stop signal, that is, a Ctrl+C in most operating
systems or a kill command from the command line. We can start it from the command
line, and if that port is free (why wouldn't it be), we can use it. We can in fact create a
small client, using Cro, just the way we did in Chapter 9:

```
use Cro::HTTP::Client;
my $ingredient = @*ARGS[0] // "water";
my $cro = Cro::HTTP::Client.new(base-uri => "http://localhost:31415/
Ingredient/" );
my $response = await $cro.get( $ingredient );
say  await $response.body;
```

As we are using a standard interface, we don't need to include the class that we
are extracting the information from. We just need to know how to build the URL to

access a resource. This will print the JSON representation to the console, since it's only channeling access to the microservice. But as long as we don't need to worry about the implementation of the microservice, we could create a client in a different language as well. Python, for instance:

```python
import requests
import sys

if len(sys.argv) > 1:
    ingredient = sys.argv[1]
else:
    ingredient = "Rice"

with requests.get('http://localhost:31415/Ingredient/'+ingredient) as r:
    if (r.status_code == 200):
        print(r.text)
```

The main difference here is that we don't decode the resulting JSON. Also, we check for the status code to be correct, but essentially it's the same. At the end of the day, a REST API is a standard way to access any kind of microservice.

We can use yet another way of accessing content, using a web downloader such as curl (or wget):

```
curl http://localhost:31415/Type/Vegan
["Olive Oil","Green kiwi","Sundried tomatoes","Apple","Orange","Kale",
"Kidney beans","Lentils","Rice","Tomato","Potatoes","Cashews","Chickpeas",
"Beer"]
```

But things can go wrong, and they will, and Chapter 8 taught you a lesson (or two) on how to deal with that. We need, at least, to react in some sensible way when we try to access an ingredient that does not exist. The best way to deal with an error is to avoid it altogether, and we can use Raku's signatures to do it (again). This is just the route definition, and the rest of the script is the same as before:

```
my $recipes = route {
    get -> "Ingredient", Str $ingredient where $rrr.is-
    ingredient($ingredient) {
        content 'application/json', $rrr.calories-table{$ingredient};
    }
```

```
get -> "Ingredient",
        Str $ingredient where !$rrr.is-ingredient($ingredient) {
    not-found;
}
}
```

As we have said, Cro routes get different blocks, and the calling convention doubles as a block signature. We can do type checking in the signature: $ingredient is a real one, so it's okay. It gets a block where it answers with the data we have about it. However, we can catch the fact that it's not also in the signature: the second route will fire when it's not an ingredient, and it will just use the not-found command, which will make Raku generate the correct response. This is shown in Figure 11-2, as seen from the Postman API testing application.

Figure 11-2. *A 404 response from the microservice as seen from the Postman application, at the bottom of the image*

This mechanism is quite flexible, and it also shows in a more clear way the execution path the application is following. But even so, it's not convenient to have all the routes lumped together in a single place. Besides, we'd like our microservice, as long as it includes an efficient web server, to double up as a server for the static web pages we generated in the previous chapter. We'll also add some more routes—for instance, a route that returns all ingredients with a characteristic, such as being part of vegan dishes. This is the result. Once again, just the routes are shown:

```
sub static-routes {
    route {
        get -> *@path {
            static 'build/', @path, :indexes<index.html index.htm>;
```

```
        }
    }
}

sub type-routes {
    route {
        get -> Str $type where $type ∈ @food-types {
            my %ingredients-table = $rrr.calories-table;
            my @result =  %ingredients-table.keys.grep: {
                %ingredients-table{$_}{$type} };
            content 'application/json', @result;
        }
        get -> Str $type where $type ∉ @food-types {
            not-found;
        }
    }
}

sub ingredient-routes {
    route {
        get -> Str $ingredient where $rrr.is-ingredient($ingredient) {
            content 'application/json', $rrr.calories-table{$ingredient};
        }
        get -> Str $ingredient where !$rrr.is-ingredient($ingredient) {
            not-found;
        }
    }
}

my $recipes = route {
    include "content"    => static-routes,
            "Type"       => type-routes,
            "Ingredient" => ingredient-routes;

}
```

There are several improvements here, from the point of view of the structure of the program and also the general architecture. Routes have been divided into blocks, which are then included in a single set of routes that will be served by the microservice.

We define a new *static* route that will take care of static content. The `static` command will return the file, and in the same command we also define that `index.htm` or `index.html` is going to be the default index. These files were created in the build subdirectory, so that's used to build the route. The URL will be defragmented to a `@path`, and this path will be reconstructed as a file path, which will be returned.

The route we created to respond to ingredients of a certain type follows the same pattern we used before. It returns a list of ingredients if the type does exist (`@food-types` is imported from `Raku::Recipes`), and `404` if it does not. The other route block, `ingredient-routes`, is the same as in the previous version, except for a little detail: the route itself.

This way of expressing routes allows for decoupling of the logic from the route it's going to be hanged on to, which gives the designer much more flexibility when fixing them. Where are route names defined then? We do that in an `include` statement: it's a hash that takes the route URI fragment as a key, and the `sub` it's going to be routed to as a value. So `Ingredient` is going to be routed to the same code as before, except now this path is not baked into the code, but is totally independent.

In these examples, we used only `GET` routes, since they are simple enough and do not change the content. Originally, we didn't intend for our set of recipes to be changed from anywhere but the file. In a more general setting, however, `PUT` and `POST` can be used from `Cro` to create new resources, as well as `DELETE` to delete them. It's simply a matter of changing the `get` statements in the route to `post`, `put`, or `delete`. This is a short example of a "pantry" web service that introduces ingredients in a pantry, shows the ingredients that are stored, and can also delete one of them.

```
sub keep-routes is export {
    route {
        put -> Str $ingredient where $rrr.is-ingredient($ingredient) {
            $pantry ∪= $ingredient;
            say $pantry;
            content "application/json", $pantry.list;
        }
```

```
    get -> {
        content "application/json", $pantry.list;
    }

    delete -> Str $ingredient where $rrr.is-ingredient($ingredient) {
        if $ingredient ∈ $pantry {
            $pantry \= $ingredient;
        }
        content "application/json", $pantry.list;
    }
  }
}
```

The content of the request is retrieved in exactly the same way. It will be handled to the route as a parameter, and we can add signature checks to it in the same way we have done before. The $pantry variable has been defined as a set, and we use set operations on it in order to add a new ingredient, or delete it using the \ set difference operator. In every case, the request will return the current state of the pantry, converting it to list, since content only takes data structures that can actually be converted to JSON. We can also make requests using curl:

```
% curl -X PUT http://localhost:31415/pantry/Rice
[{"Rice":true}]
% curl -X PUT http://localhost:31415/pantry/Tuna
[{"Tuna":true},{"Rice":true}]
% curl http://localhost:31415/pantry
[{"Tuna":true},{"Rice":true}]
% curl -X DELETE http://localhost:31415/pantry/Tuna
[{"Rice":true}]
```

When a set is converted to a list, it's converted to a list of pairs ("Element" => True), and that is why it's shown that way here. If we want to show just the elements, we can simply extract just the keys of the pairs.

This recipe gives you a hint at the possibilities of Cro. We'll see more of them in the next recipes. But before those recipes, you might want to hopscotch your way to the last recipe in the chapter, about testing this very microservice. Because testing is important.

Recipe 11-2. Work with Websockets to Connect to a Client

Problem

You want to create an interactive service on your site, for instance, a bot, by providing a websocket interface.

Solution

Cro is a general-purpose network-computing framework. It can route your websocket calls and create a supply to which you can react. A specific module, Cro::WebSocket, is used to work with websockets, from the client or from the server side. We'll focus more on the server side.

How It Works

Websockets are a relatively recent technology that can be used to make sites more dynamic and responsive. Since they open a permanent connection, as opposed to the stateless connection that the plain vanilla HTTP uses, they can be used to implement iterative services such as chats or little bots.

We are going to create an iterative service, a little calorie computer that gets the amount of an ingredient and returns the number of calories in it. For example, the user might enter a 250g apple and would get back the calories in that amount of apple.

We'll create a websocket server for this purpose. We will use the cro command-line tool to generate a stub for the implementation. This tool is installed independently of the other modules Cro has, from the Raku ecosystem, and once that's done, it can be used from the command line. After placing yourself in the directory where you want the module to reside, write something like the following:

```
cro stub http calories calories ':!secure :websocket'
```

We are going to generate an HTTP service called calories, in a subdirectory called calories, that is going to use HTTP (instead of HTTPS, that is, !secure, meaning "not secure") and it's going to be a websocket server (hence the flag in the shape of an adverb). All options are written in single quotes.

This will generate a whole lot of files, including a `Dockerfile` and a `META6.json` file, as well as a script that launches the server and includes a module called `Routes`, which will include the services. We'll use the server as is, and we will work on the `Routes` module, which also includes a boilerplate for responding to requests and serving results. This will be a module in a `lib` subdirectory. It will also generate a `Cro` configuration file like this one:

```
---
name: calories
env:  []
entrypoint: service.p6
links:  []
endpoints:
  -
    id: http
    port-env: CALORIES_PORT
    name: HTTP
    host-env: CALORIES_HOST
    protocol: http
id: calories
cro: 1
...
```

The main points here are that it uses a series of environment variables, specifically defined with this service. This is the standard best practice in microservices. It also defines the `Cro` version (1) (in the `"cro"` key) and an ID for this service, also `calories`. In principle, we don't need to worry further about this file, although we might want to change the name of the environment variables or the name of the entrypoint. This file will be used by the `Cro` command line to launch the service, too.

Anyway, that's the extent of work the command line is going to do for us. We still have to write the routes. First we will have to take care of parsing the "commands" that are going to be sent to us via the socket. In the previous chapter, we parsed a part of the ingredient rows of the recipe files. However, we stopped short at actually processing the full ingredient description itself. We need to do that now, so we can produce a new grammar that will take care of that for us.

Let's first reuse what we can. Grammars have been created by the meta-object protocol, same as the rest of the type objects in Raku. They are similar, in many ways, to classes. Are they similar to roles too? Well, yes, they are. So let's spin off two tokens to their own role, a *grammarole*, so to speak, so that we can reuse them:

```
unit role Raku::Recipes::Grammar::Measures;

token quantity { <:N>+ }
token unit     { "g" | "tbsp" | "clove" | "tbsps" | "cloves" }
```

Okay, been there, done that. This looks like a grammar and acts like a grammar, but is actually defined as a role. As a role, we can mix it in a grammar like so:

```
use Raku::Recipes::Roly;
use Raku::Recipes::Grammar::Measures

my @products;
BEGIN {
    @products = Raku::Recipes::Roly.new.products;
}

unit grammar Raku::Recipes::Grammar::Measured-Ingredients does
Raku::Recipes::Grammar::Measures;
token TOP      { <quantity> [\h* <unit> \h+ <ingredient> | \h+
<ingredient>]}
token ingredient {:i @products }
```

There are several interesting things in this new grammar, besides the fact that it composes a role. We are using a BEGIN block to initialize a variable that is going to be used inside it. We need to know which products are available in the class to properly do the parsing. BEGIN is what is called a *phaser*, that is, a block that is guaranteed to run in a certain phase of the compilation procedure. This will run at compile time and will run only once, assigning a value to @products that will be baked into the precompiled binary that's stored.

But then the two tokens are also interesting. One uses this variable and is actually equivalent to "product1" | "product2" ... and so on for every product in the array. Arrays can be interpolated in regexes (token are just regexes, remember) to that effect. We also have an adverb at the beginning, to indicate that it will be case-insensitive. We don't care if people write pasta or Pasta or PaStA. It will still check out.

The TOP token also uses alternation: either we have something like 1 egg (quantity + ingredient) or we have something like a 100g apple (quantity + unit + ingredient). That alternation takes care of that and is able to match both.

Note   We also solved this problem in a slightly different way in the `Raku::Recipes` module, using regular expressions and multiple schedule. Remember, there is always more than one way to do things in Raku.

Let's get to the websocket server itself. First, we need to build a client, or we will have nothing to check it with. One option is websocat (`https://github.com/vi/websocat/releases`), but, to exemplify once again the interoperability of this kind of server with all kinds of clients, we will use the following script. It's adapted from the `ws` example, written in JavaScript, and runs using the deno runtime:

```
import {
  connectWebSocket,
  isWebSocketCloseEvent,
  isWebSocketPingEvent,
  isWebSocketPongEvent,
} from "https://deno.land/std/ws/mod.ts";
import { encode } from "https://deno.land/std/encoding/utf8.ts";
import { BufReader } from "https://deno.land/std/io/bufio.ts";
import { TextProtoReader } from "https://deno.land/std/textproto/mod.ts";
import { blue, green, red, yellow } from "https://deno.land/std/fmt/
colors.ts";
const endpoint = Deno.args[0] || "ws://127.0.0.1:31415/calories";
/** simple websocket cli */
try {
  const sock = await connectWebSocket(endpoint);
  console.log(green("«Calories» webservice connected! (type 'close' to
  quit)"));
  const messages = async (): Promise<void> => {
    for await (const msg of sock) {
      if (typeof msg === "string") {
        console.log(yellow(`< ${msg}`));
```

```
      } else if (isWebSocketCloseEvent(msg)) {
        console.log(red(`closed: code=${msg.code}, reason=${msg.reason}`));
      }
    }
  };
  const cli = async (): Promise<void> => {
    const tpr = new TextProtoReader(new BufReader(Deno.stdin));
    while (true) {
      await Deno.stdout.write(encode("> "));
      const line = await tpr.readLine();
      if (line === null || line === "close") {
        break;
      } else {
        await sock.send(line);
      }
    }
  };
  await Promise.race([messages(), cli()]).catch(console.error);
  if (!sock.isClosed) {
    await sock.close(1000).catch(console.error);
  }
} catch (err) {
  console.error(red(`Could not connect to WebSocket: '${err}'`));
}
Deno.exit(0);
```

This script will present a prompt, will send what you type via the websocket, and will close the connection if you write either close or an empty line. It's using the URL of the websocket we'll be starting with by default, which is ws://127.0.0.1:31415/calories (but you can change that using an argument in the command line). Websockets use the ws (or wss, for secure ones) protocol, with addresses, ports, and fragments being pretty much the same as for HTTP URLs. We'll wait until our webservice is set up to run it.

Here are the routes defined for the calories websocket, expanded from the boilerplate generated previously:

```
use Cro::HTTP::Router;
use Cro::HTTP::Router::WebSocket;
use Raku::Recipes::Grammar::Measured-Ingredients;
use Raku::Recipes::Roly;

my $rrr = Raku::Recipes::Roly.new;

sub routes() is export {
    route {
        my $chat = Supplier.new;
        get -> 'calories' {
            web-socket -> $incoming {
                supply {
                    whenever $incoming -> $message {
                        $chat.emit(await $message.body-text);
                    }
                    whenever $chat -> $text {
                        # Compute calories here
                        my $item =
                                Raku::Recipes::Grammar::Measured-
                                Ingredients
                                .parse( $text );
                        my $calories = $rrr.calories( ~$item<ingredient>,
                                +$item<quantity>);
                        emit "Calories: for $text ⇒ $calories";
                    }
                }
            }
        }
    }
}
```

Although there's a certain curly brace overload here, the gist of it is in the last non-closing-braces lines. We get the text, we parse it using the grammar, and then we extract ingredient and quantity from the parse object.

Note   We could, and in fact should, verify that the units are the same. This script will pass as good 100tbsp of pasta, 33g of egg, and things like that. We could try to catch those errors at the grammar level, or at this one, but let's for the time be happy with the fact that the correct strings are parsed correctly.

Those are fed to the routine computing calories, and a string with the result is returned. The name of the service, or the route to it, is given as an argument to get, which is why we use the /calories URL above to access this service.

Looking at the big picture, it's a bit more complicated than that, involving a couple of supplies. But essentially, from the point of view of Raku, a websocket server route is a supply whose emissions will get to the client. We emit the result string, and that string will be received through the websocket, by the client. But what actually happens is that the socket receives an incoming message through a websocket, that websocket parses the message and re-emits the body though a specific supply we created for the websocket, which allows asynchronous processing of incoming requests. The actual processing is done by the receiving end of that second supply, which we still call $chat as it was called in the boilerplate code. All in all, a slightly more convoluted processing than what happens with REST APIs, but essentially something similar to what other languages do, only using Raku-standard data structures and capabilities.

We haven't changed the server script, so we run it directly from there. Comma IDE includes a special facility for running web services; we'll use it in this occasion. We create an execution configuration, as shown in Figure 11-3.

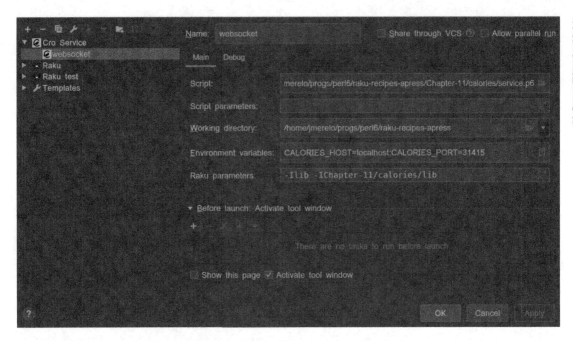

this figure will be printed in b/w

Figure 11-3. *Running the websocket from Comma IDE*

Observe that we are defining in Figure 11-3 the two environment variables we are going to run. We'll use localhost and the usual port for running. The Raku parameters show the path to the libraries that we need to include, the Raku::Recipes ones, which are at lib, and the routes, which is in the shown path.

We can now launch our client and type requests, getting the answers shown in Figure 11-4.

```
→ Chapter-11 git:(master) ~/.deno/bin/deno  run --allow-net ws-client.ts
«Calories» webservice connected! (type 'close' to quit)
> 2 apple
> < Calories: for 2 apple ⇒ 104
3 egg
> < Calories: for 3 egg ⇒ 234
133g sardines
> < Calories: for 133g sardines ⇒ 276.64
4 green kiwi
> < Calories: for 4 green kiwi ⇒ 168
close
```

this figure will be printed in b/w

Figure 11-4. *Consuming websocket from a deno client*

We use the command line:

```
deno  run --allow-net ws-client.ts
```

deno needs to explicitly allow the use of the net, since it runs in a sandbox similar to the browser. As you can see, it returns the computed calories, showing them in a different color, and opening the prompt back again. The word close will effectively close the connection.

For websockets, you can also use plain JavaScript from the browser developer console, which you can access usually by pressing Shift+Ctrl+C. The result in Firefox is shown in Figure 11-5.

```
>> var exampleSocket = new WebSocket("ws://localhost:31415/calories");
<- undefined
>> exampleSocket.onmessage = function (event) {
     console.log(event.data);
   }
<- ▶ function onmessage(event)
>> exampleSocket.send("80g skyr drink")
<- undefined
   Calories: for 80g skyr drink ⇒ 43.2
```

Figure 11-5. *Working with a websocket from the Firefox developer console*

We open the connection, then set an event that will fire every time a message is received. We log the data attached to the message, and then send a message to the socket by hand, getting the response in the console.

In general, these websocket services will be implemented within a website as a widget, or as a microservice to serve other microservices. At any rate, this recipe has shown you how to create a websocket microservice from scratch, how to run it from Comma IDE, and how to verify that it works using different client services.

Recipe 11-3. Create a Mini-Bot for a Messaging Application Such as Telegram

Problem

Messaging applications such as Telegram and Slack provide an alternative user interface, a conversational one, that can be used to answer simple queries, store information, or even create mini-games. These requests can arrive at any time and the responses to them must be immediate, not blocking the program, and also as fast as possible. We need an agile program to be able to respond quickly to those requests.

Solution

With the microservice we have created in Recipe 11-2, we can create another layer that taps it to serve the information in this way. We can also directly use the business logic in the classes if needed. In any case, both Telegram and Slack have an open source API. Slack is not as well covered in the Raku ecosystem, with a single module usable only for sending messages. There are at least two Telegram modules that we can use, so we'll create a Telegram bot with one of them.

How It Works

We will create a Telegram bot that computes the number of calories, given the amount and unit of an ingredient. The first thing this implies is parsing the string so that we obtain the unit, quantity, and name of the ingredient. But we have done that before, right? Right, although it allowed wrong units. Let's give this a twist for this recipe. After all, we kinda have a higher standard for bots than for other types of services, right?

There are many ways to achieve this fix; for instance, we could simply issue a syntax error from the grammar and refuse to parse incorrect strings. That's easier said than done, however. In the way the grammar is constructed, we have already parsed the unit and the quantity when we arrive at the ingredient. In that moment, we could try to match the ingredient to the unit and refuse to parse it if there's no match, but the error wouldn't be in the ingredient itself, but in the unit, so we would need to backtrack. We would have to reorganize the whole grammar, and make the whole process much slower by backtracking.

Tip   By the way, grammars at all levels are awesomely explained in a book by this same publisher, *Parsing with Perl 6 Regexes and Grammars*, by Moritz Lenz. If you are curious about them, or want to use them much more extensively, give it a go.

Fortunately, we can catch that error at a different level, using Raku mechanisms, and that would be via an action. While a grammar will give you an abstract syntax tree (AST), an action that's attached to a grammar will *compile* that AST into an object you can readily use. So far, we have been extracting parts of the AST to get to the ingredients, or whatever. Now we will, in one fell swoop, solve two problems: get a parsed object that does not involve knowing the parsed structure, and check if there's anything incorrect at some level. We will create this action for that two-step process:

```
use Raku::Recipes::Roly;
use X::Raku::Recipes;

my $rrr = Raku::Recipes::Roly.new();

unit module Raku::Recipes::Grammar::Actions;

class Measured-Ingredients {
    method TOP($/) {
        my $unit = $/<unit>.made // "Unit";
        my $ingredient = $/<ingredient>.made;
        if ( $rrr.check-unit( $ingredient, $unit ) ) {
            make $ingredient =>  $unit => $/<quantity>.made;
        } else {
            X::Raku::Recipes::WrongUnit.new( desired-unit => 'Other',
                    unit => $unit ).throw;
        }
    }

    method ingredient($/) {
        make tc ~$/;
    }
    method quantity($/) {
        make +val( ~$/  ) // unival( ~$/ )
    }
    method unit($/){
        make ~$/;
    }

}
```

A grammar action is, at one level, simply a class. Instances of that class will be embedded in the corresponding grammar and produce the result. Its denomination needs to be coupled somehow to the grammar they serve, which is why in this case it's called Raku::Recipes::Grammar::Actions::Measured-Ingredients. By putting this class in a module, we have put all actions we would create here in the same Raku::Rec ipes::Grammar::Actions namespace, and we can also load them together by using a single use clause.

The class itself has got methods for every token in the grammar; those methods get as an argument the match object, $/, that is matched at that point. Methods take that object and generate another object that is attached to the abstract syntax tree at that point. The make command attaches its argument to $/ at that point; make is equivalent to $/.make. If we attach something to $/ at the unit token, that result will be available anywhere on top of that token at $/<unit>.made.

Remember that $/ is a match object. We need to coerce it into something else, which is why we convert the match object in unit into a string, and in ingredient we convert and also capitalize it using the tc (title case) command (remember that ingredients are always capitalized). For measurements, we do something similar to what we did before when we parsed the CSV: We use different methods to convert it to a number depending on val working (ASCII numbers) or not (for things like ⅔).

But the key of this action is in the TOP method; this is where we check that the unit is correct, using the appropriately called check-unit method of Raku::Recipes::Roly. If it's correct, we return a pair whose key is the ingredient, and whose value is another pair—unit and quantity. We have also conveniently used Unit when there's no unit, for instance, in the string "3 Apple".

Note   As long as we're nitpicking, we could also try to coax plurals into the grammar. However, we would need to add more information to the original data to avoid things like 3 tablespoons olive oils or 300g tunas (tunae?) behaving as false positives. We will go there if needed, but for the time being let's be lenient with those kinds of errors.

We can use this action in this way:

```
my $item = Raku::Recipes::Grammar::Measured-Ingredients.parse("2 egg",
        actions =>
        Raku::Recipes::Grammar::Actions::Measured-Ingredients.new);
```

It will produce an object of this kind: Egg => Unit => 2. This is quite convenient, and we can use it for our Telegram bot.

In case you are not using it already, Telegram is a messaging application created originally by a Russian programmer, and it has become incredibly popular thanks to its security features, flexibility, and ability to create bots, which is lacking in other commercial chat apps such as WhatsApp. Unlike WhatsApp, it can also work with your phone off, and it's got a nice, open source, desktop application for all platforms. Creating a bot is quite easy and is done (how else?) via a dialogue with a bot called BotFather. Figure 11-6 shows how we created this one.

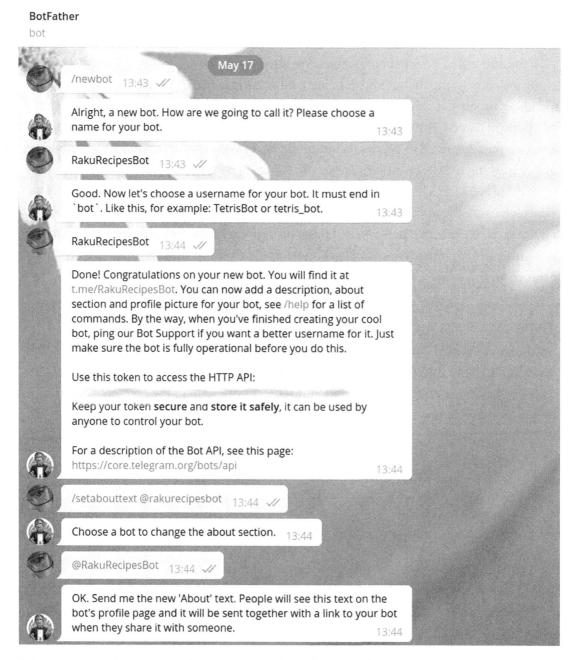

Figure 11-6.   *Creating RakuRecipesBot by talking with the BotFather*

This dialogue will give you a key, which I have blurred here. It's a long string that is going to be your token for starting your bot microservice.

A bot works in a way that is similar to a microservice: it gets a message and answers to it. It needs to parse that message to look for specific commands, or to understand it to give an answer. In this case, we will make our bot respond with the calorie content in measures of ingredients, such as the ones we've used in the websocket server (or websocker). So in essence, it will be tapping a supply of messages and responding to them using the API. This is what we do in this program.

```perl6
#!/usr/bin/env perl6
use Telegram;
use Raku::Recipes::Grammar::Measured-Ingredients;
use Raku::Recipes::Grammar::Actions;
use Raku::Recipes::Roly;

my $bot = Telegram::Bot.new(%*ENV<RAKU_RECIPES_BOT_TOKEN>);
my $rrr = Raku::Recipes::Roly.new;

$bot.start(1);

react {
    whenever $bot.messagesTap -> $msg {
        my $item =  Raku::Recipes::Grammar::Measured-Ingredients.parse(
                $msg.text,
                actions =>
                    Raku::Recipes::Grammar::Actions::Measured-Ingredients
                        .new).made;

        if $item {
            my $calories = $rrr.calories( $item );
            $bot.sendMessage($msg.chat.id,
            "{$item.value.value} {$item.value.key} of {$item.key} has
            $calories calories");
            say "{ $msg.sender.username }: { $msg.text } in { $msg.chat.id
            } → $item";
        } else {
            say "There's something wrong with the input string; can't
            compute calories";
```

```
        $bot.sendMessage( $msg.chat.id,
                "Sorry, can't compute '{$msg.text}'");
    }
}
whenever signal(SIGINT) {
    $bot.stop;
    exit;
}
}
```

We start the program by creating an object that uses the API token we've acquired. As usual, API tokens and all kinds of secure information must be read from environment variables. We need to create a `Roly` object to compute calories, and then we start the bot by telling it to poll every second. We can change that interval at will.

The `react` block will be run when an event occurs. When a message is received and placed into the $msg variable, it's parsed to an object via the action and `.made` method. If no object is created, something has gone wrong, and the `else` clause is activated. We send a message saying that we can't work with that; `$msg.text` returns the actual text in the message.

Tip Always remember to be helpful with your messages, including explaining the origin of the misunderstanding.

However, if we have a parsed ingredient object, we can compute calories from it. We can just give it to the calorie method in `Roly`, which has a new `multi` that takes that kind of thing directly, a `Pair` whose value is also a `Pair`.

```
multi method calories( Pair $ingredient ) {
    return self.calories( $ingredient.key, $ingredient.value.value );
}
```

Since we already know that the unit is okay, we don't need to give that information to compute the calories. It will return a number, which we will send as a message, responding to the specific user who issued the command; `sendMessage` takes the chat ID as an argument to make sure the message routing is done correctly. In both cases, we also print something to the console to check that everything is okay. That information will not be received by the user.

The script is run from the console, or anywhere else. It needs to be running for it to respond to the messages. Some people use el cheapo Raspberry Pis to have a bot farm at home, running all the time, but you can also use a cloud service with free tiers to have it running permanently, running inside a container, for instance. It will work as shown in Figure 11-7.

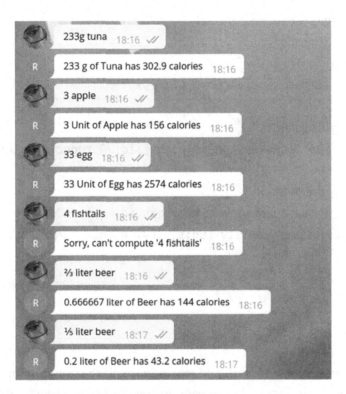

Figure 11-7. *Getting the calories of different dishes*

The amount of things a bot can do is, in principle, unlimited. You can add authentication, for instance. All configuration is done via BotFather. You can also do heavy tasks in which case you want to add concurrency for doing other tasks in the background.

One of the things Telegram can do is respond to commands. These are "slash" commands with a / in front, that are issued from the message box by typing in it. There's nothing special about these commands, except that you can define them using the BotFather and the UI will list them when you type a slash. You will have to parse them anyway. It's convenient, however, because it gives you an easy way to explain what the bot is about and how it works. Let's work with three commands—/about, /products, and /calories—in this second version of the script (just the react block is included, since it's the only thing that has changed):

```
whenever $bot.messagesTap -> $msg {
        $msg.text ~~ /\/$<command> = (\w+) \h* $<args> = (.*)/;
        say "$msg $<command>";
        given $<command> {
            when "calories" {
                gimme-calories($msg,$<args>)
            }
            when "products" {
                $bot.sendMessage($msg.chat.id, @products.join("-"));
            }
            when "about" {
                $bot.sendMessage($msg.chat.id, q:to/EOM/);
To query, use /calories Quantity [Unit] Ingredient or /products for the list
of products
EOM
            }
        }
    }
}
```

We need to parse the command, and we use a regular expression for that. A command will always be a string composed of characters, and then it might or might not have some more text. It will be captured in $<args> if there is more text.

Depending on the command, we will send different messages back. The previous code that computes the calories has been spun off to its own routine, called gimme-calories. For the message that will be returned for the about command, we use the so-called here-to syntax, which we used for the first time in Chapter 3. The result is shown in Figure 11-8.

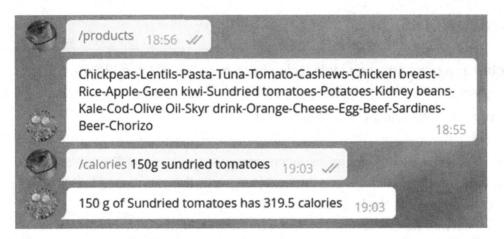

this figure will be printed in b/w

Figure 11-8. *Dialogue with the bot using slash commands*

While I was at it, I gave the bot a funny face. It looks much more friendly now. And efficient.

Providing services via Telegram can be a nice and handy way to enhance your business, as well as to do all kinds of home automation tasks, or even as an addition to web-only based services. With an adequate backend, you can serve them all, and given that you can create concurrent backends using Cro, you could embed this alongside websockers or web services sharing the same cloud instance, as well as data services, if needed. You will learn more about these options in the next chapters.

Recipe 11-4. Test Your Microservice
Problem

If it's not tested, it's broken. This also applies to microservices. At the end of the day, they are another type of function whose result you need to check. So it's essential to test every aspect of them, in the same way you do any other function in any other module.

Solution

Cro includes a testing framework, called Cro::HTTP::Test. It will do this job nicely.

How It Works

Note   If you are arriving at this recipe fresh from the first one (Recipe 11-1), excellent choice. If not, that recipe contains the microservice we are going to test, so you might want to work through it first.

First, you need to do this alongside the first recipe in this chapter. The API and its tests need to be developed at the same time, and have only been separated in this book for the sake of dealing with a single concept in every recipe.

In theory, routes are simply functions, so there should be a way to test them simply by *calling* them and observing the result. However, in practice they are a bit more complex than that, since they are invoked via HTTP requests and return HTTP responses. We could then, in theory, just fire up the service and create a series of tests for them, blackbox style. Postman, which we have used before, can also be programmed and with it we can create a blackbox test suite in several different languages.

We are more interested in whitebox testing, because we might want to know which code paths are taken, and do so without actually needing to fire up a server, occupy a port, and so on. So we will use a *native* testing library: `Cro::HTTP::Test`. In the same way as other API-testing libraries work, it just needs to access the routes that need to be tested. Internally, it produces the requests and the responses, but without actually running a server. Here's a simple test using that:

```
use Cro::HTTP::Test;

require "ingredients-microservice-v3.p6" <&static-routes>;
test-service static-routes, {
    test get('/'),
            status => 200,
            content-type => 'text/html',
            body => /recipes/;
}

done-testing;
```

After including the testing library, we need to "`require`" the program that implemented the microservices, with its correct path. Unlike `use`, `require` does not automatically import symbols, so we need to declare them at compile time. We are only testing `static-routes` for the time being, so we need to import that. Declaring route blocks as independent routines, as we did, also pays off here: `Cro::HTTP::Test` tests routes by calling the routing block. We couldn't have done that if they were directly written into a single variable. Or, could we? Actually, we could, since the variable we assign routes to in the second version is actually a subroutine.

But wait. What does `require` do? And how come it is able to import routines, if I didn't remember to actually export it? Well, we are cheating a bit. We have to change the previous program this way (with parts unchanged suppressed for readability):

```
sub static-routes is export { ... }
sub type-routes is export { ... }
sub ingredient-routes is export { ... }
# Route block definition here
if ( $*PROGRAM eq $?FILE ) {...} # Fire up service
```

So we have to explicitly declare the routines as exportable so that they can be imported for testing. But, more importantly, `require` compiles and runs what it loads.

Note   The same thing happens when you load a module via `use`; any code between definitions will be run, as well as blocks that are run in that phase—BEGIN blocks, for instance. That's a side effect of every load, and one that we don't really need in this case, because it will start the event loop for serving pages and block running anything else in the script.

So, as usual in other languages, we check if the file is being run directly or loaded as a module. `$*PROGRAM` and `$?FILE` are system-defined variables that take the value of the path the current script is using, and the handle of the current file. If they are the same, well, we are actually running *from* the same file. `$?FILE` is automatically converted to a string in string context. If we are testing, `$*PROGRAM` will be the name of the testing program and `$?FILE` will not change. They will be different in that case, and it will not run.

So, back to the test itself. The module introduces the `test-service` command, which takes as arguments the name of the routing routine, or, wait for it, *routingine*, and the block that effectively launches the test. Inside it, we'll need a test command for every test, and that one uses first the HTTP command and the route. Since that route has not been attached to any URL fragment, the paths used here will start at the root, `/`.

In this case, we are testing the static part of the route, the one that should return the static pages; / should return the index. In the response, we check that the status code is correct (200), the type is also correct (text/html), and that the content, in the body, is right. It should include the regex /recipes/, which is included in the name of the css file, raku-recipes.css.

The result printed by the program is as follows:

```
    ok 1 - Status is acceptable
    ok 2 - Content type is acceptable
    ok 3 - Body is acceptable
    1..3
ok 1 - GET /
1..1
```

Testing is the process of ensuring software quality, and good testing is not only the one that tells you that everything is okay, but the one that indicates some quirks that could be fixed. In this case, although we have shown the flexibility of Raku by modifying a script, there are more ways to do this, and one of them is simply creating a module for routes. This first testing has produced a refactoring, which is good.

Here's the module that we've created for routes:

```
use Cro::HTTP::Router;
use Raku::Recipes::Roly;
use Raku::Recipes;

unit module My::Routes;

our $rrr = Raku::Recipes::Roly.new();

sub static-routes is export {
    route {
        get -> *@path {
            static 'build/', @path, :indexes<index.html>;
        }
    }
}
```

```
sub type-routes is export {
    route {
        get -> Str $type where $type ∈ @food-types {
            my %ingredients-table = $rrr.calories-table;
            my @result =  %ingredients-table.keys.grep: {
                %ingredients-table{$_}{$type} };
            content 'application/json', @result;
        }
    }
}

sub ingredient-routes is export {
    route {
        get -> Str $ingredient where $rrr.is-ingredient($ingredient) {
            content 'application/json', $rrr.calories-table{$ingredient};
        }
    }
}
```

As a matter of fact, we eliminated the not-found commands, which were used for illustration purposes, since if no route is found with that name, the same content is returned. This is part of the refactoring, and of course, we will have to test it. We have called this My::Routes and placed it into the lib/ subfolder of the Chapter-11 folder.

Here's the new test script:

```
#!/usr/bin/env perl6

use Cro::HTTP::Test;
use My::Routes;

test-service static-routes, {
    test get('/'),
            status => 200,
            content-type => 'text/html',
            body => /recipes/;
```

```
    test get('/index.html'),
            status => 200,
            content-type => 'text/html',
            body => /"Recipes: index"/;
    test get("/foo"),
        status => 404;
}

test-service type-routes, {

    test get("Dessert"),
        status => 200,
        content-type => "application/json",
        body => /Apple/;

    test get("foo"),
            status => 404;
}

test-service ingredient-routes, {
    test get("Apple"),
            status => 200,
            content-type => "application/json",
            body => *<Vegan> == True;
    test get("Fishtails"),
        status => 404;
}

done-testing;
```

We have a test block for every *routingine*, and in every one, we test for something
that should be there, but also for something that shouldn't. In microservices, it's always
important to return the correct status when things are okay, but also when they are not.
The test command uses a positional argument, which is the route we are testing. Since
these routes are independent, they will all start at /, as they did in the static route we
tested in the previous iteration of this recipe. The rest of the named arguments will check
the status and the MIME type that was returned, and then run checks on the body. Since
it's very common to get JSON responses, testing that it's that type and the body can be
done at the same time, like this:

```
test get("Dessert"),
    status => 200,
    json => /Apple/;
```

Tests for success are similar to the ones we have seen before. They check the status, the type, which in the case of the two dynamic routes will be `application/json`, and something that should be in the body. In the case of JSON responses, it will be available as the default variable, so we can run other checks on it, for instance, if they are vegan; that's what we do for `Apple`.

The 404 tests are much simpler: You just need to check that they return that code. Status codes are in the header, so there's no need to check the body. This is also a bit of defensive programming: `"not found"` should always be returned in this unequivocal way, not via some error code in the body of a 200-successful response.

These whitebox tests cover all possible code paths. They might not cover all possible data paths, although in this case there are no possible corner cases to worry about. One issue could be how to handle ingredients with two words (hence, a space), but it's only a matter of URI encoding the space to %20 to get it right:

```
test get("Olive%20oil"),
        status => 200,
        content-type => "application/json",
        body => *<Vegan> == True;
```

With this module, you can easily insert these tests into continuous integration services and ensure the quality of all pieces of the software you'll be deploying.

Recipe 11-5. Respond to Web Hooks
Problem

Web hooks are simply programs that listen to events happening elsewhere on the web, and to which they are listening, reacting to them when they occur. External programs such as source code management sites or continuous integration sites will *activate* a hook when some internal event happens and will expect a response from those events. In the same fashion as a messaging application, we need to respond to every event in such a way that doing so does not block the application, and also in a timely and efficient way.

Solution

Essentially an application responding to web hooks is a web service, except it has some specific format and needs to respond following specific guidelines. Again, a web service with `Cro` can be crafted to work that way. Since we need real-time, or at least fast enough, responses, a good solution will be to create concurrent programs that respond to hooks in independent threads. That way, the response to further incoming hooks is not blocked, and computing power is leveraged to provide fast response to events.

How It Works

Essentially what we are looking for is an action that is triggered via some API request. For instance, since we have a script for rebuilding the website from its documents, we could trigger a rebuild if any of the files it depends on change. We would need to create a route that analyzes the request and responds to it adequately.

It's important that these web hooks work asynchronously. These actions can take a long time, so they can't hang the server and prevent it from responding to any other requests, so we'll create a task that waits for a signal to start rebuilding the site.

Concurrency is a nice concept: it allows you to work with parallelism, but at a high level. Not too many languages include these kinds of facilities. Go would be one of them, along with Scala and Erlang. Raku's facilities for concurrency are similar to those we see in Go: it's an implementation of Hoare's Concurrent Sequential Processes, where different processes communicate state via channels, with no direct communication or (ideally) access to shared memory.

In the previous chapter, we generated the site using templates. In this chapter, the whole site-generation routine has been incorporated using a method in the `Raku::Recipes::Texts` class, and we simply invoke it from this program. That will trigger builds via messages in a channel:

```
use Raku::Recipes::Texts;

my $builder = Channel.new;

my $p = start {
    react {
        whenever $builder {
            say "Building...";
```

```
            my $recipes-text = Raku::Recipes::Texts.new();
            $recipes-text.generate-site()
        }
    }
}

await (^3).map: -> $r {
    start {
        sleep $r;
        $builder.send($r);
    }
}

$builder.close;
await $p;
```

This program, which is heavily inspired by the example in the documentation, tries to illustrate how concurrent operation works.

First, we have channels; a channel we call $builder will be used to trigger builds. Actual messages do not really matter; we will use the *existence* of a message to trigger a build. We start a thread to do that, a thread that includes a react block, which will "wake up" whenever the $builder channel gets a message and builds the site.

Any interaction with the filesystem would probably have to be accompanied by locking, to avoid race conditions. In this case, two threads might want to modify a single file at the same time. We'll come back to this a bit later. For the time, we're focused on the basic concurrency mechanism.

We of course need to generate those messages. We create a loop that starts three threads, every one of them emitting a message in increasing number of seconds (thanks to the sleep delay). Since await is at the front of the loop, it will not end until all three promises have finished, that is, after three seconds. Then the program flow will proceed to the next instruction, closing the channel, which will propagate to the thread that was started by looking at that channel and close it too, fulfilling that promise. We wait once again for that promise in the last instruction, so that the program will eventually exit.

The basic idea is that the response to the messages doesn't hog a single sequential program, or even wait for the event loop to get to it, as it would happen in an asynchronous system. Threads will wake up in parallel if one of them has not finished yet. They also need to avoid working on the same filesystem fragment at the same time.

But once we have the conceptual scaffolding, we can set this up in a real route, like this one:

```
use Cro::HTTP::Router;
use Raku::Recipes::Texts;

my $lock = Lock::Async.new;
my $builder = Channel.new;
my $p = start {
    react {
            whenever $builder {
                say "Waiting for lock...";
                $lock.protect: {
                    say "Rebuilding";
                    my $recipes-text = Raku::Recipes::Texts.new();
                    $recipes-text.generate-site();
                    say "Rebuilt";
                };

            }
    }
}

unit module My::Rebuild;

sub rebuild-route is export {
    route {
        get -> {
            $builder.send(True);
            content 'application/json', my %result = %( :building("Started") );
        }
    }
}
```

What we have added is a lock. A lock ensures that no two threads will be running that piece of code at the same time, so no race conditions will happen on its watch. We use an asynchronous lock, which will wait until it's released to work. So this *routingine* (routing routine) will set up the lock, the channel, and the thread that will respond to the rebuilding orders.

Note   And I so missed to the opportunity to use lock, stock, and barrel here somehow. Okay, never mind.

These orders will be issued from the route, which is down below. The web hook will be something like `http://localhost:31415/rebuild` and will send a message, any message, to the channel—it could be `"Be kind, rebuild"` for instance. The channel will then immediately return with a message indicating that it's rebuilding. Rebuilding will happen behind the scenes, and the server will immediately be ready to respond to other requests.

The whole microservice, integrating all routes, is shown here:

```
use Cro::HTTP::Server;
use Cro::HTTP::Router;
use My::Routes;
use My::Rebuild;

my $recipes = route {
    include "content"    => static-routes,
            "rebuild"    => rebuild-route,
            "Type"       => type-routes,
            "Ingredient" => ingredient-routes;
}

if ( $*PROGRAM eq $?FILE ) {
    my Cro::Service $µservice = Cro::HTTP::Server.new(
            :host('localhost'), :port(31415), application => $recipes
            );

    say "Starting service";
    $µservice.start;
```

```
react whenever signal(SIGINT) {
    $µservice.stop;
    exit;
}
}
```

This includes all spun-off routes, as well as this one, in a single showing how this web hook integrates seamlessly with the rest of the microservice. The log in the console from which we are running the server will show something like this:

```
Starting service
Waiting for lock...
Rebuilding
Rebuilt
Waiting for lock...
Rebuilding
Rebuilt
Waiting for lock...
Rebuilding
Rebuilt
```

In this way, we have integrated a web hook in a microservice architecture. This web hook can be integrated into a workflow by, for instance, invoking it every time a push is received from a Git server. Once the code has been pulled, the hook can be invoked to rebuild the server. This could be, for instance, in a context where you have this recipe site with text, but also services for other frontends (or even the web itself), or you might want to have a microservice that serves a series of web hooks. The essential point is that web hooks are generally *fire-and-forget* events that perform heavy-duty tasks, which is why they must be done concurrently if possible and must learn to work well with themselves by using locks.

CHAPTER 12

Working with Data Sources

Most applications use some kind of permanent storage, from a very simple, and maybe unstructured system such as text files, to a more complex, but also more efficient, media such as databases, either old-style relational databases or new ones that work with any data structure. These databases offer their own APIs, but it's convenient to have abstract layers that allow you to focus on your business logic and not worry about specific data access languages. Raku offers different ways of interfacing with all kinds of databases, but also has a very nice object relational manager called RED. You will learn how to use them in this chapter.

Recipe 12-1. Work with Relational Databases

Problem

You need to permanently store and access data, so you choose a relational database such as MariaDB, PostgreSQL, or SQLite3.

Solution

Use the generic DBIish interface to access relational, SQL-based databases.

How It Works

DBIish is a module in the ecosystem, thus named because it has the same functionality as the Perl DBI (DataBase Interface) module. The main idea of this module is to offer an

© J.J. Merelo 2020
J.J. Merelo, *Raku Recipes*, https://doi.org/10.1007/978-1-4842-6258-0_12

abstract layer for all database managers, so that Raku code can be created independently of the system that will eventually be used to manage data.

After having stored all our data in a (immutable) CSV file up to now, we'll upgrade our data handling to a data store. This will give us concurrency in the access, more speed, and much more flexibility when doing searches, insertions, and massive updates. Modern data stores can also be cloud-based, reducing the hassle (and the cost) of maintaining them on-premises.

There are roughly two kinds of data management services, broadly grouped into *traditional* ones using SQL and NoSQL ones. The SQL ones describe and query data and are also called relational database managers (RDBMs). NoSQL initially meant *NoSQL*, but now more broadly means *not only SQL* and includes more traditional services like PostgreSQL. NoSQL generally refers to key-value stores like Redis or document stores like MongoDB. We'll see a bit of all of them in this chapter.

Creating a Database and a Table

Let's start with relational databases. They all use SQL to model the data that you are going to include in your database. So up front, we need a description of the data we formerly included in the CSV table. As a matter of fact, databases store information in tables, and those tables have different items in rows, so every CSV column will become a table column. This SQL will define that table:

```
create table recipedata (
  name varchar,
  unit varchar,
  calories float,
  protein float,
  main BOOLEAN,
  side BOOLEAN,
  vegan BOOLEAN,
  dairy BOOLEAN,
  dessert BOOLEAN
);
```

Varchars are the equivalent of strings, but with a variable number of chars to store. calories and proteins will generally be floating point numbers, while the other characteristics are Boolean.

We will use sqlite3 here, since it's simply stored in a file, so it's much simpler to set up and also test. In production, it is probably better to use MariaDB or PostgreSQL, although it's perfectly fine to use SQLite, as long as there are not many concurrent read or writes, or there's a high volume that needs database replication and load balancing. In general, however, only the driver or command-line interface will have to be changed, and that's orthogonal to the language, which is Raku in this case, so we'll stick to it. You obviously need to install sqlite3 using the preferred method in your platform, or from its website at https://sqlite.org/index.html.

In sqlite3, a database is simply a file, and you can create this table in this database by simply using this as input for the command-line interface:

```
sqlite3 test.sqlite3 < recipedata.sql
```

With this, the table and the database have been created, but now we have to migrate the current database to this. In fact, we can import the CSV file directly into sqlite3:

```
sqlite> .separator ;
sqlite>.import ../data/calories-chapter12.csv recipedata
sqlite> select name, unit, calories, protein from recipedata;
Rice;100g;130.0;2.7
Chickpeas;100g;364.0;7.0
Lentils;100g;116.0;7.4
Egg;Unit;78.0;13.0
Apple;Unit;52.0;0.3
Beer;⅓ liter;216.0;0.3
Tuna;100g;130.0;23.5
Cheese;100g;128.0;25.4
Chorizo;100g;455.0;24.0
Potatoes;100g;82.0;2.0
Tomato;100g;24.0;0.9
Olive Oil;1 tablespoon;119.0;0.0
Pasta;100g;131.0;6.6
Chicken breast;100g;101.0;32.0
Kidney beans;100g;127.0;8.7
Kale;100g;28.0;1.9
Sardines;100g;208.0;25.0
Orange;Unit;65.0;1.0
```

```
Green kiwi;Unit;42.0;0.8
Beef;100g;217.0;26.1
Cashews;100g;553.0;18.0
Sundried tomatoes;100g;213.0;5.0
Cod;85g;90.0;19.0
Skyr drink;100g;54.0;7.4
```

We need to arrange the column names in exactly the same way as they appear in the CSV file. In this case, we've grouped them in another way for clarity, so either we change the definition or change the CSV file, which is why we created this alternative CSV file with the columns in the right order.

Inversion of Dependences and Single Source of Truth

We need our recipes application to work with data stores. And while our initial version, baked in the Raku::Recipes::Roly class, used tight coupling between data storage (in CSV files) and business logic (such as checking things about data, or computing calories), we need to make the business logic totally independent of where we store and manipulate data. We need to follow the principle of *inversion of control:* instead of making the business logic control the data access logic, the data-access logic will control the business logic. This has many advantages, the main of which is to be able to easily implement a single source of truth. The data access layer will be able to control how data is accessed, and whichever copies of our business logic we have, they will all work with the same, consistent data.

By spinning off data access, we can work with a single data interface and let someone else decide where to store our data and how to work with it. As long as it respects the interface, we can work with it.

So let's design a role that defines this interface. We will call this role Dator, as in data accessor.

```
unit role Raku::Recipes::Dator;

method get-ingredient( Str $ingredient ) {...}
method get-ingredients() {...}
method search-ingredients( %search-criteria ) {...}
method insert-ingredient( Str $ingredient, %data ) {...}
method delete-ingredient( Str $ingredient) {...}
```

This role has the basics of a CR(U)D interface. We create (with insert), read (a single ingredient via `get-ingredient`, all of them via `get-ingredients`), don't offer the possibility of updating it, since some ingredients can't just get calories on the fly or become suddenly non-dairy, and then delete. In this case, we don't use the ellipsis as a way of hiding code: it's a real ellipsis, which makes these methods stubs. Any class mixing this role needs to implement these methods, or it will not be instantiable.

Note   Some of these methods can throw an exception, however, if we think it's not reasonable to support them.

Originally we read all this data using CSV. Let's then create a class that implements this logic and that's able to read via CSV:

```
use Text::CSV;
use Raku::Recipes::Dator;
use Raku::Recipes;
use X::Raku::Recipes::Missing;

unit class Raku::Recipes::CSVDator does Raku::Recipes::Dator;

has %.ingredients;
method new( $dir = "." ) {
    # Suppressed implementation for brevity. It can be found in the book
    GitHub repository.
}

method get-ingredient( Str $ingredient ) {
    return %!ingredients{$ingredient}
            // X::Raku::Recipes::Missing::Product.new( name => $ingredient
            ).throw
}

method get-ingredients() {
    return %!ingredients;
}
```

```
method search-ingredients( %search-criteria ) {
    %!ingredients.keys.grep:
            { self!check(  %!ingredients{$_},%search-criteria) };
}

method !check( %ingredient-data, %search-criteria) {
    my @criteria = do for %search-criteria.keys {
        %search-criteria{$_} == %ingredient-data{$_}
    }
    return all @criteria;
}

method insert-ingredient( Str $ingredient, %data ) {
    die "Ingredients are immutable in this class";
}

method delete-ingredient( Str $ingredient) {
    die "Ingredients are immutable in this class";
}
```

As far as implementation goes, these are relatively simple. Since we are holding them in memory using a hash, we can't allow the clients of this class to change them. We preserve the *single source of truth principle,* because that source will be the original file. We use a private method called !check to check that an ingredient meets the criteria, but other than that it's simply working with the stored data, reproducing what we already did in Raku::Recipes::Roly with its own attributes. Note the use of exceptions (covered in Chapter 8) to relay the message that there's an ingredient missing.

We can use this, for instance, for a command-line script that prints data we have on an ingredient in JSON.

```
use Raku::Recipes::CSVDator;
use X::Raku::Recipes::Missing;
use JSON::Fast;

sub MAIN( $ingredient ) {
    my $dator = Raku::Recipes::CSVDator.new;
    say to-json( $dator.get-ingredient( tc($ingredient) ));
    CATCH {
```

```
    when X::Raku::Recipes::Missing {
        "We don't have info on $ingredient".say }
    default { say "Some error has happened"}
    }
}
```

The implementation is pretty straightforward. We need, of course, to take care of possible missing ingredients. Using MAIN will reject usage without an argument, and use the argument, which we capitalize using tc, to check the data store.

The interesting part of this is that, except for the declaration of the data store we're using, the rest is totally decoupled from the specific implementation. So let's try now to make an actual implementation using SQLite.

Implementation of a Relational Data Store

Okay, let's return to actually implementing a *dator* that can work with SQLite. In this case, the single source of truth is the data store, so we will be able to insert and delete. Every object using this class will see the same version of the data. Here is the implementation in full.

```
use DBIish;
use Raku::Recipes::Dator;
use Raku::Recipes;
use X::Raku::Recipes::Missing;

#| Basic calorie table handling role
unit class Raku::Recipes::SQLator does Raku::Recipes::Dator does Associative;

has $!dbh;
has @!columns;

method new( $file = "Chapter-12/ingredients.sqlite3" ) {
    my $dbh = DBIish.connect("SQLite", :database($file));
    # This is SQLITE3 specific
    my $sth = $dbh.prepare("PRAGMA table_info('recipedata');");
    $sth.execute;
    my @table-data = $sth.allrows();
```

```
    my @columns = @table-data.map: *[1].tc;
    self.bless( :$dbh, :@columns );
}

submethod BUILD( :$!dbh, :@!columns ) {}

#| Retrieves a single ingredient by name
method get-ingredient( Str $ingredient ) {
    my $sth = self!run-statement(q:to/GET/,$ingredient);
SELECT * FROM recipedata where name = ?;
GET
    with $sth.allrows()[0] { return self!hashify($_) }
    else { return []};
}

multi method AT-KEY( Str $ingredient ) {
    return self.get-ingredient( $ingredient );
}

method !hashify( @row is copy ) {
    my %hash;
    for @!columns -> $c {
        %hash{$c} = shift @row
    }
    %hash<name>:delete;
    return %hash;
}

method !run-statement( $stmt, *@args ) {
    my $sth = $!dbh.prepare($stmt);
    $sth.execute(@args);
    return $sth;
}

method get-ingredients {
    my $sth = $!dbh.prepare(q:to/GET/);
SELECT * FROM recipedata;
```

```
GET
    $sth.execute;
    my %rows;
    for $sth.allrows() -> @row {
        my $name = @row[0];
        my %this-hash = self!hashify(@row);
        %rows{$name} = %this-hash;
    }
    return %rows;
}

method search-ingredients( %search-criteria ) {
    my @clauses = do for %search-criteria.kv -> $k,$v {
        lc($k) ~ " = '" ~ $v ~ "'";
    }
    my $query = "SELECT name FROM recipedata WHERE " ~ @clauses.join( "
    AND ");
    $query ~~ s:g/<|w>True<|w>/Yes/;
    $query ~~ s:g/<|w>False<|w>/No/;
    my $sth = $!dbh.prepare($query);
    $sth.execute;
    return $sth.allrows().map: *[0];
}

method insert-ingredient( Str $ingredient, %data ) {
    my $stmt = "INSERT INTO recipedata (" ~ @!columns.join(", ")
        ~ ") VALUES (" ~ ("?" xx @!columns.elems ).join(", ") ~ ")";
    my @values = $ingredient;
    for @!columns[1..*] -> $c {
        with %data{$c} { @values.push: %data{$c} }
        else { X::Raku::Recipes::Missing::Column.new( :name($c) ).throw }
    }
    my $sth = $!dbh.prepare($stmt);
    $sth.execute( |@values);
}
```

```
method delete-ingredient( Str $ingredient) {
    my $sth = $!dbh.prepare(q:to/DELETE/);
delete FROM recipedata where name = ?
DELETE
    $sth.execute( $ingredient);
}
```

Probably the longest recipe we've seen so far. We declare a class that mixes in the Dator, but also the Associative role. The result we will obtain will work as an associative array, at least in some sense. This is quite convenient, syntax wise, and, as a matter of fact, we could have introduced it in the base role. However, this is an additional role client that classes might or might not want, so we've simply left the implementation to those who do. We'll have two attributes in the class: the database handle with which we will access the class, and the columns, which we will need in several places, and also for error checking.

The values of these two attributes are assigned in the new method that takes as default the database file, which has been created above, and contains the values imported from the CSV file. This part is SQLite specific, and some changes would have to be made. Mainly we're selecting that specific driver to use when we connect using DBIish, but we also use a PRAGMA to obtain the names of the columns. That PRAGMA returns information on tables. Using bless, we actually call BUILD, where we bind the variables to the attributes.

Most methods do as follows: they prepare a SQL statement and then bind values and execute it. We created a private method, called run-statement, that does it sequentially, but it will not always work, so in those cases we simply issue the SQL statements directly in the method. Using prepared statements is always safer than directly creating the SQL statement and running it, among other things.

Most methods call hashify, which returns the result as a hash, excluding the name column, which will be used as a key to the hash.

In order to make it work as associative, that is, use {} or <> to access one of the ingredients, we define the AT-KEY method. It actually calls get-ingredient, but allows us to access it in another way.

We also added the X::Raku::Recipes::Missing::Column exception, which will be issued when we try to create a new row when columns are missing.

In general, DBIish is minimalistic: it provides a few methods to issue SQL commands and massage the result. It does its job and does not really get in the way. Most of the complexity comes from creating the SQL statements and converting the result to what we were expecting.

Using It in Practice

We need to use it now. The whole point of using this kind of structure is to be able to use it interchangeably with other data access classes. So let's change the previous command-line command that JSONifies the data on an ingredient so that it can use either of them interchangeably. Here it is:

```
use Raku::Recipes::CSVDator;
use Raku::Recipes::SQLator;
use X::Raku::Recipes::Missing;
use JSON::Fast;

sub MAIN( $ingredient, $data-source = "Chapter-12/ingredients.sqlite3" ) {

    my $dator;
    if ( $data-source ~~ /\.sqlite3$/ ) {
        $dator = Raku::Recipes::SQLator.new( $data-source );
    } else {
        $dator = Raku::Recipes::CSVDator.new;
    }
    say to-json( $dator.get-ingredient( tc($ingredient) ));
    CATCH {
        when X::Raku::Recipes::Missing {
            "We don't have info on $ingredient".say }
        default { say "Some error has happened"}
    }
}
```

Different `dators` will be used whether we give a second argument to the command line that ends in `sqlite3` or if we use anything else. `CSVDator` uses the directory, and `data/calories.csv` will be in its default place, so we're okay if we use it like this.

The rest is the same: we can obtain the data we have about the ingredient using the same API. We can also inject these kinds of objects into higher-order objects that will need to access the data. It does not even matter if the data store is totally different, Redis for instance. We'll work with it in the next recipe.

Recipe 12-2. Interface with Redis

Problem

Redis is a fast in-memory data store with a high throughput, which makes it useful for caches, queues, and of course storage, as long as it's not permanent. You need to use it in the context of an application needing to retrieve data very fast.

Solution

Redis is probably overkill for an application that does not have lots of hits a second, but it's useful anyway to see how to use it from Raku. Cro has a plug-in that allows you to store session information in Redis, but we will use a simple Redis wrapper library to work with it.

How It Works

Redis is an in-memory key-value store which, thanks to its speed, has been employed in all kind of things, from simple caches to messaging queues. It's extremely convenient to use, and if used right, it can result in significant speed improvement over disk-bound data stores. It's also open source, and you can install it on your operating system using any of the options available at https://redis.io/download, including downloading it as a Docker container.

Note   As any other thing used here, it's included in the "official" Docker container for this book at docker.pkg.github.com/jj/perl6-recipes-apress/ rakurecipes:latest.

In general, what is going to be stored in Redis are key-value pairs, as indicated. However, Redis allows several kinds of values, including hashes. These hashes can be set all at the same time, or individually. Instead of using a standard language for handling stored data, Redis uses its own language, which is composed of (generally uppercase) commands such as HMSET and a series of arguments behind them. Every instance can access every single item in the instance, which is why keys generally use *namespaces*, which are colon-separated prefixes for the keys. We'll use recipes: here, to separate what we have created from any other data.

As a data store, we'll again mix in the Raku::Recipes::Dator role, as well as the Associative. Here's the resulting class, called Raku::Recipes::Redisator:

```
use Redis;
use Raku::Recipes::Dator;
use Raku::Recipes;
use X::Raku::Recipes::Missing;

#| Basic calorie table handling role
unit class Raku::Recipes::Redisator does Raku::Recipes::Dator does
Associative;

#| Contains the table of calories
has $!redis;

method new( $url = "127.0.0.1:6379" ) {
    my $redis = Redis.new($url, :decode_response);
    self.bless( :$redis );
}

submethod BUILD( :$!redis ) {}

#| Retrieves a single ingredient by name
method get-ingredient( Str $ingredient ) {
    $!redis.hgetall( "recipes:$ingredient");
}

#| To make it work as Associative.
multi method AT-KEY( Str $ingredient ) {
    return self.get-ingredient( $ingredient );
}
```

247

```
#| Retrieves all ingredients in a hash keyed by name
method get-ingredients {
    my @keys = $!redis.keys("recipes:*");
    my %rows;
    for @keys.first<> -> $k {
        $k ~~ /<?after "recipes:">$<key>=(.+)/;
        %rows{~$<key>} = $!redis.hgetall("recipes:" ~ $<key>)
    }
    return %rows;
}

#| Search ingredients by key values
method search-ingredients( %search-criteria ) {
    my %ingredients = self.get-ingredients;
    %ingredients.keys.grep:
            { search-table(  %ingredients{$_},%search-criteria) };
}

method insert-ingredient( Str $ingredient, %data ) {
    $!redis.hmset("recipes:$ingredient", |%data);
}

method delete-ingredient( Str $ingredient) {
    $!redis.del("recipes:$ingredient")
}
```

We use the Redis module to access Redis; this module is in charge of issuing commands to Redis and includes most, but not all, the Redis commands. As you can see, this is much simpler than the one we used for SQLite3. The connection is straightforward, with a local IP and a flag that indicates that we want to get results as strings, and not as blobs. Most commands behave the same way: they issue the corresponding h* command to Redis and return the result. The hmset command creates a key-value set and can set several hash keys at the same time. We always add the namespace (or eliminate it). The del command deletes by key and hgetall returns all the keys in the hash that match a value for a certain key.

We use the keys command to search; keys looks up the whole key space and returns only those that match the pattern, which in this case are the ones that have the recipes: prefix. We use it again for search-ingredients. Redis has a command for that, scan (and hscan, in this case), but that's not implemented in the Redis Raku driver. No big deal, we simply retrieve all ingredients by issuing search requests for every key and then perform the search using Raku commands.

It's not terribly useful if we don't already have data in memory, or available in some way as we did for CSV and SQLite3. That's the problem with in-memory databases, you need to populate them. Let's use the same module to create a script that fills it up.

```
use Redis;
use Raku::Recipes::Redisator;
use Raku::Recipes::SQLator;

my %data = Raku::Recipes::SQLator.new.get-ingredients;
my $redisr = Raku::Recipes::Redisator.new;

for %data.kv -> $ingredient, %data {
    $redisr.insert-ingredient($ingredient,%data);
}

say $redisr.get-ingredients;
```

It's simple enough: it gets the data using one data accessor and inserts it using the other. It finally prints the whole set of data, to check that it's effectively the same as it was in the initial data store, which we have chosen in this case to be SQLite3. It would work in the same way if we used CSVDator.

Refactoring Higher-Level Classes

Once we have enough support for all the data stores, we can refactor high-level classes and create a new Raku::Recipes::Roly, which will be decoupled from data access, whose objects will receive an *injection* of a data access object. This is the rewritten role, which we call Raku::Recipes::Base:

```
use Raku::Recipes;

unit role Raku::Recipes::Base;

has $!dator;

submethod BUILD( :$!dator ) {}

method products () { return $!dator.get-ingredients.keys };
```

```
method calories-table() { return $!dator.get-ingredients };

proto method is-ingredient( | ) {*}
multi method is-ingredient( Str $product where $product ∈ self.products -->
        True) {}
multi method is-ingredient( Str $product where $product ∉ self.products -->
        False) {}

method check-type( Str $ingredient where $ingredient ∈ self.products,
                   Str $type where $type ∈ @food-types --> Bool ) {
    return so $!dator.get-ingredient($ingredient){$type} eq "Yes" | True;
}

method check-unit( Str $ingredient where $ingredient ∈ self.products,
                   Str $unit where $unit ∈ @unit-types --> Bool ) {
    return $!dator.get-ingredient($ingredient)<parsed-measures>[1] eq
    $unit;
}
```

This is the same role externally; any access has to be done through the $dator, which takes care of all the data traffic. But using it this way guarantees that no matter what kind of data access we need to use, we can use its higher-level interface to work with it. We can write this data-source-independent script using that role (punning it to a class) to check if an ingredient is of some specific type:

```
use Raku::Recipes::CSVDator;
use Raku::Recipes::SQLator;
use Raku::Recipes::Redisator;
use Raku::Recipes::Base;

use X::Raku::Recipes::Missing;
use JSON::Fast;

sub MAIN( $ingredient, $type, $data-source = "Chapter-12/ingredients.sqlite3"
        ) {

    my $dator;
    if ( $data-source ~~ /\.sqlite3$/ ) {
        $dator = Raku::Recipes::SQLator.new( $data-source );
```

```
    } elsif ($data-source ~~ /\d+\:\d+/) {
        $dator = Raku::Recipes::Redisator.new( $data-source );
    } else {
        $dator = Raku::Recipes::CSVDator.new
    }
    my $checker = Raku::Recipes::Base.new( :$dator );

    say "$ingredient is ",
            $checker.check-type( $ingredient, $type ) ??""!!"not ",
            "of type $type";

}
```

The bulk of the script checks the data source and selects a dator. If it has a sqlite3 extension, let's use SQLator; if it includes a colon surrounded by numbers, it might be an IP plus the port, so Redisator will be instantiated, and if it's neither, tried-and-true CSVator is best. Running it with this command line:

```
raku Chapter-12/check-ingredient.p6 Rice Vegan 127.0.0.1:6379
```

Will return this:

```
Rice is of type Vegan
```

This is exactly the same as if we had used the default one, or the path to a SQLite data store. $checker has been injected into the data store, inverting dependencies, and totally decoupling our business logic (which is simply checking routines, in this case) of our data storage. We have a single source of truth, and we can proceed to add more abstract layers above it, choosing the data store as the most convenient one, and testing our business logic in a way that is totally independent of the implementation.

One problem, however, is that with these new data access layers, data representation is decoupled from the data structure, and we match them by hand. A higher-level way of doing this is possible, and we will use it in the next recipe.

Recipe 12-3. Use an ORM for High-Level Data Description and Access

Problem

You need to work with data without having to deal with the complexities of writing SQL sentences, or in such a way that code and data structures mirror the data in a closer way.

Solution

Use RED, the Raku object-relational manager, which offers a Raku idiomatic interface for creating data-access programs.

How It Works

"Look, ma, no SQL" is the motto of object relational managers, which provide an object-oriented interface to data stored in relational databases. Data is described as native classes, and the API to access data reflects a more *natural* approach to dealing with data, without worrying about the intricacies of the SQL syntax. Thus, objects are created using a *natural* object-instantiation syntax, and relationships between objects are simply attributes of the class.

So far, the main class in our recipes application has been the list of the recipes. However, the *natural* object here is clearly a single ingredient and the data we have about it. Let's use that as a basis for our Red class, which is shown here:

```
use Red:api<2>;

model Raku::Recipes::IngRedient is rw is table<Ingredient> {
    has Str       $.name      is id;
    has Str       $.unit      is column{ :!nullable };
    has Int       $.calories  is column{ :!nullable };
    has Num       $.protein   is column{ :!nullable };
    has Bool      $.dairy     is column{ :!nullable };
    has Bool      $.vegan     is column{ :!nullable };
```

```
    has Bool        $.main      is column{ :!nullable };
    has Bool        $.side      is column{ :!nullable };
    has Bool        $.dessert   is column{ :!nullable };
}
```

The first thing you might observe is that ORMs means no SQL, but also little or no code. This is a high-level description of the object, and there are a few differences with simply declaring it as a class. Differences are the key, however.

First, we use the second version of the API, since Red has two of them so far. We have already seen how to use this adverb in the chapter about exceptions, so we'll not delve further into this. The class is declared as a *model*. This is a Red-defined syntax for declaring classes that will be stored in a database. Raku has a programmable metaobject protocol, and what the author of the Red distribution, Fernando Correa de Oliveira, does here is a superb example of creating new kinds of objects using it. Models, in Red, are stored classes, but how they behave is programmed precisely in the metamodel.

Red usually derives the name of the table in storage from the name of the model itself. But in this case the name includes colons, so it's better if we give it an actual name with the trait "is table". We will simply call it ingredient. By default, it's an in-memory database, which will disappear as soon as we leave the program.

For instance, every model needs to have an ID, either a field named $.id or a column that gets the "is id" trait, indicating that it's unique and will be used to retrieve the whole row.

The rest of the columns get the correct type, so we can type-check them when assigning them, something we had been unable to do so far. They are not nullable, since all of them need to have a definite value; calories is an integer, since they are usually rounded, while proteins is a floating-point number, since they are usually a smaller amount that takes fractions of a gram as possible values.

We can use this class already; let's use it to fill a (different) database from the data we already have and retrieve just the vegan ingredients:

```
#!/usr/bin/env perl6
use Red;
use Raku::Recipes::IngRedient;
use Raku::Recipes::SQLator;

my $*RED-DB = database "SQLite";
Raku::Recipes::IngRedient.^create-table;
```

```
my %data = Raku::Recipes::SQLator.new.get-ingredients;

for %data.kv -> $ingredient, %data {
    my %red-data;
    %red-data<name> = $ingredient;
    for %data.kv -> $key, $value is rw {
        given $value {
            when "Yes" { $value = True }
            when "No"  { $value = False }
        }
        %red-data{lc $key } = $value;
    }
    Raku::Recipes::IngRedient.^create: |%red-data;
}

say "Vegan ingredients →",
    Raku::Recipes::IngRedient.^all.grep( { .vegan } ).map( { .name  } )
```

What we do here is use one of the existing data sources, in this case SQLator, with all ingredients stored in a database, and then fill this database, which will be in the same format, using it as an origin.

Red uses the $*RED-DB dynamic variable to establish the database driver that's going to be used; SQLite will be used again, since it's easier to set up and test and it's already installed.

We mentioned that Red uses the meta-object protocol; this is clearly shown when we use a HOW method, with a caret in front, to physically create the table in storage. Rak u::Recipes::IngRedient.^create-table does that, and it creates a table in memory by default. That way it will be faster, but of course you need to fill it up every time you start the program.

The loop will run over all elements that are stored in the primary SQLite database. We create a hash out of them; since the name is the hash's key, we include it there as well. We need to convert Yes and No to its Boolean equivalents, since if we use them raw they will be stored as "True", as any non-null string is truish.

To search the database for vegan ingredients, we obtain a handle to all elements using ^all. Again, a method is going to access the HOW (higher order working) of the model, and it will return a lazy Seq with all individuals. We don't need to invent a new method to search: grep will do nicely, and we filter to retain only the vegan elements (with :vegan, which will be true only when the vegan attribute of the object is true). Finally, we map to just the names of the ingredients, obtaining the following:

Vegan ingredients →(Cashews Lentils Kidney beans Green kiwi Orange Olive Oil Apple Beer Tomato Chickpeas Potatoes Rice Kale Sundried tomatoes)

Using Red, we can yet again refactor the relational-database bound dators that we worked with before. However, besides producing cleaner code, it's not going to earn us much in this case. ORMs really show their value when big systems, with complex relationships, are used, since they can easily express those relationships and retrieve whole sets of related objects from storage without needing to write complex JOINs or other kinds of SQL queries. For us, Red is probably one of the top ten Raku modules you need to know about and use, so we encourage you to try it.

Recipe 12-4. Work with MongoDB
Problem

Some semistructured data is better stored in a NoSQL database, because it can work with efficiently with such data. MongoDB is probably one of the most popular and better covered by existing tools, so let's try it.

Solution

Use the MongoDB driver in the ecosystem.

How It Works

MongoDB has become very popular as a document store, and it's even become part of what is known as *the MEAN stack*: Mongo, ExpressJS, AngularJS, and Node. That's does not mean that it's compulsory to work with those tools: there are libraries for most languages, and Raku is no exception.

MongoDB excels when we use it for semi-structured documents, that is, documents that are composed of several key-value pairs, every one of which can have any amount of text in it. Since it does not force a particular schema, you can store any kind of information there, which is why we are going to use it for these recipes. Recipes have been already fleshed out and have ingredients, or they can have any number of them. In any case, they will include a description, a title, and a list of ingredients (which can be null). We will store the list we already have in a MongoDB database, using this script:

```
#!/usr/bin/env perl6

use MongoDB::Client;
use MongoDB::Database;
use BSON::Document;
use Raku::Recipes::Texts;

my $recipes-text = Raku::Recipes::Texts.new();

my MongoDB::Client $client .= new(:uri('mongodb://'));
my MongoDB::Database $database = $client.database('recipes');

my @documents;
for $recipes-text.recipes.kv -> $title, %data {
    %data<title> = $title;
    if %data<ingredients>.elems > 1 {
        for %data<ingredients>.kv -> $k, $v {
            %data{"ingredient-list-$k"} = $v.trim;
        }
    }
    %data<ingredients>:delete;
    @documents.append: BSON::Document.new((|%data)),
}

say "Inserting docs";
my BSON::Document $req .= new: (
insert => 'recipes',
documents => @documents
);
my BSON::Document $doc = $database.run-command($req);
if $doc<ok> {
    say "Docs inserted";
}
```

Before running this, we must have a MongoDB installation ready to use; use your preferred method to install it. It uses default settings in the connection: the `mongodb://` URI that will connect, without a username or password, to the database. Remember not to do this in a production environment.

Mongo creates different *databases*, every one of which has *collections* of *documents*. Every document is a data structure, and as long as we consider a document similar to a row in a relational database, a collection would be a table. We need to select both before inserting a set of documents; we'll call both of them recipes because, why not.

Mongo uses a format called BSON; this format is a "binary JSON" and includes JSON as well as a way to work with binary data such as images. Since this is the format that Mongo uses, we need to convert other data structures to this format using the BSON distribution, which is also in the ecosystem.

This format has certain peculiarities. For instance, it does not admit nested data structures. This why we convert the list of ingredients to a set of keys of the type `ingredient-list-<number>`. That way we "flatten" the list, and what we will have is a BSON document with title, description, and a bunch of ingredient-list-n keys. We only create it if there's an actual list; it will be empty otherwise.

Commands in MongoDB are also executed via the same format. A BSON document with the key called `insert` and a value with the name of the collection we will be creating. Another key, `document`, will point to the list of documents that we are going to be inserting, which is the array of BSON documents that we created previously.

That's basically it: Mongo will return another BSON document with the key `ok` if, well, everything is okay. That will insert all documents, and we can work with them using the client or the command line, as we can see in Figure 12-1.

```
> use recipes
switched to db recipes
> show collections
Buckwheat pudding
recipes
system.indexes
> recipes.find()
2020-06-01T13:56:29.134+0200 ReferenceError: recipes is not defined
> db.recipes.find()
{ "_id" : ObjectId("5ed4ea9521d755424fbf1925"), "path" : "recipes/desserts/buckwheat-pudding.md", "description" : "An original twist on the traditional rice pudding.", "ingredients" : [ ] }
{ "_id" : ObjectId("5ed4ea9521d755424fbf1926"), "description" : "A healthy way to start a meal, or to munch between them.", "ingredient-list-0" : "250g carrots", "ingredient-list-2" : "4 wheat tortillas", "path" : "recipes/appetizers/carrot-wraps.md", "ingredient-list-1" : "200g cottage cheese or cheese spread", "title" : "Carrot wraps" }
{ "_id" : ObjectId("5ed4ea9521d755424fbf1927"), "ingredient-list-2" : "200 grams bell pepers", "ingredient-list-3" : "1 jalapeño pepper", "path" : "recipes/main/vegan/chilentils.md", "ingredient-list-1" : "100 grams texturized soy", "title" : "Chilentils", "description" : "A nutritious comfort dish, that can be as spicy as you like it.", "ingredient-list-0" : "250 grams lentils" }
{ "_id" : ObjectId("5ed4ea9521d755424fbf1928"), "description" : "An avocado cream that can be used on the side with all kind of desserts, from fruit to cakes.", "title" : "Guacustard", "path" : "recipes/dessert s/guacustard.md" }
{ "_id" : ObjectId("5ed4ea9521d755424fbf1929"), "path" : "recipes/desserts/rice/rice-pudding.md", "title" : "Rice pudding", "description" : "A sweet and tangy, as well as nutritious, recipe, that can be taken a lso for breakfast. " }
{ "_id" : ObjectId("5ed4ea9521d755424fbf192a"), "ingredient-list-0" : "500g tuna", "description" : "A relatively simple version of this rich, creamy dish of Italian origin.", "ingredient-list-4" : "1 tbsp extra virgin olive oil", "ingredient-list-5" : "4 cloves garlic", "ingredient-list-2" : "X onion", "ingredient-list-1" : "250g rice", "ingredient-list-3" : "250g cheese (parmegiano reggiano or granapadano, or manche go)", "path" : "recipes/main/rice/tuna-risotto.md", "title" : "Tuna risotto" }
{ "_id" : ObjectId("5ed4ea9521d755424fbf192b"), "title" : "Buckwheat pudding", "path" : "recipes/desserts/buckwheat-pudding.md", "description" : "An original twist on the traditional rice pudding." }
{ "_id" : ObjectId("5ed4ea9521d755424fbf192c"), "title" : "Tuna risotto", "ingredient-list-2" : "X onion", "ingredient-list-0" : "500g tuna", "ingredient-list-5" : "4 cloves garlic", "ingredient-list-4" : "1 tb sp extra virgin olive oil", "ingredient-list-3" : "250g cheese (parmegiano reggiano or granapadano, or manchego)", "path" : "recipes/main/rice/tuna-risotto.md", "ingredient-list-1" : "250g rice", "description" : "A relatively simple version of this rich, creamy dish of Italian origin." }
{ "_id" : ObjectId("5ed4ea9521d755424fbf192d"), "description" : "An original twist on the traditional rice pudding.", "path" : "recipes/desserts/buckwheat-pudding.md", "title" : "Buckwheat pudding" }
{ "_id" : ObjectId("5ed4ea9521d755424fbf192f"), "title" : "Guacustard", "description" : "An avocado cream that can be used on the side with all kind of desserts, from fruit to cakes." }
{ "_id" : ObjectId("5ed4ea9521d755424fbf192f"), "path" : "recipes/main/vegan/chilentils.md", "ingredient-list-1" : "100 grams texturized soy", "ingredient-list-3" : "1 jalapeño pepper", "ingredient-list-0" : "2 50 grams lentils", "title" : "Chilentils", "ingredient-list-2" : "200 grams bell pepers", "description" : "A nutritious comfort dish, that can be as spicy as you like it." }
{ "_id" : ObjectId("5ed4ea9521d755424fbf1930"), "description" : "A healthy way to start a meal, or to munch between them.", "path" : "recipes/appetizers/carrot-wraps.md", "ingredient-list-1" : "200g cottage che ese or cheese spread", "title" : "Carrot wraps", "ingredient-list-2" : "4 wheat tortillas", "ingredient-list-0" : "250g carrots" }
{ "_id" : ObjectId("5ed4ea9521d755424fbf1931"), "title" : "Rice pudding", "path" : "recipes/desserts/rice/rice-pudding.md", "description" : "A sweet and tangy, as well as nutritious, recipe, that can be taken a lso for breakfast. " }

bye
→ raku-recipes-apress git:(master) ✗ git status
```

Figure 12-1. *Querying the recipes collection in the database*

We can, for instance, use regular expressions, as shown in Figure 12-2.

```
> use recipes
switched to db recipes
> db.recipes.find( { "title" : { $regex: /Tuna/ } } )
{ "_id" : ObjectId("5ed4ea6321d755424fbf192a"), "ingredient-list-0" : "500g tuna", "description" : "A relatively simple version of this rich, creamy dish of Italian origin.", "ingredient-list-4" : "1 tbsp extra
virgin olive oil", "ingredient-list-5" : "4 cloves garlic", "ingredient-list-2" : "½ onion", "ingredient-list-1" : "250g rice", "ingredient-list-3" : "250g cheese (parmegiano reggiano or granapadano, or manche
go)", "path" : "recipes/main/rice/tuna-risotto.md", "title" : "Tuna risotto" }
{ "_id" : ObjectId("5ed4ea9521d755424fbf192c"), "title" : "Tuna risotto", "ingredient-list-2" : "½ onion", "ingredient-list-0" : "500g tuna", "ingredient-list-5" : "4 cloves garlic", "ingredient-list-4" : "1 tb
sp extra virgin olive oil", "ingredient-list-3" : "250g cheese (parmegiano reggiano or granapadano, or manchego)", "path" : "recipes/main/rice/tuna-risotto.md", "ingredient-list-1" : "250g rice", "description"
: "A relatively simple version of this rich, creamy dish of Italian origin." }
>
```

Figure 12-2. *Querying using a regular expression*

The query lists the key we will using to search for `"title"` and the regular
expression, simply including the word Tuna:

```
db.recipes.find( { "title" : { $regex: /Tuna/ } } )
```

```
use MongoDB::Client;
use MongoDB::Database;
use BSON::Document;

my MongoDB::Client $client .= new(:uri('mongodb://'));
my MongoDB::Database $database = $client.database('recipes');
my MongoDB::Collection $recipes = $database.collection('recipes');

my $regex = BSON::Regex.new( regex => @*ARGS[0]) ;
my MongoDB::Cursor $cursor =
        $recipes.find( criteria => ["title" => '$regex' => $regex ,],
                       projection => [ "title" => 1,] );

while $cursor.fetch -> BSON::Document $d {
    say $d<title>;
}
```

The MongoDB distribution includes classes to work with collections; since search is
done in a collection, we will be using that here. The three first statements are a cascade
that eventually creates an object that represents that collection.

We are going to search using a regular expression; we can't use it directly, so we
need to create a `BSON::Regex` document. Since all queries become BSON documents,
it's better if we do it in advance. The regex will include the word that we will use as an
argument, for instance Tuna.

A `find` command needs only a criteria, which is a named argument, but the value is also a pair. The key is the field where the search is going to be done, and the value is the criteria. If it's a *crisp* value, there is no need to do anything further, but we can use search operators such as regular expressions. In that case it will also be a `Pair`, with the operator and the regular expression we defined before. This search would return the documents (in BSON format) that match it. But we can go a bit further and define a *projection,* which build up the fields that we are interested in, in this case only the title. We pair `title` with a 1, indicating a truish value. By default, all other fields will be dropped.

This returns a `MongoDB::Cursor`; we need to fetch every item from that cursor to find the result, which we do in the following `while` loop. The document returned is associative, so we can directly print its title as if it were a hash. This will print:

```
Tuna risotto
Tuna risotto
```

This is because we have two versions of the tuna risotto recipe in the database, one of which is low cost. No need to say that in the title, though.

You can build on this recipe to create, for instance, a `dator` which could be used as a data access layer, but also create a whole `recipes` database that would be easily accessible and searchable. In either case, depending on your data and business case requirements, you can choose distributions from the Raku ecosystem that suit your needs and provide a good bridge between Raku capabilities and data store functionalities.

Recipe 12-5. Extract Information from Wikidata Problem

Wikidata is a little-known corner of the Wikipedia universe that stores facts about pieces of data and relationships between them. You need to query Wikidata to obtain information about a particular food ingredient or recipe.

Solution

In Chapter 9, we used `Wikidata::API`, a wrapper around a Wikidata query service. Here, we focus more on creating queries in the SPARQL language that will let us download the information we're looking for.

How It Works

What if we could have, at our fingertips, a veritable cornucopia of information and it would be easy to tap? Can you imagine that? Not needing to check and store every single piece of information that's in there, but simply query it when you need it. Well, that's Wikipedia for you, and its data arm, Wikidata. We've already encountered it in the past and used its API, and now we're going to really put it to work.

For instance, we need additional data about the ingredients we already have; we need to have their descriptions, at least. We might, for instance, want to store that information in our databases to go along with what we have collected. Or we might want to have information about allergens that's collected automatically. Does it contain nuts? Does it have gluten? That sort of thing.

For the time being, let's stick to the description. Every item on Wikidata has one, so if it's there, there will be a description to go with it.

Note   All the information in Wikidata is either collected from an individual data source (say, the USDA food tables) or inserted by volunteers. This means that coverage is not as complete as it should be. At the least, what's there is verified and can be, in general, trusted.

Let's try to create a script that finds the description of the ingredients that are already in our database with this script:

```
use Wikidata::API;
use Raku::Recipes::SQLator;

my $dator = Raku::Recipes::SQLator.new;

for $dator.get-ingredients.keys -> $ingredient is copy {
```

```
    $ingredient = lc $ingredient;
    my $query = qq:to/END/;
SELECT distinct ?item ?itemLabel ?itemDescription WHERE\{
  ?item ?label "$ingredient"\@en.
  ?item wdt:P31?/wdt:P279* wd:Q25403900.
  ?article schema:about ?item .
  ?article schema:inLanguage "en" .
  ?article schema:isPartOf <https://en.wikipedia.org/>.
  SERVICE wikibase:label \{ bd:serviceParam wikibase:language "en". \}
\}
END

    my $result = query($query);
    if $result<results><bindings> -> @r {
        say "$ingredient ⇒\n\t", @r.first<itemDescription><value>;
    }
}
sub utf8y ( $str ) {
    Buf.new( $str.ords ).decode("utf8")
}
```

This script runs over the names of the ingredients in the database and creates a SPARQL query that looks up its description. After lowercasing the name, which is the way it's usually stored in Wikidata, we do a complex query with two parts:

```
?item ?label "$ingredient"\@en.
```

This query finds the item whose name (or label) (in English, @en) is the contents of the $ingredient variable. Note that we're interpolating the variable inside this string. We need to be careful to escape everything else that could be interpreted as code, such as the curly braces and the at sign before en.

There are many things with the name rice. So we have to add the following:

```
?item wdt:P31?/wdt:P279* wd:Q25403900.
```

So that only food ingredients are returned. In order to find data IDs and relationships, you can either use the search slot at `wikidata.org` directly or use the Wikidata interactive query service, which is a very helpful pop-up window that gives you search options.

Note   Of course, tweaking the examples just the tiniest bit to make them work for you is also okay, as it's always been the way for programmers to go forward.

The relationship we express as `wdt:P31?/wdt:P279*` means "being an instance of or a subclass of" and the asterisk implies that that relationship could be anywhere, so it need not be a direct relationship, as in "rice is a food product." It will also include "rice is a cereal and cereals are food products." All together, this would return only rice, the food staple, and not Rice, Minnesota. The last one, wd:Q25403900, is again "food ingredient," with the `wd` prefix indicating it's a "wikidata," not a wikidata relationship (as would be indicated by `wdt`).

Note   And here's me surprised that this totally made-up city *actually exists*. Now I wouldn't be surprised if Potato, Idaho is also a real thing as well.

Not all of the items in the database will actually have an entry in Wikidata; just a few of them do, as a matter of fact. So we examine what the query returns and print the description only of those. The query is always going to return a list, and we stick to the first one; even if there are several items called, say, rice, any one of them is good enough for us. The name of the key that contains the description will be `itemDescription`, which is the term we used in the SPARQL query. The result contains more data, such as the URI of the wikidata item.

The result will be something like this:

```
cheese ⇒
        generic term for a diverse group of milk-based food products
cod ⇒
        fish
egg ⇒
        animal egg eaten as food
```

rice ⇒
        cereal grain and seed of different Oryza and Zizania species
olive oil ⇒
        liquid fat extracted by pressing olives
chorizo ⇒
        pork sausage originating from Italy and typical of the Iberian
        Peninsula, spread to Latin America of raw minced pork, seasoned
        with spices and dried
orange ⇒
        citrus fruit of the orange tree
kale ⇒
        form of cabbage with green or purple leaves
apple ⇒
        fruit of the apple tree
beef ⇒
        meat from cattle

These queries take a while, so it's better if you use them when you build the database, or else store them in a cache such as Redis so that it's handy when you need it. Being as it is data with an open license, you can use it any way you like it.

Creating Desktop Applications

When your application is addressed to a non-technical audience, you need to design it so that the users can move around and get their jobs done with only a keyboard, and maybe mouse. There are many ways to achieve that, from using a simple console UI to a more complicated, and if possible portable, window-based application. That functionality is not available by default in Raku, so in most cases you will need to use distributions in the ecosystem, and these will probably use native libraries, so this chapter also focuses on them.

Recipe 13-1. Use Full-Console UI
Problem

Create a frontend that adapts itself to a console, so it can be run anywhere without having to worry about the intricacies of local windowing systems.

Solution

We could use `Terminal::Choose`, which is simpler, but we have already done so in Chapter 6. Or we could use `Terminal::Print`, a module for CUIs (console user interfaces) with a straightforward API. However, Termbox was recently released, and it has a simple API. We'll use it to create a full-console application.

© J.J. Merelo 2020
J.J. Merelo, *Raku Recipes*, https://doi.org/10.1007/978-1-4842-6258-0_13

How It Works

User interfaces are, in general, more suitable for end users than command-line interfaces. For user-facing applications, and even for applications that do not need to be replicated a lot, like games or mini-apps, consoles have the advantage that they are always present, very lightweight, and relatively simple. A console is composed of a series of cells that can be occupied by a single character, and these cells have a background and foreground color (as well as a position).

These user interfaces generate events; generally key click events. We already know how to deal with event streams in Raku, so a UI application will consist of drawing the initial screen and processing the events, reacting to them and possibly moving things around.

For instance, let's create an application that selects a series of ingredients. We can then try to determine the calories in a dish that uses them (as we did in Chapter 11), or look up a recipe that uses them via Wikidata (following the recipe in Chapter 12). This will simply be a screen that selects those ingredients. This can be done via the following program.

```
#!/usr/bin/env perl6

use Termbox :ALL;
use Raku::Recipes::SQLator;

my %data = Raku::Recipes::SQLator.new.get-ingredients;
my Set $selected;

if tb-init() -> $ret {
    note "tb-init() failed with error code $ret";
    exit 1;
}

END tb-shutdown;

my $row = 0;
my $ingredient-index = 0;
my @ingredients = %data.keys.sort;
my $max-len = @ingredients.map: { .codes };
my $split = @ingredients.elems / 2;
print-string("Select with ENTER, move with space or cursors",1,1,
        TB_WHITE, TB_BLACK);
```

```
for @ingredients -> $k {
    my ($this-column,$this-row ) = ingredient-to-coords( $row );
    uncheck-mark( $row );
    print-string( $k , $this-column + 5, $this-row, TB_BLACK, TB_WHITE );
    $row++;
}
draw-cursor($ingredient-index);
tb-present;

my $events = Supplier.new;
start {
    while tb-poll-event( my $ev = Termbox::Event.new ) { $events.emit: $ev }
}

react whenever $events.Supply -> $ev {
    given $ev.type {
        when TB_EVENT_KEY {
            given $ev.key {
                when TB_KEY_SPACE | TB_KEY_ARROW_DOWN {
                    undraw-cursor($ingredient-index);
                    $ingredient-index =
                            ($ingredient-index+1) % @ingredients.elems;
                    my ( $this_column, $this_row ) = ingredient-to-coords
                            ($ingredient-index);
                    draw-cursor( $ingredient-index );
                    tb-present;
                }
                when TB_KEY_ARROW_UP {
                    undraw-cursor($ingredient-index);
                    if $ingredient-index {
                        $ingredient-index–
                    } else {
                        $ingredient-index = @ingredients.elems - 1;
                    }
```

```
                    my ( $this_column, $this_row ) = ingredient-to-coords
                            ($ingredient-index);
                    draw-cursor( $ingredient-index );
                    tb-present;
                }
                when TB_KEY_ENTER {
                    if @ingredients[$ingredient-index] ∈ $selected {
                        uncheck-mark($ingredient-index);
                        $selected ⊖= @ingredients[$ingredient-index];
                    } else {
                        check-mark($ingredient-index);
                        $selected ∪= @ingredients[$ingredient-index];
                    }
                    tb-present;
                }
                when TB_KEY_ESC {
                    print-string("Selected " ~
                            $selected.map( *.key ).join("-" ),
                            1,2,
                            TB_BLUE, TB_YELLOW);
                    tb-present;
                    sleep(5);
                    done
                }

            }
        }
    }
}

subset RowOrColumn of Int where * >= 1;

sub uncheck-mark( $ingredient-index ) {
    my ($this-column,$this-row ) = ingredient-to-coords( $ingredient-index
);
    print-string( "[ ]", $this-column + 1 , $this-row, TB_BLACK, TB_BLUE );
}
```

```
sub check-mark( $ingredient-index ) {
    my ($this-column,$this-row ) = ingredient-to-coords( $ingredient-index );
    print-string( "[X]", $this-column + 1 , $this-row, TB_BLACK, TB_BLUE );
}

sub draw-cursor( $ingredient-index ) {
    my ($cursor_c, $cursor_r) = ingredient-to-coords( $ingredient-index);
    tb-change-cell( $cursor_c, $cursor_r, ">".ord, TB_YELLOW, TB_RED );

}

sub undraw-cursor( $ingredient-index ) {
    my ($cursor_c, $cursor_r) = ingredient-to-coords( $ingredient-index);
    tb-change-cell( $cursor_c, $cursor_r, " ".ord, 0, 0 );

}

sub print-string( Str $str, RowOrColumn $column,
                  RowOrColumn $row,
                  $fgcolor,
                  $bgcolor  ) {
    for $str.encode.list -> $c  {
        state $x;
        tb-change-cell( $column + $x++,
                $row,
                $c,
                $bgcolor, $fgcolor );
    }
}

sub ingredient-to-coords( UInt $ingredient-index) {
    return 1 + ($ingredient-index / $split).Int * ($max-len + 5),
           (3 + $ingredient-index % $split).Int;
}
```

This program uses Termbox, as has been indicated. The Termbox distribution is a NativeCall wrapper (check the next chapter on how to create these) around a library that has the same name. The library can be downloaded from https://github.com/nsf/termbox and it has a free license. It has bindings in many popular languages, including, obviously, this one. You don't need to install any additional packages when you install Termbox with `zef`. It will build what it needs for you on the fly.

The program is rather long, because code needs to be written for every little thing. But it has several blocks.

1. Initialization of different data structures and the console UI. The `tb-init` command will initialize it and create a blank canvas we can draw on.

2. Draw the initial screen.

3. Set up an event stream. The `termbox` event stream is polled, and for every one, another one is emitted to the stream. This event stream will be closed when the user requires it.

4. A block sets up what is done when different key events occur; every one must be addressed individually.

5. An `END` phaser, which fires when the program is exited (because it's run out of instructions, for instance), takes care of shutting down the canvas when the program is over.

At a low level, the workhorse of this CUI/TUI (console or terminal user interface) is `tb-change-cell`. It takes five arguments: column and row, in this order, a single character code, and then foreground and background color. These have also been predefined as Raku constants by Termbox.

Since the simple act of printing a string involves some code, we wrap our own `print-string` subroutine around it. It takes pretty much the same arguments, but the row and column will be the initial ones, and it takes a whole string. In it, we extract the character code via `encode.list`. The first command converts a string into a blob, and the second one turns that blob into a list of characters. We increment the column number with each character. We use a state variable, `$x`, so that its value is conserved from one invocation of the iteration block to the next.

The other important variable is `ingredient-index`. The cursor will be placed in the value indicated by `ingredient-index`, which is simply the position in the array of ingredients, an alphabetized list of ingredients extracted using SQLator. All other positions revolve around it. From the `ingredient-index`, we compute the row and column for `cursor`, `checkbox`, and `ingredients`. The `ingredient-index` will be a global variable, although to take care of when and where it's changed, most routines do not change it. If we need to check or uncheck a checkbox or draw or undraw the cursor, this is the only value we need to know. Figure 13-1 shows how the UI will look onscreen.

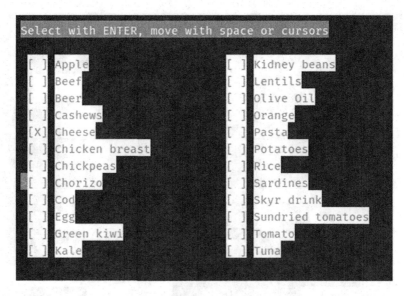

Figure 13-1. *CUI for selecting ingredients. Cheese has been marked, and the cursor is in front of Chorizo*

The `ingredient-to-coords` routine converts the `ingredient` index (or row, in the initial drawing) to coordinates, placing the ingredients in two neat rows. It takes into account the maximum length of the ingredient names, which is stored in the global variable $max-len.

The wrapping also includes type checking. We defined a `RowOrColumn` subset to note that values must be over one. Termbox is a very practical library, but its operation is brittle in the sense that any error will simply make the program exit, since it's happening in C code and not propagating up to Raku to generate a proper exception. We need to catch these errors within our code, to avoid user frustration.

The `react` block will respond to key presses. We first filter key events and then we differentiate between different keys. The spacebar and key down will behave in the same way. We use a junction (|). So `TB_KEY_SPACE | TB_KEY_ARROW_DOWN` will fire whenever any of them has been fired. This will move the cursor step by step by undrawing and then drawing it. After every change, we need to call `tb-present` to update the UI. This and arrow-up will wrap around the ingredient index, going back to 0 if it exceeds the number of ingredients, or going up to the final index in the number of ingredients if it goes below 0. The Enter key will toggle the checkmarks, and finally, Escape will print the selected ingredients and then, after waiting five seconds, exit. This screen is shown in Figure 13-2.

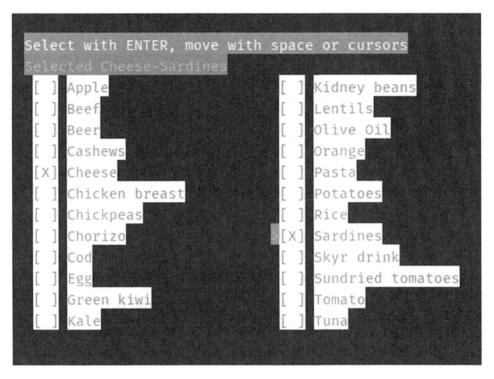

Figure 13-2. *Printing the selected ingredients*

The command after sleep, done, will close the supply and then bring the program to an end, triggering the END phaser, which shuts down the canvas.

This program does what's required of it, without many bells and whistles. It's quite handy when you have to connect to a cloud system, or to a system via limited bandwidth (that still happens). Console UIs are still preferred over window-based ones for system administration tasks. As a matter of fact, this kind of interface can also run in consoles inside the browser. In some cases, however, you will want to create a full-fledged window-based application. We'll see next how to do that.

Recipe 13-2. Create an Application That Uses System Windows

Problem

You need to create a desktop application that uses a mouse and windows and is portable to different operating systems.

Solution

GTK3 is a portable library that is used throughout the open source world to create desktop interfaces; `GTK::Simple` is a Raku binding to that library, and you can use it to build interfaces. It's community maintained and updated frequently, as its underlying library is, so it can provide a stable foundation for your desktop application.

How It Works

Designing graphic user interfaces goes way beyond throwing buttons and other widgets together in a rectangular surface and reacting when something happens. The GUI needs to focus on the users (which is the, well, the "user" in "user interface") to make as easy as possible for them to know what's available, what can be done, and what can't be done. I won't even pretend I know something about the subject, but the art of GUI is a very interesting topic, and you should be informed (or have some expert on your team). I will try to respect simple principles (like informing the users about what can be done), and show how it can be done in GTK3, channeled through Raku.

GTK3 is a popular GUI library, already in its late 3.xx versions, which was originally developed as a base for the GIMP image-processing program (as a matter of fact, GTK means Gimp ToolKit). It has lately spread to all kinds of multi-platform desktop applications, including Gnome. Many applications, including the one I'm using, LibreOffice, use it. Its original language is C, so it needs some scaffolding to be used in languages like Raku. Before installing the distribution we'll be using, `Gtk::Simple`, we have to install the development version of the library using the instructions in `https://github.com/raku-community-modules/gtk-simple` (`sudo apt install libgtk-3-dev` in the case of Ubuntu or Debian). In the case of Windows, the shared libraries are downloaded and installed with the installation of the Raku module.

The basic concept of GTK3 are boxes. You pile widgets horizontally in Hboxes and vertically in Vboxes, and these, in turn, are also embedded in each other until the final window rectangle is created. For instance, if you want to create two widgets on top of another widget, you need to embed the two widgets within a horizontal box, and then that horizontal box is inserted, together with the new widget, into a vertical box.

As in the previous recipe, a UI application will consist essentially of two parts: designing the layout of the UI and creating reactions to events in it. We'll create an application that lists the three types of ingredients—main, side, or dessert—along with Vegan and Dairy buttons, that will allow us to toggle ingredients of that type.

Here goes:

```perl6
#!/usr/bin/env perl6

use GTK::Simple;
use GTK::Simple::App;
use GTK::Simple::RadioButton;
use Raku::Recipes::SQLator;

my $app = GTK::Simple::App.new( title => "Select ingredients" );

my $dator = Raku::Recipes::SQLator.new();
my @all-radio;

my @panels = do for <Main Side Dessert> {
    create-type-panel( $dator, $_)
};

for @all-radio -> $b {
    $b.toggled.tap: &grayout-same-name;
}

$app.set-content(
        GTK::Simple::VBox.new(
            create-type-buttons( @panels ),
            GTK::Simple::HBox.new( |@panels )
        )
    );
```

```
$app.border-width = 15;
$app.run;

END {
    say "Selected ingredients →";
    say @all-radio.grep(  *.status ).map( *.label ).join(" | ");
}

sub create-type-buttons( @panels ) {
    my $button-set = GTK::Simple::HBox.new(
            my $vegan = GTK::Simple::Button.new(label => "Vegan"),
            my $dairy = GTK::Simple::Button.new(label => "Non-Dairy"),
            my $exit = GTK::Simple::Button.new(label => "Exit"),
            );
    $vegan.clicked.tap: { toggle-buttons( $_, "Vegan" )};
    $dairy.clicked.tap: { toggle-buttons( $_, "Dairy" )};
    $exit.clicked.tap({ $app.exit; });
    return $button-set;
}

sub create-radio-buttons ( $dator, @labels is copy ) {
    my $label = shift @labels;
    my $first-radio-button =
            GTK::Simple::RadioButton.new(:$label )
            but $dator.get-ingredient($label);
    my @radio-buttons = ( $first-radio-button ) ;
    while @labels {
        $label = shift @labels;
        my $this-radio-button =
                GTK::Simple::RadioButton.new(:$label)
                but $dator.get-ingredient($label);
        @radio-buttons.append: $this-radio-button;
        $this-radio-button.add( $first-radio-button );
    }
    @all-radio.append: |@radio-buttons;
    @radio-buttons;
}
```

```
sub create-button-set( $dator, $title, @labels ) {
    my $label = GTK::Simple::TextView.new;
    $label.text = "→ $title";
    my @radio-buttons = create-radio-buttons( $dator, @labels );
    GTK::Simple::VBox.new( $label, |@radio-buttons);
}

sub create-type-panel( Raku::Recipes::Dator $dator,
                       $type where $type ∈ <Main Side Dessert> ) {
    my @ingredients = $dator.search-ingredients( { $type => "Yes" });
    create-button-set( $dator, $type, @ingredients );
}

sub toggle-buttons( $button, $type ) {
    state $clicked = False;
    if $clicked {
        $button.label = "Non-$type";
        for @all-radio -> $b {
            if $b.Hash{$type} eq "Yes" {
                $b.sensitive = False;
            } else {
                $b.sensitive = True;
            }
        }
        $clicked = False;
    } else {
        $button.label = $type;
        for @all-radio -> $b {
            if $b.Hash{$type} eq "No" {
                $b.sensitive = False;
            } else {
                $b.sensitive = True;
            }
        }
```

```
        $clicked = True;
    }

}


sub grayout-same-name( $b ) {
    state $toggled = False;
    if $toggled {
        for @all-radio -> $other {
            if $b !=== $other and $b.label eq $other.label {
                $other.sensitive = False;
            }
        }
        $toggled = False;
    } else {
        for @all-radio -> $other {
            if $b.WHICH ne $other.WHICH and $b.label eq $other.label {
                $other.sensitive = True;
            }
        }
        $toggled = True;
    }
}
```

Let's see how the different parts of this program work.

Creating the Layout

The window has the following:

- A top row with three buttons: Vegan and Dairy toggle buttons, as well as an Exit button. We call these *type* buttons.

- A panel with three columns, every one with a label indicating their type. They contain a list of ingredients that work as radio buttons in that you can select only one of them. These are the *type panels*.

The layout is framed in this command:

```
$app.set-content(
        GTK::Simple::VBox.new(
            create-type-buttons( @panels ),
            GTK::Simple::HBox.new( |@panels )
        )
    );

$app.border-width = 15;
```

So it's a vertical box with the type buttons on top, and a horizontal box with the type panels on the bottom. Figure 13-3 shows how this looks.

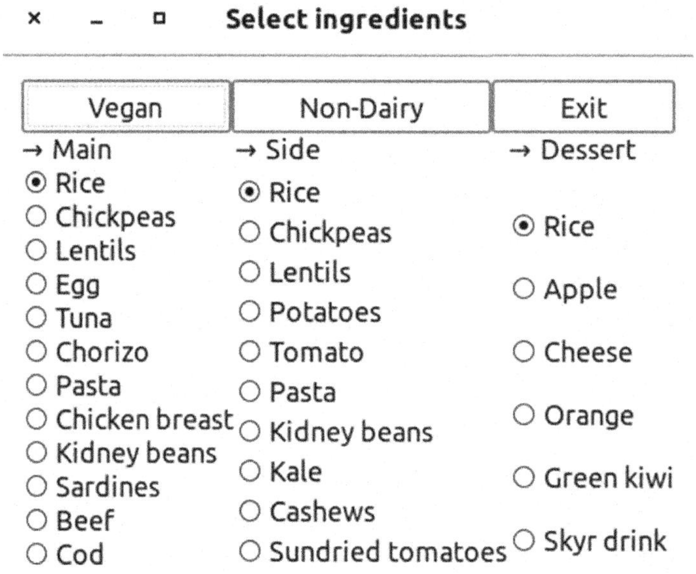

× – □	**Select ingredients**	
Vegan	Non-Dairy	Exit
→ Main	→ Side	→ Dessert
⦿ Rice	⦿ Rice	
○ Chickpeas	○ Chickpeas	⦿ Rice
○ Lentils	○ Lentils	
○ Egg	○ Potatoes	○ Apple
○ Tuna	○ Tomato	
○ Chorizo		○ Cheese
○ Pasta	○ Pasta	
○ Chicken breast	○ Kidney beans	○ Orange
○ Kidney beans	○ Kale	
○ Sardines	○ Cashews	○ Green kiwi
○ Beef	○ Sundried tomatoes	○ Skyr drink
○ Cod		

Figure 13-3. *Initial application window*

The length of every component is automatically set, although we give the whole window 15 pixels all around.

We also need to have some information for every radio button. A button widget simply contains the information required to display it. But we will need to check if a button contains information on a vegan or dairy ingredient or not; there's a payload we need to add to the button. We do this using *mixins*:

```
my $first-radio-button =
        GTK::Simple::RadioButton.new(:$label )
        but $dator.get-ingredient($label);
```

The $first-radio-button (and other button) variables contain a GTK RadioButton *but* also the data we have on the ingredient. $first-radio-button is a *mixin*. When we call methods on the "first" object, it will behave as such. However, if we cast the object (by just using it in a context where the other object makes more sense) to the type of the mixed-in class, in this case Hash, we will be able to access that part of the mixin. $first-radio-button will behave as a RadioButton, but $first-radio-button.Hash will contain information on that part. This is a very clever way of adding a *payload* to variables without needing to cross-referencing them with another hash or array or whatever. And we can mix payload when we create it or afterward. You'll find this quite useful later.

All windows are contained in an App variable. We set the content of this variable via set-content, and start the event loop using $app.run. $app.exit will exit the application, and we bind that to the Exit button.

We'll see in a bit more detail about how the actions work. Every widget creates a *clickstream*, which in Raku terms is a supply you can tap. Taps are subscriptions to that clickstream; the tap block will be executed every time an event is received. We used them extensively in Chapter 2. We need to set these taps explicitly so that something is done every time a button is clicked. By default, the status of the widget will change, but we will probably need something else to be done about it. For instance, if we click on Vegan, we need to deselect all ingredients that are not vegan, but we also need to toggle its state to indicate where they are. In GUIs, showing state is always important and it should be clearly stated. If we click on Vegan, Figure 13-4 illustrates what will be shown in the window.

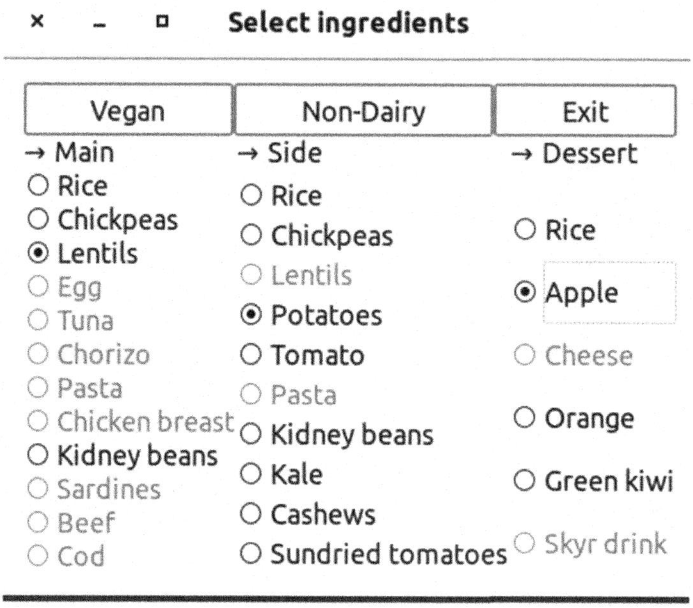

Vegan	Non-Dairy	Exit
→ Main	→ Side	→ Dessert
○ Rice	○ Rice	
○ Chickpeas	○ Chickpeas	○ Rice
⊙ Lentils		
○ Egg	○ Lentils	⊙ Apple
○ Tuna	⊙ Potatoes	
○ Chorizo	○ Tomato	○ Cheese
○ Pasta	○ Pasta	
○ Chicken breast	○ Kidney beans	○ Orange
○ Kidney beans		
○ Sardines	○ Kale	○ Green kiwi
○ Beef	○ Cashews	
○ Cod	○ Sundried tomatoes	○ Skyr drink

Select ingredients

Figure 13-4. *Vegan option selected*

By graying out those options that do not follow the selected criteria, we show what can and can't be done. The `toggle-buttons` routine takes care of that. But in order to toggle these buttons, we need to know what kind of type they are. This is where the mixin mentioned above comes in handy:

```
for @all-radio -> $b {
    $b.sensitive = $b.Hash{$type} eq "No";
}
```

We have stored all the buttons in a global variable, `@all-radio`, to be able to do this kind of thing. `$b.Hash<Vegan>` will tell us if the button refers to a vegan ingredient, and ditto for dairy.

These radio buttons also have their own taps, but these only gray out other buttons with the same name.

```
for @all-radio -> $other {
    if $b.WHICH ne $other.WHICH and $b.label eq $other.label {
        $other.sensitive = False;
    }
}
```

Whenever we toggle a radio button, we check if there are others with the same name. First we check if they are different: .WHICH is an unique ID for every object, and it will be same if it's the same button. Then we need to check if the labels are exactly the same; in that case, we gray it out by toggling the sensitive property to False (or True, if the opposite is happening). That way, if we select rice in any of the columns, the other two columns will be grayed out, as shown in Figure 13-5.

Vegan	Non-Dairy	Exit
→ Main	→ Side	→ Dessert
◯ Rice	◉ Rice	
◯ Chickpeas	◯ Chickpeas	◯ Rice
◉ Lentils	◯ Lentils	
◯ Egg		◉ Apple
◯ Tuna	◯ Potatoes	

Figure 13-5. *Grayed-out rice after selecting it in another column*

What you actually do with the selected ingredients is beyond the scope of this recipe, but anyway, we print them using an END block. Again, having all buttons in a single variable comes in handy: we simply filter those buttons whose status is True, meaning clicked, and then extract the label using .map(*.label). Something like this will be printed (to the console) when we exit:

```
Selected ingredients →
Lentils | Rice | Apple
```

We could do something different with it, displaying information interactively. Text is displayed in TextView widgets, which we use here for the column titles. This, however, would follow the same principle: set up the widget, store it somewhere so that you can use it, and change the status of the widget in a tap when you need it.

More complicated applications can be created on top of this: there's a whole series of Gnome::* distributions in the ecosystem, recently updated, with which you can create applications with drawing panels, even small editors. Gnome::Gtk3 is a fork, which is frequently updated, and has a very liberal Apache license.

In general, if you need to create a full-fledged, windowed, multi-platform application, there are many different ways of doing so in Raku.

Recipe 13-3. Create a Mini-Game

Problem

You need to create an animation or a desktop mini-game.

Solution

Use SDL2::Raw and SDL2, low-level, object-oriented wrappers around the SDL2 library, which is a multi-platform, optimized, framework for creating video games.

How It Works

Games might seem complex enough to be left for video game developers to create, but at the end of the day, a game is a narrative media that can be used to transmit a message, encourage behaviors, or simply show something in an animated, and certainly entertaining, way.

In a game, you have to take many things into account, but as a person who cut his gaming teeth on Pong, which was essentially two lines and a thumbnail-thick pixel, I can tell you that the most important things are the narrative and the mechanics, not the graphical aspects.

SDL, or Simple DirectMedia Layer, is a multiplatform library that can help you with any of these things. It contains multiple primitives for drawing shapes, points, getting clickstreams from the window, and anything needed when creating a game. As a matter of fact, many professional games have been created using SDL. It helps that there are bindings to many languages, including Raku. At any rate, follow the instructions at http://www.libsdl.org/download-2.0.php to download a development version of the library, or simply issue this command from the command line if you are using Ubuntu:

```
sudo apt install libsdl2-dev
```

So let's use that for our program. Our game will be called *DIVCO* and it's intended to show how an infection spreads in Flatland. If the squares are contiguous (even corner by corner), there's a 0.5 possibility that they will infect each other. If there are two sick squares next to a healthy one, infection will always happen. We can infect any square at any time, and every second we will check if new infections occur. The users can infect as many initial squares as they want, just by clicking on one square.

We need to define the square, and we will use an independent class to do so:

```
use SDL2::Raw;

enum unit-state <HEALTHY INFECTED>;
constant OPAQUE = 255;

constant @infected = (255,0,0,OPAQUE);
constant @healthy = (0,255,0,OPAQUE);
constant GRID_X = 25;
constant GRID_Y = 25;

unit class My::Unit;

has $!renderer;
has $!x;
has $!y;
has unit-state $.state = HEALTHY;
has $!rect;

submethod BUILD( :$!renderer, :$!x, :$!y ) {}

submethod TWEAK {
    $!rect = SDL_Rect.new: x => $!x*GRID_X, y => $!y*GRID_Y,
                w => GRID_X, h => GRID_Y;
}

submethod flip() {
    $!state = $!state == HEALTHY ?? INFECTED !! HEALTHY;
    self.render;
}

method render {
    if $!state == HEALTHY {
        $!renderer.draw-color(|@healthy);
    } else {
        $!renderer.draw-color(|@infected);
    }
    $!renderer.fill-rect($!rect);
}
```

Every square has coordinates in a grid, the renderer object it's passed at birth, the state, and a rectangle defined as an SDL_Rect. Since its position is not going to change, we can as well generate the primitive here and reuse it when we need it. The only public attribute is the state; this will prevent any client from changing the rest after the inception of the object.

The Unit can flip from infected to healthy and back, and it uses SDL2::Raw primitives to draw itself onto the grid. We use draw-color to *draw* them in different colors—green for healthy and red for infected. We use the fill-rect primitive to draw the precise shape. As you can see, it's done in three steps: we set the color, we create a shape, and we fill the shape. This has a lot of flexibility (we can use textures, for instance), but it's certainly verbose when you need to draw a simple rectangle. It's not really rendered, but instead it's in a "shadow canvas" that will be presented only when we require it.

Okay, this is going to be our basic unit, but we need to define the rest of the game in a main program. Here it is:

```
#!/usr/bin/env perl6

use SDL2::Raw;
use lib <lib Chapter-13/lib>;
use SDL2;
use My::Unit;

LEAVE SDL_Quit;

my $occupied =  @*ARGS[0] // 0.5;

my int ($w, $h) = 800, 600;
my $window = init-window( $w, $h );
LEAVE $window.destroy;

my $renderer = SDL2::Renderer.new( $window, :flags(ACCELERATED) );
SDL_ClearError;

my @grid[$w/GRID_X;$h/GRID_Y];
say "Generating grid...";
for ^@grid.shape[0] -> $x {
    for ^@grid.shape[1] -> $y {
        if ( 1.rand < $occupied ) {
            @grid[$x;$y] = My::Unit.new( :$renderer, :$x, :$y );
```

```
        @grid[$x;$y].render;
        }
    }
}
sdl-loop($renderer);

#------------------ routines ------------------------------------------

#| Init window
sub init-window( int $w, int $h ) {
    die "couldn't initialize SDL2: { SDL_GetError }" if SDL_Init(VIDEO) != 0;
    SDL2::Window.new(
            :title("DIVCO"),
            :width($w),
            :height($h),
            :flags(SHOWN)
            );
}

#| Rendering loop
sub sdl-loop ( $renderer ) {
    my SDL_Event $event .= new;
    loop {
        state $last-update = now;
        while SDL_PollEvent($event) {
            handle-event( $renderer, SDL_CastEvent($event) );
        }
        if now - $last-update  > 1 {
            infection-loop($renderer);
            $last-update = now;
        }
    }
}

#| Handle events
proto sub handle-event( | ) {*}
```

```
multi sub handle-event( $, SDL2::Raw::SDL_MouseButtonEvent $mouse ) {
    my ( $grid-x, $grid-y ) = gridify( $mouse.x, $mouse.y );
    given $mouse {
        when (*.type == MOUSEBUTTONUP ) {
            with @grid[$grid-x; $grid-y] {
                .flip;
            }
        }
    }
}

sub gridify ( $x, $y) {
    return ($x / GRID_X).Int, ($y/GRID_Y).Int;
}
multi sub handle-event( $, SDL2::Raw::SDL_KeyboardEvent $key ) {
    given $key {
        when (*.type == KEYDOWN )
        {
            if $key.sym == 27 {
                exit;
            }
        }
    }
}

multi sub handle-event( $, $event ) {
    given $event {
        when ( *.type == QUIT )
        {
            exit;
        }
    }
}

sub infection-loop( $renderer ) {
    say "Infection loop…";
    for ^@grid.shape[0] -> $x {
```

```
    for ^@grid.shape[1] -> $y {
        with @grid[$x; $y] {
            if .state == HEALTHY {
                my $prob=0;
                for max($x - 1, 0) .. min($x + 1, @grid.shape[0] - 1) ->
                $xx {
                    for max($y - 1, 0) .. min($y + 1,
                            @grid.shape[1] - 1) ->
                    $yy {
                        if @grid[$xx;$yy] && @grid[$xx;$yy].state ==
                        INFECTED {
                            $prob += 0.5
                        }
                    }
                }
                if 1.rand < $prob {
                    @grid[$x;
                    $y].flip;
                }
            }
        }
    }
}
$renderer.present;
}
```

Again, a bit verbose, as is usual with GUI applications. It proceeds to build up the application in this way.

1. It creates the low-level primitives needed for the game—the window (800 x 600) and the renderer, which is the object that takes care of the *shadow canvas* and paints it on the screen. As a matter of fact, these use the two SDL2 high-level classes. One of them is used to create a renderer object, which will be passed along many other methods, since it's used to draw on the screen. SDL2 is not too complete, and in most other cases we will use the SDL2::Raw procedural equivalents.

287

2. It then creates the flatland grid. The probability is by default 0.5 (50% of the squares will be occupied), but it can be changed via the command line, using a number between 0 and 1. The higher the density, the higher the probability of infection. Every `Unit`, or square, gets a copy of the renderer, which it needs to define rectangles and draw onto the *shadow* canvas. The units are stored in a shaped array. Shaped arrays are n-dimensional arrays that remember the size of every dimension. They are adequate for representing a grid. As an added advantage, running a loop over them is quite easy thanks to the `.shape` method, which returns an array with the number of elements in every dimension.

3. Then it enters the `main` loop. The loop runs forever, or until the correct key is pressed, and it does two things—it checks for anything in the clickstream and processes it, and it runs the infection loop every second. This infection loop will move, square by square, checking its neighbors and flipping them from healthy to infected according to the stated probability. This probability is hardcoded in this line `if @grid[$xx;$yy] && @grid[$xx;$yy]`. `state == INFECTED { $prob += 0.5 }`, but it's left to you to use different probabilities to see how they affect the infection probability.

4. A `LEAVE` block will quit from the SDL engine in an orderly way. This will be called right before the program shuts down.

An example of how it works is shown at `https://youtu.be/zzw9XSOX5-Q`, and in Figure 13-6. No instructions are shown on the screen, but clicking somewhere feels *natural* and encourages users to explore the game. No score is shown either: what it's trying to transmit is how closeness makes the infection spread more quickly.

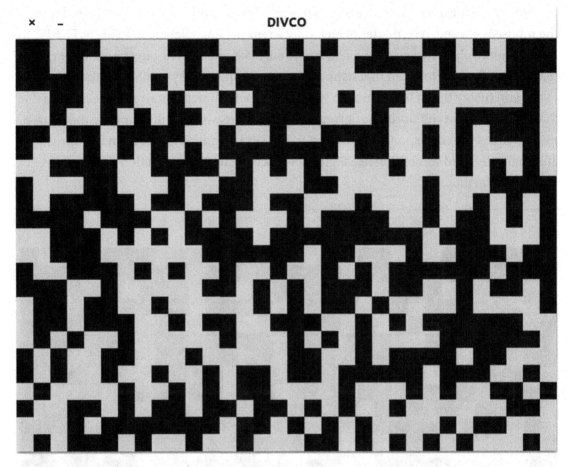

Figure 13-6. *Initial screen, before infection*

The main loop is exclusive, that is, it prevents other event loops from taking place, including asynchronous loops. This is not the best way to work in Raku, but we can still simulate asynchronous events in some other way. Some languages use event loop integrators, but in our case, we'll have to use the available means. The loop subscribes to the clickstream, capturing the clicks in the $event variable. We create a `multi` to handle this event, so that we can unclutter the program and work with different types of clicks in different ways. The generic `multi` will deal with `QUIT` events, basically when we close the window. We could, for instance, print a closing message when this happens. The next one up handles keyboard events, but it just *listens* to the key whose value is 27, that is, the Escape key, and it also reacts when the key has been pressed, not when we have stopped pressing it. The clickstream in SDL captures all kinds of events, so that we can react to different gestures using keys, the mouse, or even joysticks and other input devices.

Finally, the next `multi` up deals with mouse events, but we are only interested when the mouse is clicked. As a matter of fact, only when we stop clicking it: `MOUSEBUTTONUP`. Every time we click, two events will be captured, `DOWN` and `UP`. We can choose either to react to it. What we do when that happens is convert the x and y position of the cursor to the grid (using the `gridify` sub) so we can use them directly as array indices. With that computed, we will *infect* the corresponding square, which will simply be the square that occupies the corresponding position in the `@grid` array. The infection will spread automatically until something like Figure 13-7 occurs, with the infection unable to spread any farther.

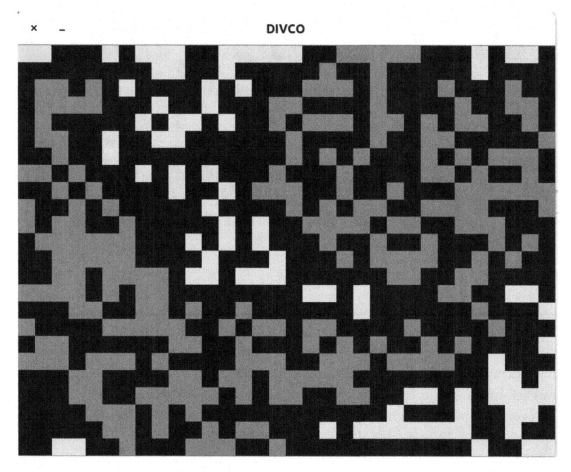

Figure 13-7. *The final stage of the infection with 0.4 initial density and two seeded squares*

We can experiment with different densities to see how the infection would proceed. With a density equal to 0.5 (which is the default), it's very likely that, starting with a single infection, it will spreads to all but maybe a few isolated squares. As soon as the density is lowered to 0.4, there are already disconnected islands and a single contagion will not spread to the rest of the blocks, showing that social distancing is a way to stop spreading.

At the end of the day, programming game mechanics involve two types of actions: a periodic action (movement, appearance of new objects, whatever) and a reactive action (reacting to a keypress, making *enemy* objects react to your actions). In Raku and using SDL, it's a question of combining the basic event loop, and making different reactions to events in the clickstream. Those can be combined creatively with scoring methods, different game plays, or even creating client-server combinations that allow people to work together.

In the current state, however, it's playable and already conveys the message, and it's taken only a few dozens lines of Raku. Be creative and create your own games, even if they are for your friends and family only.

CHAPTER 14

Interfacing with Library and Code in Other Languages

The world is full of (open source) code to be reused in your applications. If only it were already written in Raku... No worries! Raku was designed to embed other languages, from calling libraries that use C or C++ calling conventions to full-fledged code in other languages such as Perl, Python, or even subsets of JavaScript. In this chapter, this will be the main theme: working with code written in a variety of other languages. You can extend that to higher levels and even extend it to languages that are embeddable and written in C, like Perl.

Recipe 14-1. Embed Perl Programs
Problem

Either you really love Perl regexes, you have some hairy code in Perl that you need to access from your Raku program, or you simply have some legacy code you'd better not touch *because it works* but you still need to extend its functionality. In any case, there's some Perl code you need to run alongside Raku.

Solution

Use `Inline::Perl`, or in some, limited, cases, use one of the Butterfly Project's p5* modules, which extend Raku using routines with the same name as in Perl so that you can use native Raku code all the way.

© J.J. Merelo 2020
J.J. Merelo, *Raku Recipes*, https://doi.org/10.1007/978-1-4842-6258-0_14

How It Works

Perl is, despite reports to the contrary, a popular language that, as of 2020, fetches some of the highest wages among current languages. This also means that it has a very rich ecosystem consisting on thousands of CPAN (Comprehensive Perl Archive Network) modules, and a huge installed base that has to be maintained in production. In any case, you might need to use Perl code to include it in your application.

Note   You probably know that Raku was originally called Perl 6. The fact that it's not compatible at all with Perl led to the name change. However, this `Inline::Perl` module is well maintained, so they are still not worlds apart from each other. In fact, they share a big community, and many arrive at Raku after learning about it at a Perl (and Raku) event.

Additionally, Perl has been stable for a long time, with an unchanging API, which means that libraries published 10 or even 15 years ago (or *modules*, in Perl parlance) are perfectly usable nowadays. In addition, Perl is a popular language and, for some time, was probably one of the top three, which means that there's a library in CPAN for everything. With `Inline::Perl5` you can use these libraries pretty much natively in Raku.

First, you need to install the distribution, and in order to do so, you have to prepare a special, shared, version of the Perl interpreter. Using `perlbrew`, the Perl version manager, you can do it this way:

```
perlbrew --notest install stable -Duseshrplib
```

Many OS-packaged Perls come with `-Dusershrplib -fPIC` (like Ubuntu's or Debian's Perl), in which case there is no need for this.

This will install, without testing (because there might be one or two errors with minor importance) the latest version of Perl, which at the time of this writing is 5.30.2.

Since Raku was formerly called Perl 6, Perl remains stuck at the 5.xx version, producing evenly numbered versions yearly by the middle of the year, in time for the annual Perl (and now Raku) conventions. The stable version by the time you read this will be at least 5.32, but the last stable version will be activated with this command:

```
perlbrew use 5.30.3
```

That is necessary for `Inline::Perl5` as well as the installation of the modules we are going to use here. Once that is done, install `Inline::Perl5` in the usual way using `zef`; or, if that fails, following the instructions at `https://github.com/niner/Inline-Perl5/`.

We will try to find a module that allows us to work with recipes; that will help us import them as well as convert them to HTML if necessary. And that module could be MealMaster, `https://metacpan.org/pod/MealMaster`, a module that allows the import of recipes in a format called MealMaster. You can find a gazillion recipes on the web page, which comes straight from the early 90s: `http://www.ffts.com/recipes.htm`. Apparently, the format was used by a desktop program called "Now you're cooking".

It looks a bit like this:

```
MMMMM----- Recipe via Meal-Master (tm) v7.07

      Title: Freezer Log
 Categories: Appetizers
   Servings:  6

     1/2 lb Sharp Cheddar cheese
       8 sl Cooked bacon
     1/2 ts Worcestershire sauce
       1 ts Dry mustard
       2 ts Mayonnaise

  Combine in food processor - 1/2 lb. sharp yellow cheese, 8 slices bacon,
  1/2 tsp. Worcestershire sauce, 1 tsp. dry mustard, 2 tsp. mayonnaise.
  Blend until bacon is minced. Form into a log shaped like party rye bread.
  Wrap in plastic wrap or foil and freeze til firm. To serve, slice, put on
  rye bread,
MMMMM
```

It's not a difficult format to parse, using whitespace for different parts, five `M`s to mark the beginning and the end of every recipe, and fixed metadata such as Servings or Title. Still, you need to parse that format, and the MealMaster module has been doing it since 2005. Before using it in the Raku program, we need to install it to make it available to the Perl (within Raku or without) interpreter. We use a `cpanfile` to express these requirements:

```
requires 'MealMaster';
requires "Text::Markdown";
```

This format has been lately extended as the best way to show the requirements to our system. We can then install these requirements via the following:

```
cpanm --installdeps .
```

This is cpanm (or CPAN minus), a command-line utility that installs the requirements. After doing this, we are ready to run this program. It imports recipes from a file in the MealMaster format, imports them to instantiate an object of type Raku::Recipes::Recipe, and then exports them in HTML, using again a module from Perl, called Text::Markdown.

```
#!/usr/bin/env perl6

use Inline::Perl5;

use MealMaster:from<Perl5>;
use Text::Markdown:from<Perl5>;

use Raku::Recipes::Recipe;

my $parser = MealMaster.new();
my @recipes = $parser.parse("Chapter-14/appetizer.mmf");

my $md = Text::Markdown.new();

for @recipes -> $r {
    my $description = "Categories " ~ $r.categories().join( " - ");
    my $title;
    if $r.title ~~ Str {
        $title = $r.title
    } else {
        $title = $r.title.decode
    }
    my $recipe = Raku::Recipes::Recipe.new(
        :$title,
        :$description,
        ingredients => $r.ingredients().map: {.product }
            );
    say $md.markdown( $recipe.gist );
}
```

To use Perl modules, the clause is exactly the same, except we add the adverb `:from<Perl5>` to the end, to clarify that they need to be installed and instantiated through the `Perl5-Raku` bridge. We also use `Text::Markdown` from Perl 5. Even if there are several distributions for markdown in the Raku universe, none is as mature as this one, which was published in 2010, and is based on the original markdown implementation, which was written in Perl.

Those symbols are installed into the program and can be run using native Raku commands. We instantiate, for instance, a recipe reader and a markdown parser. `MealMaster.parse` will create an array of objects, every one of them a MealMaster recipe, or an object of the `MealMaster::Recipe` kind. We extract properties of that object to instantiate our object. In the conversion from Perl to Raku, some things might get a bit altered. For instance, the title will return a `Str` if it's simple ASCII, but a `Blob` if it somehow includes other symbols, such as º or é (we should have to do this for ingredients too, since they have the same problem, but for now it's not as evident and we'll let it pass). This is why we smart-match the result of `$r.title` to a `Str`, decoding it to such a type of object if it's a `Blob`.

Since the MealMaster format has no place for a description, we create one out of the categories that are listed in the format. And finally, we create an array of ingredients. MealMaster will return every one in its own format, `MealMaster.Ingredient`, and we obtain out of it only the product that it uses. It also includes the measure and quantity, but since they are not in a format we are using, let's just stick to the product.

Finally, we create HTML out of the gist of the product; as we saw previously, this gist is already in markdown format, so it's converted to HTML straight out, producing something like this:

```
<h1>Zucchini Fritters #2</h1>

<p>Categories: Appetizers</p>

<h2>Ingredients</h2>

<ul>
<li>Milk</li>
<li>Egg, lightly beaten</li>
<li>All-purpose flour</li>
<li>Baking powder</li>
<li>1-ounce package ranch-style dip mix</li>
```

```
<li>(8 ounces) shredded zucchini</li>
<li>Vegetable oil</li>
</ul>
```

We could use recipes in Chapter 11 and publish them to a website, or process them in some other way, but the point is that we can dig into the treasure trove of CPAN modules for anything we can imagine and import and massage data, connect to esoteric data stores, or anything else that's not so readily available in the Raku ecosystem.

As mentioned, the other alternative is to use Raku native code to create code that is as close as possible to the original. In that endeavor, Liz Mattijsen's "Butterfly Project" will help. You can find information about it at `https://modules.raku.org/dist/P5built-ins:cpan:ELIZABETH`. The main idea is to port all Perl built-ins to Raku, so that you can simply transcribe old Perl code to its Raku equivalent with a minimum effort.

We will try to do that with a Perl module called `File::Chown`, which you can find at `https://metacpan.org/pod/File::chown`. This was chosen because it was mostly a bit of added value over basic Perl, and you didn't have additional dependencies that needed to be ported. Essentially it wraps over Perl's own `chown` function and gives a programmatic interface to change the user and group of a group of files using the names of the user and groups, the IDs, or simply a file whose user and group will be used for that.

This is the module, called `Sys::Chown`, that has been created:

```
unit module Sys::Chown;

use P5getpwnam;
use P5getgrnam;
use UNIX::Privileges :USER;
use File::Stat <stat>;

subset Valid-User of Str:D where userinfo($_).uid.defined;
subset Valid-Group of Str:D where groupinfo($_).gid.defined;

proto sub chown(|) {*}

multi sub chown ( @files,
                  Valid-User $user,
                  Valid-Group $group = getgrgid(userinfo($user).gid)[0] )
        is export {
```

```
    my @result = do for @files -> $f {
        UNIX::Privileges::chown($user, $group, $f);
    }
    so all @result;
}

multi sub chown ( @files,
                  UInt $uid,
                  UInt $gid = userinfo(getpwuid($uid)[0]).gid )
        is export {
    my @result = do for @files -> $f {
        UNIX::Privileges::chown(getpwuid($uid)[0], getgrgid($gid)[0], $f);
    }
    so all @result;
}

multi sub chown (@files, IO::Path $file where .e ) {
    my $stat = stat($file.path);
    chown( @files, $stat.uid, $stat.gid);
}
```

We use two modules from the Butterfly Project, P5getpwnam and P5getgrnam.
The other two modules are used to emulate functions that have not been ported:
UNIX::Privileges is for the low-level, single-file, chown, and File::Stat is for stat,
which extracts information from a file.

We also define two subsets, Valid-User and Valid-Group, so that calling the
functions is (type-) safer. In the original (which you can check out in its repository, at
https://github.com/perlancar/perl-File-chown/blob/master/lib/File/chown.pm),
calls were made and the single chown sub bailed out with an error if that didn't work.
However, we can catch those errors at the signature level, so we do.

Additionally, we leverage the multis, instead of using a single call. The original relied
on nested ifs to find out which mode of invocation was used. If it was a reference to a
hash, then we wanted to work with a file, if we didn't, well, it was user and group. The
rest of the elements were the files we wanted to work with. We'll create three different
signatures in a multi to take care of each one.

The first one uses the name and group as strings, but it checks that they exist. By
default the group will be the first group corresponding to the user, which usually has

the same name as the user. We mix `UNIX::Privileges`' user info, which obtains a data structure with information about the user, including the group, and then we call `P5getgrnam`'s `getgrid` to obtain the name of the group from the obtained grid. The low-level (from `UNIX::Privileges`) `chown` uses the user and group name.

Finally, the one that uses a file employs `File::Stat`'s stat to find information about the `uid` and `gid` of a file. It uses an `IO::Path`, which is easily created from a string by just adding `.IO` to the end. It must be a valid file, since it's checked for existence. With this, you can use this library from a script as administrator to change file permissions, since they are privileged. But the whole point is that you can easily port Perl's `File::chown` to a new library by using Butterfly Project's modules, as well as some additional ones. By reusing the API, it will be much easier to port other Perl libraries natively to Raku; for instance, `File::Create::Layout` `https://metacpan.org/release/File-Create-Layout`, which is another Perl library that depends on `File::chown`.

Recipe 14-2. Run External Programs and Capture Output

Problem

You have a program without an API but you can run it from the command line, and you want to embed it as if it were part of your own application, thus capturing its output.

Solution

In Chapter 2 we saw how to connect input and output of external programs; we also used `etcd` from its external CLI and we ran external programs in Chapter 1. Here, we will learn how to use `Proc::Async` (`https://docs.raku.org/type/Proc::Async`) to connect asynchronously to a program that runs externally, capture its output, and provide it with input if needed.

How It Works

Many languages and utilities use an interactive REPL or a CLI, with a set of simplified commands. This REPL takes input from the standard input and produces output to the standard output or errors to the standard error output. When you work with them interactively, it's via a keyboard and console. However, a good thing about most operating systems is that those are handles to open streams. By default, those streams are connected to the console and keyboard. However, you can rewire those connections and use another program to provide them or to process output and do stuff with it.

Linux has an excellent command-line calculator called bc, for instance. You type an expression, and you get the output. No frills.

Note   You can download it for other OSs at `https://www.gnu.org/software/bc/bc.html`.

It would be nice to have some frills, however. At least keep the output of former computations or be able to refer to the result of the last line automatically. We'll use the @xx format for that, with @1 being the result of the first computation and so on. @ without a number indicates the last one available. Also, add a prompt. We will use that in the next program:

```
#!/usr/bin/env perl6

sub term:<bcp> { prompt(" " x 6 ~ "← ") }

class Bc {
    has $!bc;

    submethod BUILD( :$!bc ) {}

    method send( Str $str ) {
        $!bc.print($str.trim ~ "\n");
    }

    method get-next( @outputs ){
        my $next = bcp;
        $next.trim;
        if ! $next {
            $!bc.close-stdin;
        }
        if $next ~~ /"@" $<output> = (\d*) / {
            my $index = $<output> ne "" ?? $<output> - 1 !! @outputs.
            elems - 1;
```

```
            my $result = @outputs[$index] // 0;
            $next ~~ s/"@"\d*/$result/;
        }
        self.send($next);
    }
}

my $bc = Proc::Async.new: :w, 'bc', '-l';
my $this-bc = Bc.new( :$bc );
my @outputs;

$bc.stdout.tap: -> $res {
    @outputs.append: $res.trim;
    say "[ {@outputs.elems} ] → ", $res;
    $this-bc.get-next(@outputs);
}

$bc.stderr.tap: {
    say 'Error in input ', $_;
    $this-bc.get-next($@outputs);
}
my $next = bcp;
my $promise = $bc.start;
$this-bc.send($next);
await $promise;
}
```

The program uses an instance of Proc::Async to run bc, and then connects streams to an external program. Proc::Async rewires inputs and outputs, and not only that, but it offers them as supplies you can tap. That is asynchronous, of course, as in the name of the class. It's a standard class, so there's no need to use an external dependency.

The $bc object is a representation of the external program, and we will work with it. First, after declaring the global variable where we'll be keeping the output to every operation, we set two taps, for standard output and standard error. The first one will store the result, present it with a prompt that includes the index, and prompt for the next input. We will wrap the Bc class around it, to encapsulate the object and not carry it around calling subroutines.

The `get-next` method of `$this-bc` is called from this tap and the next, and it contains most of the added value of this program. It uses a term `bcp` to get input.

This is the first time we have faced this kind of thing. Terms are a way of defining symbols; they define a set of characters that can be used anywhere. It's essentially a routine that can use any symbol. We're not tapping its real value by using ASCII characters, so let's call it some other way.

```
sub term:<⤶> { prompt(" " x 6 ~ "← ") }
```

We can then use it by referring to it with just the symbol:

```
my $next = ⤶;
```

No matter the name, it presents six spaces and then an "input" arrow and waits for input. This will allow the input and output arrow to be aligned, at least as long as we don't have more than ten operations. The user input will be returned as the value of the variable and processed further in the tap.

The `get-next` method then proceeds to find out if there's an at sign in the string. Using a regex, it stores it in the `$<output>` variable. It's converted to an index by subtracting one (because the first output is the zeroth element in the array), or assigning to it the value of the last element in the array if that variable contains nothing. That is, if there's a bare @ in the element. Then, before sending the string to be evaluated by `bc`, we substitute it with the value we stored.

To send it to `bc`, we use `print` on the `$bc` object. While we need to tap output, we just need to provide input by "printing" or putting some values in the standard input of the utility. The `sub bc-send` does that. It also trims any excess whitespace on either side (to avoid it having two returns, for instance), and puts only one at the end, which is the format expected by `bc`.

The second tap is on the standard error output. It prints the error message and prints a prompt so that the REPL loop is entered again. The result of the session is shown in Figure 14-1.

```
/home/jmerelo/.rakudobrew/versions/moar-2020.05/install/bin/rakudo /home/jmerelo/progs/perl6/raku-recipes-apress/Chapter-14/bc.p6
      ← 8*33
[ 1 ] → 264

      ← 354 / 8
[ 2 ] → 1.340909090909090909

      ← 81 * 083
[ 3 ] → 233112

      ←
```

Figure 14-1. *A session of using bc with value added by Raku*

We could think of many other uses for this wrapper. For instance, cache results so that we don't need to compute them in bc but just return them immediately. At any rate, the degree of control Raku offers over command-line interactive programs allows us to use these programs as external APIs, even if they are not available as an external library.

However, if there is an external library, Raku offers a way to use it natively within our programs. We'll see how to do this next.

Recipe 14-3. Wrap External Libraries Written in C with NativeCall

Problem

There are several C libraries that integrate nicely into your business logic, or are tried and true high-performance modules that you could use to speed up your programs. But, well, they are written in C.

Solution

Choose a library that is mature and well developed and wrap around it using NativeCall. Always check before you sit down and write one that there's not already such thing in the ecosystem.

You don't need to wrap every single function and data structure, just choose those that are going to be useful to your business case.

How It Works

C is a mature language, with lots of libraries that have undergone many cycles of debugging and release and probably are the best at what they do. The DRY (Don't Reinvent Yourself) principle applies here, so instead of rewriting the library in Raku, you want to be able to use an existing library from it. NativeCall is a safe way, provided by Raku, to wrap around existing C (and C++) libraries and incorporate them into the ecosystem.

Most languages have a mechanism to *bind* external libraries so that they can be used natively within the language. Most modern languages also allow you to use the binary API of a shared library (.so in Linux, .dynlib in Osx, and .dll in Windows) by binding C data structures and functions to the language data structures and routines.

In Raku, there are two things you need to take into account. First, native data types, and second, how to declare a routine so that, when called, the code inside the shared library is executed.

As an example, we'll create a binding to libcmark, a C library that interprets CommonMark, a systematization of markdown. The library includes functions for parsing and converting markdown to different formats. In our case, we are just interested in the one that generates HTML from the markdown string.

In many cases, the library has been released as a libxxx-dev package by your distribution. In others, you have to build it from scratch from the source. In this case, you need to download it from https://github.com/commonmark/cmark and follow the instructions to install it. The shared library will be called something like libcmark.so.0.29.0 and it will be placed in /usr/local/lib. Make sure it ends up as /usr/lib/libcmark.so so that it can be found correctly by our module.

We are going to bind a single routine called cmark_markdown_to_html. This routine is defined in this way in the original library:

```
char * cmark_markdown_to_html(const char *text, size_t len,
                                          int options)
```

Here's the module code:

```
use NativeCall;

unit module cmark::Simple;

constant CMARK_OPT_DEFAULT is export = 0;
constant CMARK_OPT_SOURCEPOS  is export = 2;
constant CMARK_OPT_HARDBREAKS  is export = 4;
constant CMARK_OPT_SAFE  is export = 8;
constant CMARK_OPT_UNSAFE is export = 131072;
constant CMARK_OPT_NOBREAKS = 16;
constant CMARK_OPT_NORMALIZE = 256;
constant CMARK_OPT_VALIDATE_UTF8 = 512;
constant CMARK_OPT_SMART = 1024;

sub cmark_markdown_to_html(Str $text,
                           int32 $len, int32 $options
      --> Str )
   is native("cmark") is export {*};

sub commonmark-to-html( Str $text ) is export {
    cmark_markdown_to_html( $text, $text.encode.elems, CMARK_OPT_DEFAULT);
}
```

Note   This was released as `cmark::Simple` in the ecosystem. A few days before, another binding of the same library, `Cmark`, was released into the ecosystem too. You can check it out at `https://github.com/khalidelboray/raku-cmark` to check the differences in implementation, as well as a more complete binding.

NativeCall is a Rakudo library, not a Raku one. This means that it's part of the Rakudo implementation of Raku, but not part of the specification. In practice, it means that it needs to be explicitly used, same as Test, for example, which is also part of the default Rakudo (and thus Raku) distribution.

Check back to the original `cmark_markdown_to_html` above. The first thing we need to do is to convert the types in the declaration to equivalent Raku types. The `char *` is simply a `Str` type. As a matter of fact, it would be more accurate to use a `CArray[uint8]`, or a native type array of unsigned integers with eight bits. However, `char *` is so pervasive, and so commonly converted to `Str`, that these, even if they are a non-native type, can be used directly. The `size_t` type is an integer that can be represented with 32 bits, which is what we use in the declaration. And the last argument, which is used for options, can have values up to 2^17 (for `CMARK_OPT_UNSAFE`), so we need 32 bits to represent it. If there were some C `struct` used here, we would also need to declare it, but it's not needed in this case.

We define this function as native, pointing to the name of the shared library. Being called `cmark`, it will look for `libcmark.so`. The prefix and the suffix are implicit. We also export it, just in case someone wants to use it directly. What will be run when this `sub` is invoked is the C function in the library with the same name, which is why we use a stub `{*}` for its code.

We will want to make this a bit easier and straightforward, so we wrap another function around it. It chooses the default options for `cmark_markdown_to_html` and and finds the length of the string by calling an `.encode` and then an `.elems`. The C routine needs the precise number of bytes, not the length in characters. `.encode` will turn the `Str` into a `Blob`, with as many elements as the number of bytes needed to encode it. So `.elems` will return the size and process correctly, as so:

```
commonmark-to-html('þor')
```

The þ in þor is two bytes long in UTF8. This will correctly return `<p>þor</p>`, as would be expected.

At the end of the day, this exemplifies how to easily create bindings for a C library in Raku. Identify the entry points or routines you want to call, convert the calling signature to an equivalent in Raku, declare the data structures, mainly `structs`, that will be used, and declare them as native. Note that there's no need to recast all routines or all data structures, just the ones you're interested in.

In many cases, these external C libraries are used for speed and performance. And nowhere else is this more important than in graphics libraries. We'll work with one of them next.

Recipe 14-4. Work with Graphic Processing Libraries

Problem

Graphics processing is a broad area that ranges from basic 2D picture manipulation to creation and motion of 3D structures composed of many different points and that, in order to get moving, have to undergo a series of mathematical operations involving matrices and vectors. This is an area where performance is at a premium; essentially, you need a fraction of a second to perform a fragment of the movement in order for it to look fluid. This is why low-level languages like C are routinely used. They are able to perform within a wide range of hardware. But you need that capability in one of your Raku programs.

Solution

There are excellent graphic processing libraries out there, and most are written in C for speed. You don't need the full feature set, just a few routines, or even a single one. In order to incorporate their functionalities into your program, the best way to go is to use a Raku ecosystem module, if it's available. Most will probably link the corresponding C library and you'll be able to use it straight away. However, if that's not the case, you will need to use NativeCall to link, declare, and use routines from any library you're familiar with or simply have chosen for speed.

How It Works

Low-level graphics processing units are concerned mainly with applying transformations to vectors and points. If you want to move an object coherently, you will have to apply the same kind of transformation to every point of the object, considering in each one its position and orientation.

Eventually, most graphic libraries have converted to a four-component representation of a vector, usually called vec4. The three first components are the three-dimensional coordinates, the forth one, usually represented by w, is 1 for vectors, 0 for points.

Vectors are transformed by applying matrices to them; multiplying a matrix by a vector will yield another vector, the transformed one. Almost any transformation can be applied this way, but most transformations are combinations of the three: rotation, translation, and scaling. In general, a graphics library will have all these operations, as well as easy ways to create matrices that perform these kinds of operations or combine them.

If we try to find a library that performs these operations in Raku, we will find no way to do it (before kazmath was released to the ecosystem). There are many C libraries out there, such as CGLM, or the one we are going to use, kazmath (which you can obtain from its repository at https://github.com/Kazade/kazmath). This library has been extensively tested, includes optimized operations for these graphic primitives, and has a relatively simple API that includes a few, simple, data structures. So we will show you how to wrap a Raku API around these kinds of programs. The full code is at https://github.com/JJ/raku-kazmath; I show it here piecewise so that I can more easily explain the process of creating this wrapper.

The first thing we have to think about are the data structures. Essentially, we are going to need two of them, vec4 and mat4. The first one is more straightforward:

```
class vec4 is repr('CStruct') is export {
    has num32 $.x;
    has num32 $.y;
    has num32 $.z;
    has num32 $.w;

    method new( Num() $x = 0, Num() $y=0, Num() $z=0, Num() $w = 1 ) {

        self.bless( :$x, :$y, :$z, :$w )
    }

    submethod BUILD ( :$!x, :$!y, :$!z, :$!w) { }
}
```

Data structures that are going to be interchanged with C code need some specific representation. We indicate that with the repr('CStruct') trait, which indicates that it needs to be represented internally in the same way as a C struct. That way, the C part of the code will be able to pick it up directly.

Besides, the representation of the data itself needs to be native. The original data structure was like this:

```
typedef struct kmVec4
{
        kmScalar x;
        kmScalar y;
        kmScalar z;
        kmScalar w;
} kmVec4;
```

Every element is a kmScalar, which is actually defined elsewhere as a double. The problem is that a double can have different meaning in different platforms. In Raku, we have two different ways of representing that: num32 and num64. In general, num32 is equivalent to float and num64 to double, but in this case, after several tests, num32 ended up being the right one to use.

In general, choosing the right representation is a trial-and-error process, since there are several possibilities for every C data type. Eventually, through errors and segmentation faults, you will determine one which one is the best for you. These native data structures, however, cannot be used as attributes. We will use the Raku type that is closest to it, in this case Num. In the constructor we provide for automatic conversion (via Num( ) in the signature) for any other type for which that transformation is possible (like Ints or Rats)

Other than that, this data structure is also a Raku class, which is why we can provide a default constructor and a submethod BUILD to bind variables to values, including their default values.

We can then create these structs this way:

```
our $vec4-x = vec4.new( 1, 0, 0, 1);
```

This would be a vector that's oriented in the X direction. This is shown by the 1 in the first position, which corresponds to that direction, and the fact that there's a 1 in the last position, which flags it as a direction vector as opposed to a point. Every dimension needs to be a floating-point number, and as a matter of fact, literals will be converted to Raku, not native, data structures. However, we can provide a Raku equivalent, in this case 1, to the one we're looking for. Alternatively, we can use a numeric literal to represent the same, with the exponential notation as follows:

```
our $vec4-y = vec4.new( 0e0, 1, 0e0, 1);
```

If we use 0 it's going to be converted to Num anyway; this only makes it explicit.

The name we use for the structure is arbitrary. We're only giving it a name but the important part is the structure itself. The original one was called kmVec4, and we call it vec4.

Now we're ready to define a function that deals with these things; for instance, one that scales it up.

```
sub kmVec4Scale(vec4 $pOut, vec4 $pIn, num32 $s)
       returns vec4 is native('kazmath') is export {*}
```

This function is equivalent to this one in C:

```
kmVec4* kmVec4Scale(kmVec4* pOut, const kmVec4* pIn, const kmScalar s);
```

It has the same name, although we can redefine it if it clashes with any other symbol in the namespace. Then check out the equivalent signature. The kmScalar type is mapped to num32, and kmVec4 is mapped to vec4. There are no pointers in Raku, so we simply use the corresponding data structure, but Raku will not allocate memory for us. We need to allocate any memory needed in advance. In order to show it, we map it to the function with the same name in C, we say is native('kazmath'). Raku will look for the shared library file, /usr/lib/libkazmath.so, which we should have installed in advance.

We can use it as follows:

```
my vec4 $out .= new;
my vec4 $in .= new(1.Num, 0.Num, 0.Num, 1.Num);
my vec4 $result = kmVec4Scale($out, $in, 2.Num);
```

If we issue a say $result, it will print the following:

```
kazmath::vec4.new(x => 1.4142135381698608e0, y => 0e0, z => 0e0, w =>
1.4142135381698608e0)
```

The vector has been scaled to twice the size and then normalized. The two components, $x and $w, have been normalized to the square root of two so that the vector keeps the correct length.

Note   Actually, w indicates that this is a vector, but these functions do not take that into account.

Let's go a bit further up the food chain, to the mat4 data structure, which is used to transform the vectors.

```
class mat4 is repr('CStruct') is export {
    HAS num32 @.mat[16] is CArray;

    submethod BUILD( :@mat = 0.Num xx 16) {
        for ^16 {
            @!mat[$_] = @mat[$_];
        }
    }

    method gist() {
        my @arr;
        my $index = 0;
        for ^16 {
            my $index = ($_ % 4 ) * 4 + ($_ div 4 );
            @arr.append: @!mat[$index];
        }
        return (@arr.rotor(4).map: "|" ~ *.join(" ") ~ "|").join("\n")
    }
}
```

This is also a struct in C, which is defined in this way:

```
typedef struct kmMat4 {
        kmScalar mat[16];
} kmMat4;
```

That is, it's an array with precisely 16 elements, every one of which is a kmScalar and thus a float.

The way we reflect this in Raku is relatively complex. Let's start with the easy part: @.mat[16] clearly shows it's a positional with 16 elements. The num32 in front indicates that every element is going to be of type num32, or kmScalar in the C realm.

But then we need to use a trait to indicate that this needs to behave as a CArray. As its name implies, these are arrays that can be used natively in C. We can't declare it directly because CArrays can't be constrained to a size; as a matter of fact, they're more equivalent to a pointer-to-element than to an array. So we need to declare a sized array, and then slap on top of it the CArray label.

This is not enough, however. Previously, the different elements of the struct used a simple "has as" a" declaration. This, however, uses HAS in all caps. HAS is the embedded equivalent of has; when there's a complex data structure like this one, Raku (and any other language) will create a pointer to the embedded array and stash it somewhere convenient. What we're telling it here is "Don't do that". When you pass this data structure to anything, the array must be right there; it must go with it. You will need to use this whenever you have complex data structures within structs, mainly with arrays.

We also give this class an easy way to build, and this is not random but a requirement. Data structures in C need to be initialized to something, so we initialize it to 0 so that when a mat is built, we can already use it.

The gist method is simply convenient; first it shows the way these 16-component vectors are converted into arrays, in column-first fashion, elements top to bottom and then right to left. This is simply an easy way to represent it so that we can print an array when we produce it.

Let's look at the way to produce an array like this one. For instance, we want to create a matrix that rotates on the x axis. This is achieved with this function.

```
sub kmMat4RotationX(mat4 $mat, num32 $radians)
    returns mat4 is native('kazmath') is export {*}
```

The functions in kazmath always behave the same way. They get a pointer to an element and return the transformed value in the element passed by the pointer and as the result of this. Obviously, this original function:

```
kmMat4* kmMat4RotationX(kmMat4* pOut, const kmScalar radians);
```

Uses pointers for both, and the radians we rotate it by is a kmScalar.

We can now use it this way:

```
my mat4 $one-mat .= new;
my mat4 $result1 = kmMat4RotationX($one-mat, pi/2);
say $result1;
my vec4 $out .= new;
my vec4 $in  .= new(0.Num, 1.Num, 0.Num, 1.Num);
my vec4 $result = kmVec4Transform( $out, $in, $result1);
say $result;
```

Which will result in the following:

```
|1 0 0 0|
|0 -4.371138828673793e-08 -1 0|
|0 1 -4.371138828673793e-08 0|
|0 0 0 1|
kazmath::vec4.new(x => 0e0, y => -4.371138828673793e-08, z => 1e0, w => 1e0)
```

The rotation matrix will only contain the four elements in the middle plus the diagonal, which will be ones that will be multiplied by the value of the coordinates of the vector. The result will be the rotated and normalized vector, slightly rotated. It's now looking at z, and the value of y is a rounding error, but never mind. We use the kmVec4Transform function, which takes an out vector, an in vector, and then the array that we will be using as a transformation. It's defined this way:

```
sub kmVec4Transform(vec4 $pOut, vec4 $pV,
                    mat4 $pM)
     returns vec4 is native('kazmath') is export {*}
```

As the rest of the functions, it's defined as "is export" since it's actually in the kazmath module. The result will have the same value as $pOut, since all functions in the module are defined in this way.

We could achieve the same result with kmVec4Transform($out, $kazmath::vec4-y, $result1), since it's a vector that has been defined by default, and it points in the y direction.

In general, open source is built on the shoulders of giants, and it's always better to transform, adapt, or wrap existing code than to write your own, especially if it's fast, tight, and tested code as this library in C. You still need to put some work into casting the data structures as Raku ones. Once that's done, converting the functions in the API is quite straightforward. Remember that you only have to "export" those you're interested in, once the C code is called, all the functions it's calling internally do not need to have a Raku mirror.

This graphics code can, in turn, be incorporated into games (like the ones you saw in the previous chapter) or used to speed up math modules (like the ones used in Chapter 4). But in any case, it expands the possibilities of Raku to reuse legacy or code in other languages.

CHAPTER 15

Speeding Up Processing

Modern computers have much more than a single processor where instructions are run one by one; multiple cores and multiple threads can help you make stuff faster by the simple procedure of doing several things at the same time. But you need a language that gives you a nice layer of abstraction to *really* speed up programming. Raku, having been designed in the 21st Century, includes a whole array of capabilities to leverage hardware parallel-processing capabilities. We'll look at several ways of doing that in this chapter.

Recipe 15-1. Use Data Parallelism with Hyper/Race

Problem

You need to process massive amounts of data as fast as possible.

Solution

Data parallelism is a technique by which parts of a serial data structure are processed at the same time. Raku uses explicit threading via the hyper and race methods, or implicit autothreading using junctions. The hyper and race commands give you finer control over how the data structure is divided and processed.

How It Works

Modern desktop computers have a lot of power, with many-core architectures being the norm, even with low-end laptops. Using explicit concurrency, we can use that power without a lot of overhead, but still it looks like a bit of overkill if all you want to do is process several fragments of a big data structure in several cores or processor threads at once.

© J.J. Merelo 2020
J.J. Merelo, *Raku Recipes*, https://doi.org/10.1007/978-1-4842-6258-0_15

That's called *data parallelism:* instead of processing serial data one by one, several items of that structure are processed at the same time. Raku implements data parallelism mainly through two mechanisms: `hyper`/`race` and junctions. Let's leave the latter for the time being and focus on the former.

The two commands, `hyper` and `race`, can be used like methods for serial data structures (hashes and arrays) or as prefixes for loop constructs such as `for`. The main difference is the order in which the processing, and thus the output, takes place. Use `race` when you don't really care in which order the output is displayed. `hyper`, on the other hand, guarantees that the result will appear in the same order as in the original data structure.

Other than that, they work the same way. They gather elements of the data structure in batches, submit that to different threads, and gather the result as many times as is needed. In the case of `hyper`, results are ordered. This obviously involves some overhead, which means that data parallelism shouldn't be used by default. You need to use a big data structure, so we will revisit the 140MB nutrients file we processed in Chapter 3, rearranging the code a bit for this new version.

```
# Grab Nutrients.csv from https://data.nal.usda.gov/dataset/usda-branded-
food-products-database/resource/c929dc84-1516-4ac7-bbb8-c0c191ca8cec
my @nutrients = "/home/jmerelo/Documentos/Nutrients.csv".IO.lines;
my $time = now;
my @selected = @nutrients.grep: {
    my @data = $_.split('","');
    @data[2] eq "Protein" and @data[3] eq "LCCS" and @data[4] > 70 and
    @data[5] ~~ /^g/;
};
say now - $time;
say @selected.join: "\n";
```

As in the previous case, this code essentially selects nutrients (by code) whose derivation mode uses LCCS and that contain more than 70 units of protein per gram (probably milligrams, but that's not really important). If you go back to Chapter 3, you will notice several changes. First, we separated all the input and output operations. The file is read at the beginning, and the results are printed at the end. The loop in the middle is the only thing that's timed; it `grep`s (filters) over the data structure, producing a new one. On my desktop computer, it takes around 32 seconds to process the whole data structure, for a total of around 38 seconds.

Seeing as this takes a long time, let's attempt to use parallelization simply by adding race. This will, by default, divide in batches of 64 and use four threads. We will change this line:

```
my @selected = @nutrients.race.grep: {
```

The time for the loop goes down to 30 seconds. Well, not a great deal, to the point that, depending on circumstances, it's pretty much in the same ballpark. This proves there's no such thing as automatic data parallelism; you really have to take into account hardware. Since my computer has eight cores, with two physical threads per core, let's bump it up to 11 to see if there's any increase (let's leave a little juice for the rest of the programs).

```
my @selected = @nutrients.race( :11degree ).grep: {
```

Actually, no big increase is achieved. Still, the size 64 of every batch is critical. So let's change that.

```
my @selected = @nutrients.race( :batch(@nutrients/4), :4degree ).grep: {
```

Since we know in advance the size of the array, let's simply divide it by the number of threads we are going to use, and then use that many threads. That brings it down to, ta-da, 8.71, so we've shortened the initial time by four-ish. Can we maybe crank it up a little bit? Let's use a batch size of total size divided by six and six threads, changing 4 to 6 in the code. Do we get something out of that? Nope, up to nine-ish seconds. Four seems to be a sweet spot, since using three also brings it up to ten seconds.

At the end of the day, does this buy us much? If you look back at the initial version, which interspersed read-from-file operations, processing, and output, its time is on the same ballpark as the fastest data-parallel version, with degree 4. Why is that? Put simply, reading from disk is the slowest operation, and there's a certain degree of parallelism between I/O and the processor the language takes advantage of. The same goes for output operations: output to console is a serial operation, which hinders parallelism.

This implies that data parallelism can bring you performance boosts as long as the all operations can be performed in a pipeline, taking data as input and producing more data as output, with no side effects. All the data needs to be in memory without any input/output operations, and, besides, you need to adapt the degree and batch size by yourself to achieve the biggest speed boost. But the most important part is to do a substantial amount of processing for every piece of data; we'll come back to this later.

This recipe does just a few comparisons and it's nearly on the brink of benefitting from race/hyper, as we have seen. The main point, anyway, is that these commands have the *potential* for automatic parallelism, but you need to consider your actual production machine and your problem to see if they can help you or not. When you do, fine-tuning degree and batch will give you the maximum performance boost.

The final version will look like this:

```
my $degree = @*ARGS[0] // 4;
my $time = now;
my @selected = @nutrients.race( :batch(@nutrients/$degree),
:degree($degree)  ).grep: { /...
```

You can adapt the degree to the machine and OS, using by default the degree that gave the best results for me (may not be the case for you).

Recipe 15-2. Work with Asynchronous Input/Output

Problem

You need to create programs that respond to inputs immediately, without hanging while the input or output operation is taking place.

Solution

Combine data parallelism with asynchronous input or output via channels and threads, or simply rely on Raku's inherent event loop to process input in a fast and efficient way.

How It Works

In Chapter 11, we set up a web hook that immediately responded to a change message by using multiple threads working on *heavy* loads, such as building a website. We can apply that technique more generally to make I/O-bound operations much faster. For instance, network operations are notoriously slow. Consulting an external API takes time, and blocking the rest of the program while you wait for the response will take a long time. Making requests in parallel will make the whole operation as slow as the slowest one, when we will be able to collect all operations.

You need to be careful, however. An attempt to parallelize the Wikidata query example we used in Chapter 11 will result in failure. In the case of open APIs like this one, essentially making two simultaneous requests is not considered polite, and a parallel request will return the following:

There's an error in the API request: Error response 429: Rate limit exceeded.

Let's then try a different example. You probably remember using the Edamam API in Chapter 9. A single API request took around three seconds. Why not pool these requests asynchronously, so that we make as many requests as possible asynchronously, and then process the results when they arrive?

The first thing to consider is the "as many as possible" part. Most APIs have a limit, and Edamam is not an exception. It allows, in the free tier, five requests per minute (you'll get an email if you exceed this amount, and it will return a 429 status if you do). So the pool will have to be, at most, five, and then we'll have to wait for a while. Any possible speed improvement is lost when waiting for the request limit to replenish. In any case, obtaining early results as soon as possible has its value, and this is what we do here.

```
use Cro::HTTP::Client;
use URI::Encode;
use Raku::Recipes::SQLator;

my $appID = %*ENV{'EDAMAM_APP_ID'};
my $api-key = %*ENV{'EDAMAM_API_KEY'};
my $api-req = "\&app_id=$appID\&app_key=$api-key";

my $dator = Raku::Recipes::SQLator.new;
my $cro = Cro::HTTP::Client.new(base-uri => "https://api.edamam.com/");

my @responses = do for $dator.get-ingredients.keys[^5] -> $ingredient {
    $cro.get("search?q=" ~ uri_encode(lc($ingredient)) ~ $api-req) ;
}

for await @responses -> $response {
    my %data = await $response.body;
    say "⇒Ingredient %data<q>\n\t→", %data<hits>.map(*<recipe><label>).
    join:
            "\n\t→";

}
```

Most of the script is the same as the previous version. At the end of the day, it's about making requests and getting responses.

The main difference is in the request loop. By using the `do  for` structure, the result of the last instruction in the loop is returned. `$cro.get` returns a promise; as a matter of fact, what we did before was wait on that promise to obtain the result. What we do now, instead of waiting on every response individually, is create an array of response promises.

Promises need to be kept, and we need to wait on the responses anyway to get to them. But instead of stopping the program flow to wait on the first one, then proceed to the second, we wait on all five promises with `await @responses`. In this form, `await` will return the result of all the promises when every one of them has been fulfilled. This is going to be as slow as the slowest response, and all five requests are going to fire pretty much at the same time. Processing the response proceeds in the same way now, except that we loop over the result of the promises, contained in the variable `$response`.

This will print something like this:

```
⇒Ingredient chicken breast
          →Sous Vide Chicken Breast Recipe
          →Roasted Chicken Breast
          →Chicken Breast with Salsa
```

That is, a few recipes in the Edamam database for every ingredient, named in the first line. But the important part is, how long does it take? It takes around five seconds in my system, which is barely a bit over what a single request takes, and this program actually does more, since it gets information from the database and prints more lines of output.

The key here is that `Cro::HTTP::Request` works asynchronously, integrating nicely into asynchronous programs. You could obtain the same result simply by wrapping a promise around a synchronous request (like `get` from `LWP::Simple`). Using `Cro`, however, the code is much clearer and simpler.

Asynchronous programming allows you to leverage bandwidth by pooling as many requests as possible in a rapid-fire series. This is essential in user-facing applications, and will help you create responsive programs. Raku integrates very well with all kinds of facilities, offering the promise industry-standard data structure.

Recipe 15-3. Make Your Program Work Concurrently Using Channels and Threads

Problem

A single-threaded program takes a long time to run.

Solution

Remodel your problem to work as a sequence of tasks that interchange messages, or get started when they receive a message with a payload that indicates what the task will be.

How It Works

Concurrent programming is the art of having different processes working at the same time and coordinating to obtain a result. The problem, of course, is with the coordinating part. In general, you will need to get data to and/or from the processes, and the way you do that is essentially part of the problem. There are many ways to handle that; one of the worst is using a part of the memory that's shared (say, through a global variable) and have everyone read or, even worse, write in it. It can become a bit easier if there's a way to lock that shared memory so that only one process is reading/writing at a time, but there's still the problem of having every process manage its own locks and free them on time.

Another way of managing this is through a methodology called *Communicating Sequential Processes (CSP),* introduced by C.A.R. Hoare, a great computer scientist. The basic idea of CSP is simple: There will be no shared memory among processes that use a communication bus to exchange information. That communication bus is usually called a channel, and as we saw in Chapter 11, it's implemented as a basic data structure in Raku (as well as other languages such as Go and Julia).

Processes in Raku will use channels to receive the data structure they need to work on, as well as to communicate results with other channels, if needed. Specifically, we can use it to assign data to tasks in a semi-automatic way.

Let's do this in the next program, which takes a big file that contains recipes in the MealMaster format, a file that has been processed from several ones found at http://ffts.com/recipes.htm. Some of these recipes were taken from Usenet in the 80s. Long story short, these recipes seem to have no copyright and I've merged them into a single file, converted to UTF8 codification. With every recipe, we will:

- Extract the title, ingredients, and categories.

- Scan ingredients and link them to the page that we created for it (as we did in Chapter 11).

- Dump the result in markdown, and then convert it to HTML.

- Create a web page using a template (in the same way we did in Chapter 10).

We will create this script to illustrate the main principles of concurrency and communication to channels.

Warning   While this program runs in parallel most of the time, it can be very much improved, as we will see in the next recipe. Use it only for reference of overall syntax and concepts. The next recipe will expand on the methodology used in concurrent programs and will explain how they can be debugged to get the most out of them.

```
use Inline::Perl5;
use MealMaster:from<Perl5>;
use Raku::Recipes::Recipe;
use Raku::Recipes::SQLator;
use URI::Encode;
use Template::Classic;
use cmark::Simple;
my $threads = @*ARGS[0] // 4;

my Channel $queue .= new;
my $parser = MealMaster.new();
my @recipes = $parser.parse("Chapter-15/allrecip.mmf");
my %ingredients = Raku::Recipes::SQLator.new.get-ingredients;
my @known = %ingredients.keys.map: *.lc;
my &generate-page = template :($title,$content),
        template-file( "templates/recipe-with-title.html" );#Same as in Ch10
```

```
my atomicint $serial = 1;
my @promises = do for ^$threads {
    start react whenever $queue -> $recipe is copy {
                $recipe.ingredients = process-ingredients( $recipe );
        "/tmp/recipe-$serial.html".IO.spurt(generate-page($recipe.title,
                commonmark-to-html($recipe.gist)).eager.join);
        say "Writing /tmp/recipe-$serial.html";
        $serial ⚛ ++;
    }
}

for @recipes -> $r {
    my $description = "Categories: " ~ $r.categories().join( " - ");
    my $title;
    if $r.title ~~ Str {
        $title = $r.title
    } else {
        $title = $r.title.decode
    }
    my $recipe = Raku::Recipes::Recipe.new(
        :$title,
        :$description,
        ingredients => $r.ingredients().map: {.product }
            );
    $queue.send: $recipe;
}

$queue.close;

await @promises;
sub process-ingredients( $recipe ) {
    my @real-ingredients = $recipe.ingredients.grep: /^^\w+/;
    gather for @real-ingredients -> $i is copy {
        $i = $i ~~ Blob ?? $i.encode !! $i;
```

```
    if $i ~~ m:i/ <|w> $<ingredient> = (@known) <|w>/ {
        my $ing = ~$<ingredient>;
        my $subst = "[$ing](/ingredient/" ~ uri_encode($ing.lc) ~ ")";
        $i ~~ s:i!<|w> $ing <|w> ! $subst !;
    }
    take $i;
  }
}
```

This program is a bit long, but except for its novel use of channels, it's mostly a combination of techniques seen in other recipes. One of the key parts of the program is the need to generate a single serial number so that we give a unique name to every HTML file we create. We are going to need this no matter what, as long as we don't use random filenames. If we use the title, for instance, we will still need to check that it's unique and we're not clobbering old files with new ones. So we will use a unique Raku feature, atomic numbers. The atomicint data type provides a series of operations that are safe under threading. We just need to increment it, but atomicints are not normal ints, so we also atomic-increment it like this: $serial ⚛ ++. This is shared memory, but it's guaranteed to work under threading, so we're good.

We also use a channel, simply called $queue, as it's a task queue that will receive data about which operations are going to be performed.

The program includes two main parts: one part extracts recipes from the file and converts them into a Raku::Recipes::Recipe data structure. This data structure is sent, with $queue.send: $recipe; to the queue. Queues can handle any kind of data structure in Raku, with no special need to serialize/deserialize them. It just works.

The threads performing the tasks are indeed created before this emission takes place, simply because they are reactive pieces of code that will wake up when needed. And this need will arise when a message is received in the $queue. We first set up a loop over the number of threads we will work with:

```
my @promises = do for ^$threads { start ... }
```

This is built with the do statement prefix, which gathers the result of every iteration in the loop. This is the result of the last statement in it. In this case, it's a start statement, which returns a promise; @promises will then contain the promises created for every thread, which will be four by default (a reasonable number for mid-range laptops and desktops).

The promise is effectively reactive code: react whenever $queue → $recipe will wake up when something is received in the queue. Every promise will behave in the same way, and they will attempt to read from the queue as soon as they become available. Whether they run on different threads or not will depend on how many are available, but from a high-level perspective, and given the right circumstances, every promise will be fulfilled in a different thread.

Within the queue, the operation is not terribly heavy, but it consists of a series of dependent passes. First, we filter out "ingredients" of the form "---- xxx ---" which are actually badly parsed parts of the recipe. Then we go over these remaining ingredients, using a regular expression to look up the known ingredients that we are going to link. This regex <|w> $<ingredient> = (@known) <|w> will not only try to find the ingredients in that recipe, returning only those that are whole words, as stated by the word boundary markers, <|w> (so that we only link rice, and not licorice), but it will also store the name of the ingredient, which we will use to create the link and store it in the $subst variable.

If there are any of those ingredients, we also need to substitute them, which we do here:

```
$i ~~ s:i!<|w> $ing <|w> ! $subst !
```

s is the substitution operator working on $i, which has been declared as an "as is" copy so that we can change its value. The :i adverb indicates it will be case-insensitive, since the recipes have all kinds of capitalization, from all caps to first-letter cap. This s operator can use any kind of quotes. We opt for ! ! ! instead of /// simply to make the regex a bit more visible. This will add the markdown-style link.

These ingredients are in a gather/take loop; $i is "taken" to be gathered, processed or not, depending on us having found an ingredient.

The rest of the loop reassigns these ingredients to the recipe. This Raku::Recipes::Recipe has the machinery to print the whole recipe to markdown, so we leverage that for, in the next sentence, do a series of things on the recipe.

- $recipe.gist will render the recipe (including the newly minted markdown links) to markdown.

- The result goes through `commonmark-to-html`, from the `cmark::Simple` module we created in the previous chapter, to be converted to HTML.

- That goes through `generate-page`, a `Template::Simple` subroutine that will put the generated HTML fragment into a page, together with the title of the recipe. This routine generates a lazy array, which we "eagerize" to render and then join into a single string.

- That string is written, through `spurt`, to a file, which in this case will be in the `temporal` folder.

The serial is atomic-incremented, and that code goes to sleep for indeed a very short time before it wakes up, possibly in another thread. That takes a few minutes to read the original file and generate more than 4,000 files with the default number of threads; it takes around ten minutes in a run.

That's really a good mark for a 10MB file. It would probably be better if processing was a bit heavier for every one and it was not so I/O bound. If we could have mixed lazy reads from the file, it would have been even better. Adding more threads is not really an improvement. Why that's so is a task left to the next recipe.

Recipe 15-4. Monitor Concurrency Using Comma IDE

Problem

Debugging concurrent programs is especially difficult. In addition to grokking what the program does, you need to know if it's happening at the same time, that is, if concurrency is actually happening and how much of it is occurring.

Solution

The IDE for Raku, Comma, includes facilities for visualizing concurrent events and tasks. In order to use it, you must add a specific logging library to your code, called `Log::Timeline`. Comma examines these logs to visually present events and tasks from within the IDE.

How It Works

One of the most important things that you must consider in parallel programs is the balance between communication and computation. Communication (to and from channels) create a certain amount of overhead with the sequential version. If the amount of simultaneous computation you do in different threads overcomes that overhead, it's a win. If it's not, you're losing. So you need to put as much computation as possible in threads, but also verify that, effectively, these threads are acting in parallel, and that there are no gaps whereby one processor is idling while others do all the work.

The main tool to carry this out is Comma, the IDE we discussed several times already. By itself, Comma cannot monitor concurrent execution; it needs a small modification in the program to be able to do so. We'll need to add modules that mix in the Log::Timeline module. This is the one we will be using to monitor the previous program.

```
unit module Recipr::Log::Timeline;
use Log::Timeline;

class Processing does Log::Timeline::Task['Recipr', 'Backend', 'Processing']
is export { }
```

We'll put all the logger classes in a single module, called Recipr::Log::Timeline. There are two types of roles that can be mixed in: Log::Timeline::Task and Log::Timeline::Event. For the time being, we'll use the former. They are used to log what their last name indicates, either extended tasks or single events. The main objective of task loggers is to wrap around the code we need to monitor in order to check when and how much it's running. The event loggers are traditional loggers: you can log any kind of data to a common format. Both will be presented in the monitor.

Log::Timeline::Task is a parameterized role. It's been designed so that parameters are used as a kind of instantiation. Different tasks to be logged will have a different combination of the three parameters, which correspond to the module name, the category of the task, and the name of the task. Tasks will be grouped by category and then by name. We will use the same class to log all threads that will be doing the same task. The class itself is empty, because we don't need any additional processing. We also export it out of the module so that it's visible from outside.

There's not much we need to do to add this to our program. You just wrap the code of the task you want monitored with `Recipr::Log::Timeline::Processing.log: -> { }`. That is:

```
my @promises = do for ^$threads {
    start react whenever $queue -> $recipe is copy {
        Recipr::Log::Timeline::Processing.log: -> {
            #...same code here
        }
    }
}
```

Normally, all the work that is going to be done in a thread will be wrapped this way. But you can wrap any code you want represented in that way; every fragment will be given a representation in the code monitor.

We will perform an additional change to the code. We were using an atomic variable that ensured that it was not going to be modified by two threads at the same time. However, that does not guarantee that it's not going to be *used* by two threads at the same time, since it's modified after the file is written, and writing a file can take a fraction of a second. That's extremely unlikely after the first files, but it might cause a race condition at the very beginning, when threads start at the same time. So it's better to use a local variable, instead of a global variable, and put that variable into the message that initiates the task. Let's change it to this:

```
$queue.send: ($i++, $recipe);
```

This will require a change to the receiving code:

```
start react whenever $queue -> ($serial, $recipe) is copy {
```

This deconstructs the received list into the serial number and the recipe object. The rest of the code will only eliminate the atomic increment operator, keeping the filename the same.

Let's try to get this working then, with the monitor. We need to click the icon by the side of the buggy that looks like... really, I have no idea what it looks like. Two green lines with blue and yellow dots and lines. Guess it's kinda a timeline. Anyway, we need to run it that way. We will see something like Figure 15-1. Needless to say, this is not exactly what we were looking for.

At least, we see that it's parallel. The problem is that parallelism starts after a relatively long hiatus of several seconds without the threads running in parallel at all. Second, there are only two threads.

Figure 15-1. *The first iteration of the program, monitored with Comma. The parallel monitor icon is to the left of the red square "stop" icon*

Once they get going, the two threads are running in parallel alright, as shown by the bands that are being created alternatively in the two threads.

What seems to be the problem then? The sequential part, which is essentially the loop that feeds the channels, is problematic. The whole program is not running in a parallel way, since the threads start to perform their tasks a few seconds after the start, when the scheduler finds a way to let them in. It's definitely not ideal, and that explains why using more threads will not help the overall performance, as we saw before.

What can we do? We can make the code that feeds the channel concurrent as well, by starting a thread that runs it. We add that by using this code:

```
await start for @recipes -> $r { # Rest of the loop is the same.
```

That is, `start for` starts a thread and `await` proceeds only when all that has been done.

The monitor will show this very different panorama, as in Figure 15-2.

Figure 15-2. *Running Recipr in six different threads*

Let's switch to four threads. We can change the command line in Comma by editing the command-line parameters in the configuration. The result is shown in Figure 15-3.

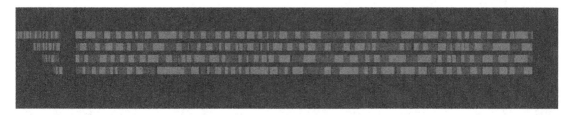

Figure 15-3. *Running with four threads*

There are several things we can appreciate here. First, the quite obvious gap (which is 1/5th second when you know the scale) that shows up in every run. Second, the fact that the tasks are initially very quick. If we hover the mouse over the stripe, we will see that they take around 0.06 seconds. Later, something that should take more or less the same time takes up to half a second. The result is in the same ballpark as the initial version, around ten minutes for four threads. Adding more threads is not really a boost, at least on my laptop.

The problem is still the balance between communication and computation. There's a single thread preprocessing the recipes and creating the objects. That thread is running all the time. Let's monitor it to check that it's running effectively while the others are processing. We've also added one thread to the total number of threads in our program, so there's not much space left.

We add another task monitor:

```
class Emitting does Log::Timeline::Task['Recipr', 'Backend', 'Emitting']
              is export { }
```

And then we wrap the loop interior in it:

```
await start for @recipes -> $r {
    Recipr::Log::Timeline::Emitting.log: -> {
        # same code as before.
    }
}
```

This will result in Figure 15-4.

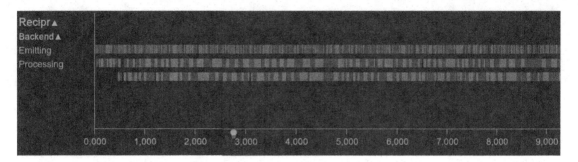

Figure 15-4. *Monitoring the emitting thread*

That additional monitoring is showing us that the emission takes very little time, and that there are many emissions that can't be processed in real time. There's still a small gap, and the problem is that processing every file takes several tenths of a second. We can try to delve a bit into that, to see where that time goes. Let's add another monitor. Since we are going to have two monitors in the same group, we'll try to split them into two groups, renaming them this way:

```
unit module Recipr::Log::Timeline;
use Log::Timeline;

class Processing does Log::Timeline::Task['Recipr', 'Processing',
'Processing']
is export { }

class Emitting does Log::Timeline::Task['Recipr', 'Backend', 'Emitting']
                is export { }

class Saving does Log::Timeline::Task['Recipr', 'Processing', 'Saving']
                is export { }
```

So whatever goes into the processing threads will have `Processing` as a name, and `Emitting` will be the single task logger in the `Backend` category. The result is shown in Figure 15-5.

Figure 15-5. *Monitoring inside a task*

The small stripe for "saving" shows that it's not taking a long time: it's the rest of the task that takes so long. Incidentally, we can also see that the emitter is sending messages much faster than they can be processed; that's only natural, anyway, but still processing every message seems to be taking a long time.

What we need to do now is profile what these slower parts do. That's outside the realm of parallel processing, but this chapter is about performance. Let's try to max out this thing. I am not going to bore you with yet another screenshot of the monitor showing how different parts of the loop perform, but working on code fragments instead of the whole loop reveals several issues. That loop over ingredients is effectively taking a long time, and in some cases, it's individual iterations that are taking up to several hundredths of a second. We can speed that up a tiny bit by taking out the creation of URLs from the loop. You lose something (that they will appear in the same capitalization as originally), but you save some speed.

We need to make it a bit faster. Maybe the regexes, which are notoriously slow, are to blame. Let's use subst instead.

```
my @promises = do for ^$threads {
    start react whenever $queue -> $recipe is copy {
        Recipr::Log::Timeline::Processing.log: -> {
            my @real-ingredients = $recipe.ingredients.grep( /^^\w+/)
            .map( { $_ ~~ Blob ?? $_.decode !! $_ } );
            $recipe.ingredients = @real-ingredients;
            my $recipe-md = $recipe.gist;
            for @known -> $k {
                $recipe-md .= subst( /:i <|w> $k <|w>/, %urls-for-known{$k} )
            }
            Recipr::Log::Timeline::Saving.log: -> {
                "/tmp/recipe-$serial.html".IO.spurt(generate-page($recipe.
                title,
                        commonmark-to-html($recipe-md)).eager.join);
                say "Writing /tmp/recipe-$serial.html";
            }
            $serial⌖++;
        }
    }
}
```

We have eliminated the loop over the ingredients, substituting it with a map over filtered ingredients. That map decodes the blobs found in the original file (mainly coming from using some non-English letters like é). As a matter of fact, we can eliminate the use of the temporary variable `@real-ingredients`.

Instead of making the substitution per ingredient, which, besides, might be prone to errors since it only substituted the first word found, we loop over all products and substitute them. We use the adverb `:i` inside the regex to make the search case-insensitive. Instead of converting the recipe using `gist`, what we use now in the rendering is this new markdown document with all the substitution.

Does this result in a real improvement? Unsurprisingly (or not), it does. It eliminates a loop, and it introduces another one whose result might be faster, since it will substitute a single product name over all its instances, and it will do so much faster. This last version of the program takes around five minutes. The main boost, however, might come from the fact that we're checking a regular expression only once, instead of twice in the cases when it resulted in a positive match.

At any rate, this shows the methodology that should be used to debug and obtain the maximum performance out of a concurrent program. First, you have to find out what's slowing it down. Your program might be fast enough, or it might spend most of the time in a tiny part. That slow part also needs to be parallelizable in some way. Then, you have to maximize concurrency: put as many serial parts of the program in their own independent threads, try to eliminate bottlenecks by checking out performance, and eventually optimize per-thread performance so that every part is as fast as possible. Always keep the number of threads flexible and test-run for several numbers until you get the best combination for your particular platform. This will depend on the number of physical threads you have, other programs and services that are running, as well as input/output performance. Maxing out the number of threads might not be the best idea; use the number that gives you the maximum boost.

Be sure to take into account the best practices discussed in the next recipe.

Recipe 15-5. Create Powerful Concurrent Programs Problem

You need to create the fastest program possible, given your specifications, inputs, and outputs.

Solution

Well, there's no one solution here. Concurrent performance depends on many things, and there's no silver bullet. Striking the balance between computation and communication, finding the right data and control structures, is a matter of systematic testing and deep knowledge of the hardware and software your program is running on. Lacking a one-size-fits-all approach, all you have is a series of best practices that you can use to improve your programs incrementally, using Raku tools such as the Comma parallel monitor and logs.

How It Works

Parallel programming is the art of making many CPUs do a lot of work together with lots of communication, when a sequential program might be all you need in the first place. Let's go back to the previous program and try a sequential version. The whole program is shown here, although most of the code is reused.

```perl6
#!/usr/bin/env perl6

use Inline::Perl5;

use MealMaster:from<Perl5>;

use Raku::Recipes::Recipe;
use Raku::Recipes::SQLator;

use URI::Encode;
use Template::Classic;
use cmark::Simple;

my $threads = @*ARGS[0] // 2;

my Channel $queue .= new;

my $parser = MealMaster.new();
my @recipes = $parser.parse("Chapter-15/allrecip.mmf");

my %ingredients = Raku::Recipes::SQLator.new.get-ingredients;
my @known = %ingredients.keys.map: *.lc;
```

```
my &generate-page = template :($title,$content),
        template-file( "templates/recipe-with-title.html" );

my %urls-for-known = | @known.map: { $_ => "[$_](/ingredient/$_)"};
@recipes.kv.rotor(2).map( { process-recipe(@_[0], @_[1]) } );

sub template-file( $template-file-name ) {
    "resources/$template-file-name".IO.e
            ??"resources/$template-file-name".IO.slurp
            !!%?RESOURCES{$template-file-name}.slurp;
}

sub process-recipe( $serial, $recipe ) {
    my $description = "Categories: " ~ $recipe.categories().join(" - ");
    my $title;
    if $recipe.title ~~ Str {
        $title = $recipe.title
    } else {
        $title = $recipe.title.decode
    }
    my $rrecipe = Raku::Recipes::Recipe.new(
            :$title,
            :$description,
            ingredients => $recipe.ingredients().map: { .product }
            );
    my @real-ingredients = $rrecipe.ingredients.grep(/^^\w+/)
            .map({ $_ ~~ Blob ?? $_.decode !! $_ });
    $rrecipe.ingredients = @real-ingredients;
    my $recipe-md = $rrecipe.gist;
    for @known -> $k {
        $recipe-md .= subst(/:i <|w> $k <|w>/, %urls-for-known{$k})
    }
    "/tmp/recipe-$serial.html".IO.spurt(generate-page($rrecipe.title,
            commonmark-to-html($recipe-md)).eager.join);
    say "Writing /tmp/recipe-$serial.html";

}
```

This program makes two relatively small changes:

- Every recipe is processed in a single function that receives the wrapped Perl 5 `MealMaster::Recipe` object, does all the filtering, and eventually saves it to a file.

- It uses a single map, instead of threads and channels, to process the array of around 10,000 recipes. This line `@recipes.kv.rotor(2).map( { process-recipe(@_[0], @_[1]) } );` generates an `index`-`element` sequence, which is chunked into (index, recipe) arrays via `.rotor`. We will use the index to create the filename as we did before.

There's no real parallelism here, only efficient data flow. In general, laying out the code so that you can apply it as a map makes it faster than using a similar approach with loops. Instead of two loops, we now have a single map. Running this takes around three minutes on the same laptop that took nearly five minutes to run the parallel version. What gives?

Well, communication is all. The latest version of the program was relatively efficient, but it could not overcome the fact that it was sending a message for every recipe, around 10,000 messages in all. And every message had its own overhead. Although we could process messages at the same time, the overhead added was more than what you gained by parallelizing the whole program.

That does not make the previous program invalid. It has its use case: when you don't want to overload a single processor, or when you effectively want to leverage low-load processors in that way. Every parallelization technique has its own niche. Besides, by improving single-threaded code, we also paved the way for this, higher performance, version.

Can we do better than that? No, we can't. We can use `hyper`, or `race`, but the result is going to be in the same ballpark. The problem here is that the amount of computation done for every recipe is not that much. The second takeaway here is that, in order to strike a good computation-communication balance, you need to have a fair amount of single-item computation to start with. Big data structures and a small amount of computation is not a good combination, although you might come up with a scheme to deal with it in parallel (for instance, batching the computation of chunks of the data structure by hand). A fair amount of computation on a small enough data structure is more like the kind of problem that is amenable to automatic (via `hyper`/`race`) or manual (via channels/start) computation.

So if the problem does not fit itself to solving, we can always change the problem. Instead of creating a single file and processing it all at once in very small chunks, let's divide the file in many smaller files, and try to parallel-process those. This Raku script will split the big file we used originally into chunks that contain 400 recipes (except for the last one).

```perl6
#!/usr/bin/env perl6

use Inline::Perl5;
use MealMaster:from<Perl5>;

my $input-file-name = @*ARGS[0] // "allrecip.mmf";

my $all-recipes = $input-file-name.IO.slurp;

my @recipes = $all-recipes.split( /^^ ["-----" | "MMMMM"] \s+ /);
my $index = 1;

for @recipes.rotor(400) -> @chunk {
    my $all-recipes = '';
    for @chunk -> $r {
        my $this-mm;
        if $r ~~ /^"-"/ {
            $this-mm = "$r\n-----\n";
        } else {
            $this-mm = "$r\nMMMMM";
        }

        "/tmp/temp.mmf".IO.spurt($this-mm);
        if MealMaster.parse("/tmp/temp.mmf") {
            $all-recipes = "$all-recipes\n$this-mm";
        } else {
            say $all-recipes;
            die $this-mm;
        }
    }
    "/tmp/all-recipes-$index.mmf".IO.spurt( $all-recipes );
    $index++;
}
```

It also makes small inroads into processing the format with Raku. As a matter of fact, the only thing it does is split the whole file in recipes, check them, and then join them back together in a single, 400 recipes file.

In order to do this, we look back again at the format. A bit weirdly, recipes are included within a format that ends either with five dashes or five Ms. In the first case, it will have a bunch of dashes followed by a statement, in the second, there are five Ms followed by dashes and the same statement. Since we split either via this regular expression `/^^ ["-----" | "MMMMM"] \s+ /` which matches five dashes or five Ms at the beginning of a line and one or more spaces, that precise information is lost. However, Ms and dashes need to be matched, so we put them back, write to a file (because the MealMaster module only reads from files, so that's a good candidate for a pull request) in order to check it via a parse, and if it's okay (the original is going to be okay, but the splitting may not), it's added to a string. Eventually, the whole string is written to a file with an index that self-increments itself. We end up with 21 files, 20 of them containing 400 recipes, one of them containing whatever is left. So now we have 21 files. Can we process them in parallel?

Well, it so happens we can't. Since the underlying code is written in Perl, it's not reentrant. Any code you call from a thread must be reentrant, or you might find race conditions that will mix code coming from two different threads. Trying to process a file via MealMaster in a thread will result in failure. So we have to make do processing them using Raku. We don't have the grammar to interpret this (for the time being). Let's try to process it as best we can. This is an example:

```
    Title: Vegetable Casserole Supreme
Categories: Casseroles, Vegetables
     Yield: 6 servings

  4 ea POTATOES, SLICED                    1 lb GROUND BEEF
  3 ea CARROTS, SLICED DIAGONALLY          1 cn MUSHROOM SOUP       *
  1 cn PEAS

  *       USE CREAM OF MUSHROOM OR TRY CHICKEN SOUP OR ?
  *-------------------------------------------------------------------*
LAYER ALL VEGETABLES AND BEEF IN A 2 QUART CASSEROLE DISH. POUR THE SOUP
(DILUTED WITH 1 CAN OF WATER) OVER THE TOP OF THE DISH.
BAKE AT 350 DEG F. UNTIL ALL LAYERS ARE DONE.
```

There are three sections, separated by double carriage returns. Processing them is beyond the scope of this book, so we will just convert the title to a heading, slap a second-level heading in the categories and yield, and convert the whole thing to HTML. This program will do it:

```
#!/usr/bin/env perl6

use Inline::Perl5;

use MealMaster:from<Perl5>;

use Raku::Recipes::Recipe;
use Raku::Recipes::SQLator;
use Recipr::Log::Timeline;

use URI::Encode;
use Template::Classic;
use cmark::Simple;

my $threads = @*ARGS[0] // 3;
my Channel $queue .= new;

my $parser = MealMaster.new();
my @recipes = $parser.parse("Chapter-15/allrecip.mmf");

my %ingredients = Raku::Recipes::SQLator.new.get-ingredients;
my @known = %ingredients.keys.map: *.lc;

my &generate-page = template :($title,$content),
        template-file( "templates/recipe-with-title.html" );
my %urls-for-known = | @known.map: { $_ => "[$_](/ingredient/$_)"};

my @promises = do for ^$threads {
    start react whenever $queue -> $recipe-file  {
        Recipr::Log::Timeline::Processing.log: -> {
            $recipe-file.path ~~ /$<serial> = (\d+)/;
            my $serial = +$<serial>;
            my @all-lines = $recipe-file.lines;
```

```
            my $recipes = @all-lines
                    .grep({ !$_.starts-with("MMMMM") })
                    .grep({ !$_.starts-with("-----") })
                    .join("\n");
            $recipes ~~ s:g/\h+ "Title:" /# /;
            for <Categories Yield> -> $c {
                $recipes ~~ s:g/\h+$c/## $c/;
            }
            process-recipes($serial, $recipes);
        }
    }
}

await start for dir("/tmp", test => /"all-recipes"/ ) -> $r-file {
    $queue.send: $r-file;
}
$queue.close;
await @promises;

# Subs
sub template-file( $template-file-name ) {
    "resources/$template-file-name".IO.e
            ??"resources/$template-file-name".IO.slurp
            !!%?RESOURCES{$template-file-name}.slurp;
}
sub process-recipes( $serial, $recipe ) {
    "/tmp/recipes-$serial.html".IO.spurt(generate-page("Recipes $serial",
            commonmark-to-html($recipe)).eager.join);
    say "Writing /tmp/recipes-$serial.html";

}
```

Essentially we are doing what has been indicated. Detecting lines that start with markers and eliminating them, adding some markup to titles and categories, and converting it to HTML. We use start-with as a search term, and we use regular expressions that include \h, horizontal space, so that carriage returns are not converted and thus the result is proper markup.

If we do this with a single thread, it takes around 50 seconds. With two threads, it goes down to 27 seconds. More threads give you marginal gain. The main problem is that processing every file takes up to several seconds; unless a thread takes a substantial part of the load off another thread, it might be stuck processing something. More threads increment the variability of time that passes between the first thread that finishes and the last thread. Let's clarify with an example. We have four tasks that take three, two, one, and seven seconds. Sequentially, we need 15 seconds. Two threads will take, at least, seven seconds, but only if we're lucky and we run that longer task first. Additional threads will always take seven seconds. Although the quantity is not the same in this case, the principle is the same. For tasks that take a long time, simply dividing them with no priorities among threads will have diminishing returns. See Figure 15-6.

Figure 15-6. *Working with four threads*

At the end of the day, what matters is raw performance, and this last version (that, admittedly, does something that is slightly different) takes just a fraction of the time of the initial versions. But it shows the many dilemmas in the design of a powerful concurrent application. Even if you manage to have a very good communication/computation ratio, you still need to have a good balance of workload among different tasks, and you need to keep the overall amount of work done by every task low, because its max value will be how much the overall program has to wait for all the tasks to end. And on top of it all, taking into account how many physical threads are available in your system is important. With fewer physical threads, every thread will slow down while they wait for the processor to be available. You will need to run your program with an increasing number of threads, and just stop when there's no significant gain. In general, the operating systems will keep for itself two to three threads. In the case shown (and on my laptop), going from sequential to two threads will result in a big boost. Anything else will amount to minimal gains.

Monitoring tools—such as a simple command-line timing and the more complex Comma monitor together with its logging libraries—will help you design the powerful concurrent program you are looking for.

CHAPTER 16

Creating Mini-Languages

Grammars are a unique feature of Raku; they are a powerful way to process text with structure in it, and they can be used to create mini-languages. You can use these mini-languages for many different purposes, from configuration to real and actual programming languages. Like regular expressions, mini-languages are the kind of thing that you will wish you would have known about before, because they will save so much trouble thanks to their expressivity. We'll dive into them next.

Recipe 16-1. Use Mini-Languages That Show Off Their Possibilities

Problem

Many problem domains would benefit from having a mini-language that would better describe them, rather than using a language with a forced syntax such as JSON. Mini-languages are, in general, natural ways of expressing things. They are closer to the natural (textual) description, with a structure that makes them easier to understand. Interpreting a mini-language gives us the structure of it, a structure that can be converted to other (mini) languages or processed in different ways.

Solution

Use a grammar to parse a (mini) language, including roles that play parts that are common to other languages.

© J.J. Merelo 2020
J.J. Merelo, *Raku Recipes*, https://doi.org/10.1007/978-1-4842-6258-0_16

How It Works

Note   Before diving deeper into grammars, you might want to check out Chapter 15 of *Perl 6 Quick Syntax Reference,* by the same author and publisher, for a more extensive reference to their functionalities and possibilities.

Languages are structured hierarchically, from the lowest rung, which are literals like words or numbers, to expressions, and finally to "programs" or "documents." Parsing involves creating these rules that go from the top to the bottom, checking that the document is correct and identifying the parts we need to identify in them. Every part will get a *token*, not as appreciation, but simply as a way to understand what the document says and what we need from it. Not every symbol needs such a token; an example would be parentheses in most normal languages. There is no "parenthesized" token, but we understand that whatever token is within them is going to be grouped together with preference given to whatever is outside.

We dealt with grammars in Chapters 8 and 11. In this chapter, we'll try to go a bit further by designing a grammar from the bottom up that interprets a recipe written in Markdown using specific constructs. That recipe would look like this:

```
# Tuna risotto

A relatively simple version of this rich, creamy dish of Italian origin.

## Ingredients (for 4 persons)

* 320g tuna (canned)
* 250g rice
* ½ onion
* 250g cheese (whatever is in your fridge)
* 2 tablespoons olive oil
* 4 cloves garlic
* 1 spoon butter (or margarine).
* ⅓ liter wine (or beer).

## Preparation (60m)
```

1. Slightly fry tuna with its own oil it until it browns a bit. You can do this while you start doing the rest. Save a bit of oil for the rice.
1. Stir-fry garlic until golden-colored, chopped if you so like, retire if you don't like the color.
2. Add finely-chopped onion, and stir-fly until transparent.
3. Add rice and stir-fry until grains become transparent in the tips.
4. Add wine or beer and stir until it's absorbed by grains.
5. Repeat several times: add fish broth, stir, until water is evaporated, until rice is soft but a bit chewy.
6. Add tuna, butter, grated cheese, and turn heating off, removing until creamy.
7. Let it rest for 5 minutes before serving.

This recipe has three parts, plus a title, which uses the common convention for Markdown headlines: a description, which is free-form text, a set of ingredients (with the title indicating how many people will be served), and instructions for preparation.

The ingredients will need to be parsed specifically: they contain an amount, a measure, the ingredient itself, and possible options. For instance, from 320g tuna (canned) we need to understand that it's exactly 320 grams of tuna, and that we can use canned tuna for that. We already processed ingredients partially before, but stopped short of doing the whole thing (including options). We'll do that here.

Finally, the preparation includes the time it will take in parentheses, and it contains an ordered list of instructions. They need to be processed in order, but the numbers in front follow the Markdown convention. They need to be a number, not even in order, which is why the two first items have number one. We might want to indicate that those things can be done at the same time. The first word is significant, since it usually indicates an activity. We might want to capture that too, so that we highlight it.

We're no stranger to grammars. We have been using them during the whole book, mainly to parse parts of recipes. We have also used external libraries to process mini-languages, such as the one used in the MealMaster application, which we used in Chapters 14 and 15. However, we weren't dealing with whole "documents" or "programs," just small grammars that helped us understand some (maybe complex) strings. Besides, we haven't so far come up with a way to process the whole recipe, described in a subset of Markdown or in any other way. Since it's based on Markdown and it's used for recipes, let's just call it *RecipeMark*.

Let's try to create a grammar that processes such a format. Bear in mind that a language needn't be a structured set of operations, executed sequentially. It need not be a Turing-complete language with which we can create complicated programs. A mini-language can be a small set of operations or a simple or complicated configuration, or simply be a way to structure a document so that it can be processed automatically. Our recipes language will be one of that kind.

Let's determine what we can reuse from before. This grammarole was defined previously:

```
use Raku::Recipes;

unit role Raku::Recipes::Grammar::Measures;

token quantity { <:N>+ }
token unit     { @unit-types }
```

It defines the minimal part of the ingredient, the quantity, and the unit. It restricts the units to the options that we are interested in, to our "language." We need to do this because if we don't know the unit, we can't compute anything about it—its weight, calories, or anything else. A language usually restricts the "key" words that are used in certain positions, and we will do that here too (or will continue doing so, since this is reused). Here's how it's defined in Raku::Recipes:

```
our @unit-types is export = <g tbsp clove tbsps cloves liters liter l
tablespoons Unit tablespoon spoons cloves clove spoon cup cups>;
```

The language won't understand any other unit (such as "a pinch" or "to taste"). By restricting these words, we also anchor the units: either we have one of these words, or we will simply be using units. If we find a word that's not one of these behind a number, we know that we are referring directly to a product.

One step up will be the grammarole that interprets the whole line that describes the ingredient.

```
use Raku::Recipes::CSVDator;
use Raku::Recipes::Grammar::Measures;
```

```
my @products;
BEGIN {
    @products = Raku::Recipes::CSVDator.new.products.map:
        {$_.ends-with("s")?? $_ !! ( $_, $_ ~ "s").Slip }
}

unit role Raku::Recipes::Grammarole::Measured-Ingredients does
    Raku::Recipes::Grammar::Measures;
token ingredient-description {
    <measured-ingredient> \h* <options>?
}

token measured-ingredient {
    [ <quantity> \h* <unit> \h+ <product> || <quantity> \h+ <product>]
}

token options {
    '(' ~ ')' $<content> = .+?
}

token product {:i @products }
```

Let's start with this last line. We will be able to create ingredients that include these products only. These are the products that we have stored elsewhere. As a matter of fact, we use one of the *dators* to extract that information from the data source. This token is essential and defines any ingredient in our data store as a keyword in the language. At the same time, it's essential to anchor the rest of the components of the ingredient. By checking a word (or, in some cases, two words) against the ingredient description, we are able to understand that whatever is to the left is a measurement, and whatever is to the right might be additional information. Without this limited choice of words, it would be very difficult to understand this particular instruction. A language, besides, is syntax and semantics. The data store provides the semantics for this syntax, and also makes it very easy to extend the language by simply adding more rows to the data store.

We will not code for capitalization. We create the product list so that it takes into account plurals (although this yields some weird mistakes, such as "Kales" and "Tunas," we cannot account for all the quirks of the beautiful English language). Plural words will be as much a part of RecipeMark as singular ones. Again, this is restrictive because we will be able to write recipes with the ingredients we know about. But this is also consistent with how languages are designed: they have a syntax and semantics. The semantics of the restricted units of measurement we will use are the ones we know about and can transform to weights. The semantics of the products will be the ones we give them—what kind of dish they can be in, as well as the quantitative data we have about them.

Since this is a role, we don't have a designated TOP rule: it's simply the one that we feel is at the top. So let's look at them now from the top down. What we have there is an ingredient-description, which will be an ingredient plus an optional part that we call options. This optional part will be in parentheses:

```
'(' ~ ')' $<content> = .+?
```

The tilde is a marker for nested content. This rule will not only check that there's some stuff (defined after) within the parentheses, it will also fail in a graceful way by pointing out that the closing parenthesis is missing, if it is. We need to capture everything inside the parentheses, so we use .+? for a non-greedy description of anything that can go there. It will generally be letters and spaces, but there could be more—a emoji indicating something is nice. We also need to assign it to a specific token, $<content>, to indicate that's the part we are interested in, not the parentheses. We've seen the measured-ingredient part elsewhere, so this is just a little reminder—two options, with or without unit. The quantity was defined in the previous grammarole as any number (1¾ will be valid, in principle). The unit will be separated or not by horizontal whitespace (again, this means that we will take things like 1cup, but we can either accept it or, later on, refine the grammar so that it takes only "sticky" units that way), followed by the product.

As you know, we can use grammaroles straight away, as long as we specify the rule we'll be using. Let's give it a spin to check if it fits everything we want:

```
use Raku::Recipes::Grammarole::Measured-Ingredients;
grammar Tester does Raku::Recipes::Grammarole::Measured-Ingredients {}

say Tester.subparse("½ onion",
        rule => "ingredient-description")<measured-ingredient>;

say Tester.subparse("⅓ liter wine (or beer)",
        rule => "ingredient-description");
```

Grammaroles are not exactly grammars, so we need to weave them in a tester grammar to check them out. Besides, this one does not include a TOP so we need to specify the entry point for the grammar and use subparse. We obviously choose the "top" rule (which, in this case, is a token; every component of a grammar is called rule by default). This works as expected, printing the following:

```
⌈½ onion⌋
 quantity => ⌈½⌋
 product => ⌈onion⌋
⌈⅓ liter wine (or beer)⌋
 measured-ingredient => ⌈⅓ liter wine⌋
  quantity => ⌈⅓⌋
  unit => ⌈liter⌋
  product => ⌈wine⌋
 options => ⌈(or beer)⌋
  content => ⌈or beer⌋
```

In the first case, there's no unit or product, and it parses the quantity and the content of the optional part in the second case correctly.

There's a small problem here: if we use "eggs" as a product, that will be effectively returned as a token. We then would have to check if there's that word, or its equivalent singular word. We can change the token to:

```
token measured-ingredient {
    [ <quantity> \h* <unit> \h+ <product> || <quantity> \h+ <product>] s?
}
```

With an optional s at the end:

```
say Tester.subparse("3 eggs (free run)",
      rule => "ingredient-description");
```

It would correctly return:

```
⌈3 eggs (free run)⌋
 measured-ingredient => ⌈3 eggs⌋
  quantity => ⌈3⌋
  product => ⌈egg⌋
 options => ⌈(free run)⌋
  content => ⌈free run⌋
```

We could look up the product in our data store directly. Unfortunately, "lentilss" would also pass muster, although we would extract the correct product out of that. Well, you earn something, you lose something, but when there are two options, it's always better to have some false positives (words that might be syntactically incorrect in your problem domain but that you can interpret correctly) rather than false negatives (words that are semantically incorrect and that you have to process further to understand what's actually happening).

As in the case of the "sticky" units, a deeper understanding of the English language would be needed. In this case, metadata on whether the word is a singular or a plural ("egg" vs. "lentils") and differentiated rules for each one. That's doable, but is left as an exercise to the reader.

Completing RecipeMark

Once the (possibly) most complicated part is out of the way, we can build our way up to create the rest of the grammar. Grammars are never easy, and in writing this, it's good advice to rely on grammar debugging tools such as the ones we saw in Chapter 8. Ideally, we would factor out any part of the grammar that could be reused as a role and build our way up to the full grammar. We might have to add some constraints to what is considered "correct" RecipeMark and what's not.

If we compare grammars with usual language-compiling or interpreting modules, they tokenize (in the appropriately named *tokens*) and then parse the whole structure so that tokens are placed in the right sequence and separated by the right separators. Every token in the grammar will actually do both, so there's no clear distinction between the two phases. However, we will usually design (and test) grammars from the simplest element to the most complicated one, which will understand the structure of the whole document.

Here's the grammar for RecipeMark.

```
use Raku::Recipes::Grammarole::Measured-Ingredients;
unit grammar Raku::Recipes::Grammar::RecipeMark does Raku::Recipes::
Grammarole::Measured-Ingredients;

use Raku::Recipes::Grammarole::Measured-Ingredients;
```

```
token TOP {
    "#" \h+ <title>
    <.separation>
    <description>
    <.separation>
    "##" \h+ Ingredients \h+ "(for" \h+ $<persons> = \d+ \h+ person s? ")"
    <.separation>
    <ingredient-list>
    <.separation>
    "##" \h+ Preparation \h+ "(" $<time> = \d+ "m)"
    <.separation>
    <instruction-list>
}

token separation { \v ** 2 }

token title { <words>+ % \h }

token description { [<sentence> | <sentence>+ % \s+] }

token ingredient-list { <itemized-ingredient>+ % \v }

token itemized-ingredient { ["*"|"-"] \h+ <ingredient-description>}

token instruction-list { <numbered-instruction>+  % \v }

token numbered-instruction { <numbering> \h+ <instruction> }

token instruction { <action-verb> \h <sentence>}

token numbering { \d+ )> "." }

token action-verb { <.words>  }

token sentence { <.words>+ % [[","|";"|":"]? \s+] "."}

token words { <[\w \- \']>+ }
```

It's structured so that simplest things are at the bottom, and the more complex things, including the whole document, are at the TOP. Let's simply look at the header, which includes the grammarole that we discussed and get down to the bottom, the most simple thing, the word.

What is and what is not a word seems intuitively clear. However, we have to separate words from punctuation and possibly consider dash-separated words or those that include an apostrophe. That is why word-like characters (which include _ and numbers) are thrown together with these two symbols to create the words we are going to use. That excludes from RecipeMark emojis, for instance. We would all like to include the eggplant emoji as an ingredient, but that will have to wait for RFC 123 (request for comments) describing the next generation of RecipeMark.

Words form sentences, with punctuation in between (semicolons, colons, and commas), and end with a period. This also excludes some punctuation (an em-dash, for instance), but again, this is by choice and will not really hurt the description of the recipe. We're also designing a mini-language and have a certain freedom imposing some restrictions (not using acronyms with dots in the middle, for instance). Besides, we use `<.words>` in sentences (as well as in `<action-verb>`). We're not so much interested in every individual word, but in the fact that they will be used to build more complex structures. So these pieces of the document will be matched and thrown away as soon as they are included in a higher-level structure.

An instruction will be an action-verb and a sentence. Actually, an action-verb is any first word, but we want to encourage people to use action-verbs (such as stir, fry, and boil) as the first word of an instruction. We could even restrict them; we're not doing it now, but we could in the future with a simple change to the rule. And an instruction will include only a sentence; the rationale being that if there're two sentences, well, they are two instructions, so just create another one. All instructions need to be numbered followed by a period. By putting the capture marker `)>` directly behind the digits, we just ditch that part and keep the number itself.

Obviously, an instruction list is a set of instructions separated by vertical whitespace. A repetition indicator (such as +) followed by % and an expression that's atomic, such as % \v means "separated by." With this, we've taken care of the last part, the set of instructions.

The description of every ingredient was created in the grammarole. Here we do, in a similar fashion, the itemization (using * or -, as is usual in Markdown) and create of a list of them. Finally we need to define the title, where words actually matter, and the separation, which is defined mainly to avoid many constants in the main rule. That's replicated here:

```
token TOP {
    "#" \h+ <title>
    <.separation>
    <description>
    <.separation>
    "##" \h+ Ingredients \h+ "(for" \h+ $<persons> = \d+ \h+ person s? ")"
    <.separation>
    <ingredient-list>
    <.separation>
    "##" \h+ Preparation \h+ "(" $<time> = \d+ "m)"
    <.separation>
    <instruction-list>
}
```

This TOP rule dutifully shows the overall structure of a RecipeMark document as we described it. Every section, or title and content of section, is strictly separated by a couple of vertical separators, and we introduce a couple of additional tokens—the number of people the recipe was designed for as well as the time in minutes it needs to cook. Again, this is strict, and the words that describe every section have to be written precisely in that way. Note that, implicitly (and as part of the ingredients), this grammar uses the data store to check what constitutes an ingredient and verify the correct measure of that ingredient.

With this and a simple program such as this one:

```
use Raku::Recipes::Grammar::RecipeMark;
use Grammar::Tracer;

my $rm = Raku::Recipes::Grammar::RecipeMark.new;

for <tuna-risotto tuna-risotto-low-cost> -> $fn {
    my $text = "recipes/main/rice/$fn.md".IO.slurp;
    say $rm.parse( $text );
}
```

Our syntactically correct recipes will be parsed to a data structure such as this one:

```
 title => ⌈Tuna risotto⌋
  words => ⌈Tuna⌋
  words => ⌈risotto⌋
```

```
description => ⌈A relatively simple version of this rich, creamy dish of
  Italian origin.⌋
  sentence => ⌈A relatively simple version of this rich, creamy dish of
  Italian origin.⌋
persons => ⌈4⌋
ingredient-list => ⌈* 320g tuna (canned)
# Ingredients here
  itemized-ingredient => ⌈* 320g tuna (canned)⌋
    ingredient-description => ⌈320g tuna (canned)⌋
      measured-ingredient => ⌈320g tuna⌋
        quantity => ⌈320⌋
        unit => ⌈g⌋
        product => ⌈tuna⌋
      options => ⌈(canned)⌋
        content => ⌈canned⌋
# Lots more ingredients
time => ⌈60⌋
instruction-list => ⌈1. Slightly-fry tuna with its own oil it until it
browns a bit, you can do this while you start doing the rest, save a bit
of oil for the rice. # and the rest
7. Rest for 5 minutes before serving.⌋
  numbered-instruction => ⌈1. Slightly-fry tuna with its own oil it until
    it browns a bit, you can do this while you start doing the rest, save a
    bit of oil for the rice.⌋
    numbering => ⌈1⌋
    instruction => ⌈Slightly-fry tuna with its own oil it until it browns a
      bit, you can do this while you start doing the rest, save a bit of oil
      for the rice.⌋
      action-verb => ⌈Slightly-fry⌋
      sentence => ⌈tuna with its own oil it until it browns a bit, you can do
        this while you start doing the rest, save a bit of oil for the rice.⌋
# Rest of instructions
```

If there's a syntax error, it will simply return Nil.

Checking syntax (and extracting parts of the document) will take you part of the way. But you need to actually process the mini-program. We will do that in the next recipe.

Recipe 16-2. Create and Process Mini-Programs Written in a Mini-Language for Recipes

Problem

Once you've created a way of ascertaining whether the text corresponds to the language standard, you need to act on it. For instance, generate a data structure with essential data that can be otherwise processed.

Solution

Use grammar actions, possibly structured with roles, to gather data and serve it in a Raku type or general data structure.

How It Works

Parsing with a grammar returns a `Match` object, which includes every token that has been matched nested in it. The Match object will contain what is matched by the TOP token. Effectively, this is a parse tree. But this parse tree, even if it contains all the information we need, might not contain it in the way we need it. Some information might be hidden two or three tokens deep, and from someone perusing the result, it might not be obvious where everything is. Besides, parse trees contain `Match` objects. We might need a piece of it in another format, from numbers to complex classes.

Raku provides a mechanism for fixing this: Grammar actions embed themselves in a grammar, checking every step in the parse tree and generating data in the format we need. Again, we used them in Chapter 11. What we will do here is use them to generate a complex RecipeMark data structure that will be easier to use.

If we look at the recipe itself, it has several parts. Three of them could be metadata: title, number of people, and preparation time. The rest is information or content: description and the list of ingredients and instructions. For starters, we can simply structure the recipe in a hash with six keys, three for metadata, and three for content, with obvious names. We can use different data structures for the ingredient and instruction list. The ingredient list can be a hash: every ingredient will be a different product, so we can use product as keys. The instruction list is an array, but we need to take into account numbers. In some cases, numbers might be repeated, so we might want to use an array of pairs. Every pair will also feature a pair as value, which will use as a key the "action verb." The ingredients will also use as a value a hash that will have "options," "unit," and "quantity" as its keys.

This data structure will be the "processed" recipe with which we can work. We will use this action to process it.

```
unit class Raku::Recipes::Grammar::RecipeMark::Actions;

method TOP($/) { make {
    title => ~$/<title>,
    description => ~$/<description>,
    persons => +$/<persons>,
    ingredient-list => $/<ingredient-list>.made,
    preparation-minutes => + $/<time>,
    instruction-list => $/<instruction-list>.made
} }

method ingredient-list( $/ ) {
    make gather for $/.hash<itemized-ingredient> ->
    $ingredient {
        take $ingredient.made
    }
}

method itemized-ingredient($/) { make $/<ingredient-description>.made }

method ingredient-description($/) {
    my %ingredient = $/<measured-ingredient>.made;
    %ingredient{%ingredient.keys[0]}{'options'} = $/<options> if
    $/<options>;
    make %ingredient;
}

method measured-ingredient($/) {
    make $/<product>.made => { unit => $/<unit>.made // "Unit",
                                quantity => $/<quantity>.made }
}

method product($/) { make tc ~$/; }
```

```
method quantity($/) { make +val( ~$/  ) // unival( ~$/ ) }
method options($/){ make ~$/; }
method unit($/){ make ~$/; }

method instruction-list( $/ ) {
    my @instructions = gather for $/.hash<numbered-instruction> ->
$instruction {
        take $instruction.made
    }
    make @instructions;
}
method numbered-instruction($/) {
    make $/<numbering>.made => $/<instruction>.made;
}
method numbering($/) { make +$/; }
method instruction($/) { make $/<action-verb>.made => $/<sentence>.made}
method action-verb($/) { make ~$/; }
method sentence($/) { make ~$/; }
```

Let's look at it from the bottom up. First a reminder of how this works: $/ is a Match object. Every method will receive a Match object produced by the token with the same name. By using make, we attach a data structure to the corresponding abstract syntax tree, so the data structure that's generated piggybacks on the match. We can access using the .made method, so make $/<action-verb>.made will retrieve the data structure we generated using the action-verb method (right below) from the action-verb token (in the RecipeMark grammar). We will then attach it to the object $/.

Most simple or low-level tokens (the "leaves" of the parse tree, so to say) simply convert the match to a string (by using the string contextualizer) or to a number (via the numeric contextualizer +). In some cases, we need additional processing. Quantity, for instance, needs a different conversion process depending on if it's a Unicode number or not. In several cases—numbered-instruction, instruction, measured-ingredient—we create pairs, as we have indicated before.

Processing lists of tokens is a bit more complex. Match is an object that by default returns a simple list of things; an alternative way to access a list of tokens is using the .hash method, keyed by the name of the token we want to access. We do a similar thing

357

in `ingredient-list` and C: we run over the list of extracted tokens, simply adding the corresponding data structure to the array that we are going to return.

The method corresponding to the TOP rule is the one in charge of generating the data structure that's going to be returned. Besides, there are tokens that are extracted only there, the ones corresponding to metadata. We create the title, description, people, and preparation-minutes directly from the token match, and the ingredient and instruction list will be obtained from the token they're attached using `.made`. This creates the data structure we can finally work with, which contains the processed recipe.

We can use it in the following script:

```
#!/usr/bin/env perl6

use Raku::Recipes::Grammar::RecipeMark;
use Raku::Recipes::Grammar::RecipeMark::Actions;

my $rm = Raku::Recipes::Grammar::RecipeMark.new;
my $action = Raku::Recipes::Grammar::RecipeMark::Actions.new;
for <main/rice/tuna-risotto
    main/rice/tuna-risotto-low-cost
    appetizers/carrot-wraps>
-> $fn {
    my $text = "recipes/$fn.md".IO.slurp;
    say $rm.parse( $text, actions => $action ).made;
}
```

Again, we slurp the file and parse it, indicating the action that we will use. We instantiate it only once and pass it to every parsing statement. The result of parsing will still be a `Match`; but calling `.made` on that `Match` object will return the data structure that is a result of processing. For instance, it will look like this for the carrot wraps:

```
{description => A healthy way to start a meal, or to munch between them.,
ingredient-list => ({Carrots => {quantity => 250, unit => g}} {Cottage
cheese => {options => [(or cheese spread)]
 content => [or cheese spread], quantity => 200, unit => g}} {Wheat
 tortillas => {quantity => 4, unit => Unit}}), instruction-list => [1 =>
 Cut => the carrots in long sticks or slices. 2 => Spread => cheese over
 tortillas, cut them in half. 3 => Put => carrot sticks on tortillas, wrap
```

them around. 4 => Add => fresh parsley, mint or coriander to taste.],
persons => 4, preparation-minutes => 20, title => Carrot wraps}

You see here the different keys: `description`, `title`, `preparation-minutes`... In general, this presents a format with an already useful, and easily-processable, version of our recipe written in RecipeMark.

We can dump this to JSON to serialize it and make it available to any language. We can work with that data, or metadata, to generate reports, which we will do in the next recipe.

Recipe 16-3. Process Recipes and Generate Reports

Problem

You need to process a group of recipes, written using a recipe mini-language, to extract the most common ingredients, or to sum the calories in a group of recipes, or simply to look at text and decide if it's a correct RecipeMark document or not. If possible, all these functionalities should be in a single command-line tool.

You also need to generate a report when there's an error in the document; a helpful error message will help the users determine what's wrong and correct it.

Solution

Grammars give you an abstract syntax tree on which you can work to extract the solutions; once you have that, you can zero in on the part that interests you. Or you can use grammar actions, which are the equivalent of program compilation, to create mini-compiles that compile to, in this case, a single count of calories or of ingredients. At any rate, you need to go beyond returning `Nil` when the document does not fit the grammar. We should collect feedback about what users don't understand, at the least, following Chapter 8's spirit of being helpful and meaningful with errors. Besides that, we will need to catch some higher-level errors, such as repetition of an ingredient.

To solve these problems, we will create a command-line tool whose different options will give you access to the different things you want to do: from a simple check, to the generation of new documents or operations with the data extracted from the document.

How It Works

A mini-language will generally include a command-line program that carries out different operations, such as checking syntax, converting to other formats, or carrying out another type of processing. The script will perform its task if the syntax is okay, but it will simply not do if it fails with no error message. It must make the best attempt to determine the mistake, giving a hint of what was improperly understood.

Grammars, in principle, are not equipped with this kind of functionality from the get go. But, at the end of the day, grammars are Raku programs, so we can treat detectable syntax errors as exceptions, which the command-line utility can capture or simply bubble up to the user.

This calls for a whole new class hierarchy to be built around the language, so one of the first things we are going to do with refactoring is create a whole new namespace, called RecipeMark, where we insert all classes exclusively dealing with this new language. The first thing we are going to do is move the existing modules into a new namespace called RecipeMark. Since our first job is to report errors to our clients, we will rework the grammar (which will be now called `RecipeMark::Grammar`) so that it takes care of errors. We need to mix `Grammar::PrettyErrors` in. Here's the result:

```
use Raku::Recipes::Grammarole::Measured-Ingredients;
use Grammar::PrettyErrors;

unit grammar RecipeMark::Grammar
        does Raku::Recipes::Grammarole::Measured-Ingredients
        does Grammar::PrettyErrors;

token TOP {
    "#" \h+ <title>
    <.separation>
    <description>
    <.separation>
    "##" \h+ Ingredients \h+ "(for" \h+ $<persons> = \d+ \h+ person s? ")"
    <.separation>
    <ingredient-list>
    <.separation>
    "##" \h+ Preparation \h+ "(" $<time> = \d+ "m)"
```

```
    <.separation>
    <instruction-list>
}

token separation { <ws> ** 2 }
# No change in the rest , except...
token ws { <!ww> \v }
```

As you can see, the main change is rewriting the ws token, which stands for whitespace, so that it works with vertical spaces, and changing the separation token so that it includes two such tokens. Grammar::PrettyErrors works by wrapping around this token. It tries to find out the last spot where everything worked and shows that in an error. It's not perfect, but at least we know where to start looking. Trying to insert an nonexistent ingredient (like piranha instead of tuna) will result in an error like the one shown in Figure 16-1.

```
--errors--
   4
   5    ## Ingredients (for 4 persons)
   6  ▶
          ^
   7    * 320g piranha (canned)
   8    * 250g rice
   9    * ½ onion
  10    * 250g cheese (whatever is in your fridge)

Uh oh, something went wrong around line 6.
Unable to parse separation.

 in block <unit> at /home/jmerelo/progs/perl6/raku-recipes-apress/t/recipemark-00-grammar.t
```

Figure 16-1. *RecipeMark error produced thanks to Grammar::PrettyError*

The error is shown in the previous separation, and it includes the line number and, even better, a type of error that can be captured and processed in another way.

Other kinds of errors could be difficult to catch in the parsing phase; for instance, the existence of two ingredients with the same product.

The new, error detecting, grammar, is going to be called RecipeMark::Grammar, and here it is:

```
use Raku::Recipes::Grammarole::Measured-Ingredients;
use Grammar::PrettyErrors;
use X::RecipeMark;

unit grammar RecipeMark::Grammar
        does Raku::Recipes::Grammarole::Measured-Ingredients
        does Grammar::PrettyErrors;

# token TOP, separation, title, description do not change.

token ingredient-list {
    :my $*INGREDIENTS  = ∅;
    <itemized-ingredient>+ % \v }

token itemized-ingredient {
    ["*"|"-"] \h+ <ingredient-description>
    {
        my $product = tc ~$/<ingredient-description><measured-ingredient>
        <product>;
        if $product ∉ $*INGREDIENTS {
            $*INGREDIENTS ∪= $product;
        } else {
            X::RecipeMark::RepeatedIngredient.new( :match($/),
                    :name($product) ).throw;
        }
    }
}

token instruction-list {
    :my UInt $*LAST = 0;
    <numbered-instruction>+  % \v
}
#Instruction, numbered-instruction do not change

token numbering {
    \d+ )> "." {
```

```
        if +$/ < $*LAST {
            X::RecipeMark::OutOfOrder.new( :match($/),
            :number(+$/),
            :last($*LAST) ).throw;
        } else {
            $*LAST = +$/;
        }
    }
}
# The rest is the same as above
```

We made changes so that the grammar can generate two different exceptions, one for every type of error we can detect. These exceptions are defined in this way:

```
use Grammar::Message;

unit module X::RecipeMark;

role Base is Exception {
    has Match $.match;
    submethod BUILD( :$!match ) {}
}

class OutOfOrder does Base {
    has $.number;
    has $.last;

    submethod BUILD( :$!match, :$!number, :$!last ) {}

    multi method message () {
        pretty-message(
                "Found instruction number $!number while waiting for number
                > $!last",
                $!match  );
    }
}

class RepeatedIngredient does Base {
    has $.name;
```

```
    submethod BUILD( :$!match, :$!name ) {}

    multi method message () {
        pretty-message("Ingredient $!name appears twice",
        $!match );
    }
}
```

We define a Base class, mainly for convenience, because the two other classes will need a Match attribute to work. X::RecipeMark::OutOfOrder needs the number that has been inserted, and X::RecipeMark::RepeatedIngredient needs the name of the ingredient that has been repeated. In both cases, a *pretty* message is created with the match and the message. This routine comes from the published module Grammar::Message, which uses the match provided to create a listing with the document that's been matched and a pointer to where last we knew everything was going okay. This is not going to be precisely where the error happened, but it will be the last position where we knew processing was going well.

The effect is similar to what Grammar::PrettyErrors did (in fact, the code is reused from that module; free software is wonderful, don't you think so?). But the good thing about this routine is that we can simply use it to generate the exception messages if we want to transmit them to the final user.

What we need, however, is to provide that Match object when we throw the exception. The modifications made over the original grammar have gone in that direction, precisely. Regexen, tokens, and rules allow execution of code by simply putting curly braces around them. That is one of the keys of refactoring grammar.

Another key are dynamic variables, those with the twigil * between the sigil and the identifier. We have been using them since the recipes in Chapter 1, where we used $*DISTRO to determine whether we were working in Windows or not. However, all the variables we have used so far have been intrinsic variables created by the Rakudo interpreter or used in one of the modules, like Red. This is, besides, the only occasion where we actually defined such a variable, used throughout the Red ORM. This shows that they are used extensively through Raku programs, usually where one would use a global variable. Unlike global variables, however, they can't be seen (and altered) throughout the whole program. They are visible only in the scope in which they are defined and whatever is called from that scope. If we define them in a routine, they can be seen and altered in all routines called from there.

Tokens are, in fact, routines (they are actually methods, not stand-alone subs), and they "call" the tokens that are mentioned in them. So if we define a dynamic variable in a token, all the tokens mentioned there will also *see* the dynamic variables defined there.

Tokens are actually regular expressions, so we need a special syntax to define their variables (including dynamic variables). The adverb :my will be used for that. When we write the following:

```
token ingredient-list {
    :my $*INGREDIENTS = ∅;
    <itemized-ingredient>+ % \v }
```

We are defining a dynamic variable, called $*INGREDIENTS, that will be seen throughout the itemized-ingredient token and in any other token called from there. We are assigning it an empty set; this variable will contain the set of ingredients that have been used so far. If itemized-ingredient was a routine, we would have used a state variable to store that state. However, lexically scoped variables are the only kinds of variables we can declare in a token/regex/rule, so we use that facility to create a dynamic variable in the token that invokes itemized-ingredients.

This variable will hold a set, with all the ingredients mentioned. The code inserted in itemized-ingredient is as follows:

```
{
        my $product = tc ~$/<ingredient-description><measured-ingredient>
        <product>;
        if $product ∉ $*INGREDIENTS {
            $*INGREDIENTS ∪= $product;
        } else {
            X::RecipeMark::RepeatedIngredient.new( :match($/),
                    :name($product) ).throw;
        }
    }
```

It canonicalizes the name of the product (by using title case – tc), inserts it into the set if it's not there already, and raises an exception if it is, using the state of the match so far, stored in $/, and the name of the product. That exception will be helpful to the user, because it will produce an exception that says something like "Ingredient Tuna appears twice," and then will point to the line where that happens.

In the case of the instructions, we use the dynamic variable to hold the last instruction number that was used.

```
{
    if +$/ < $*LAST {
        X::RecipeMark::OutOfOrder.new( :match($/),
        :number(+$/),
        :last($*LAST) ).throw;
    } else {
        $*LAST = +$/;
    }
}
```

Contextualizing to number converts the Match to a number. We compare it to the last stored and raise an exception if the number is going down (repeated numbers are allowed).

The resulting grammar will declare as correct the same documents it did before. However, it will try to show some kind of error if they are not correct (once they are called using RecipeMark::Grammar.parse). For instance, the error produced when a product has been repeated is shown in Figure 16-2.

```
→ raku-recipes-apress git:(master) Chapter-16/recipemark check bad-recipes/tuna-risotto-repeated-product.md
Ingredient Tuna appears twice
 6 |
 7 |  * 250g tuna
 8 |▶ * 250g tuna (carnaroli or arborio)
                 ^
 9 |  * ½ onion
10 |  * 125g cheese (parmegiano reggiano, granapadano or manchego)
11 |  * 1 tbsp olive oil (extra virgin)
12 |  * 4 cloves garlic

  in regex itemized-ingredient at /home/jmerelo/progs/perl6/raku-recipes-apress/lib/RecipeMark/Grammar.pm6 (RecipeMark::Grammar) line 41
  in regex ingredient-list at /home/jmerelo/progs/perl6/raku-recipes-apress/lib/RecipeMark/Grammar.pm6 (RecipeMark::Grammar) line 29
```

Figure 16-2. *Error produced with a repeated ingredient, tuna in this case (which has been written instead of rice)*

The "tail" of that error gives a bit too much information about where it's been produced. It can be useful (for instance, it might reveal the source line where it happens), but we might choose to suppress it later.

There is some overhead associated with this additional processing: code that's called every time tokens are invoked, which results in a certain delay for the final user. However, it's a small price to pay for this kind of application, as long as we make the users happier about the RecipeMark language and their interaction with it.

Processing the RecipeMark Document

Once we know everything is correct, we must generate an internal representation of the document. We have already defined a set of actions, which we can mostly reuse by just renaming it `RecipeMark::Actions`. Additionally, we'll need to change this instruction in the `ingredient-description` method:

```
%ingredient{%ingredient.keys[0]}{'options'} = ~$/<options><content> if
$/<options>;
```

Previously, it just said `$<options>`, without the contextualizer `~`. That was okay to generate an object, but `$/<options>` is a `Match` object that will make this not a pure hash, but an hash with a whole `Match` object in it. Let's just stringify it (and eliminate the parentheses while we're at it) so that the action generates serializable, pure hash objects without other objects embedded in them. Parsing with this action will generate a data structure, but we need to reuse that data structure to generate a RecipeMark object on which we can build all the processing options we need. Here's the definition of the class:

```
use RecipeMark::Grammar;
use RecipeMark::Grammar::Actions;

use JSON::Fast;

unit class RecipeMark;
has Str $.title;
has Str $.description;
has UInt $.persons;
has UInt $.preparation-minutes;
has %.ingredient-list;
has @.instruction-list;
```

```
method new( $file where .IO.e) {
    my %temp = RecipeMark::Grammar.parse(
            $file.IO.slurp,
            actions => RecipeMark::Grammar::Actions.new
            ).made;
    self.bless(| %temp );
}

method to-json() {
    return to-json self.Hash ;
}

method Hash() {
    return { title => $!title,
            description => $!description,
            persons => $!persons,
            preparation-minutes => $!preparation-minutes,
            ingredient-list => %!ingredient-list,
            instruction-list => @!instruction-list
    }
}

method product-list() {
    return %!ingredient-list.keys;
}
```

Every object of this class will have the six attributes that made up the keys of the returned hash, which is why the new method parses the content of the file and just blesses the resulting hash self.bless(| %temp). This flattens the hash, converting it to a set of named arguments that are passed directly to the BUILD submethod (implicit) of this object. We can get the object back via the .Hash method or convert it to JSON using to-json. The list of products is simply the list of keys in the %!ingredient-list hash, but the client needn't be concerned about the implementation. Let's just add a product-list method that returns it.

This makes creating the processing code quite easy. This would be the first version of the RecipeMark command line, which, for the time being, checks and produces a shopping list:

```
use lib <lib ../lib>;

use RecipeMark;

multi sub MAIN( "check", $file where .IO.e ) {
    say RecipeMark.new( $file ).to-json;
}

multi sub MAIN( "shopping-list", $file where .IO.e ) {
    say "# Shopping list\n\n",
            RecipeMark.new( $file )
            .product-list
            .sort
            .map( {"* [ ] $_."})
            .join: "\n";
}
```

Since we are using the MAIN sub to handle the different options, this has the additional advantage of free usage messages if it's used with no option or with the –help flag. In both cases, it will print the following:

```
Usage:
  recipemark check <file>
  recipemark shopping-list <file>
```

The check command-line option will print the generated structure in JSON, and it will also produce the syntax errors indicated here, since we are not capturing the output. The shopping-list option will produce the same errors if there are any. If it's able to create the object, it will extract the product-list via the method, sort alphabetically, map it to a line of Markdown code for a to-do list, and finally join all items to print the shopping list:

```
% Chapter-16/recipemark shopping-list recipes/main/rice/tuna-risotto-low-
cost.md
# Shopping list

* [ ] Butter.
* [ ] Cheese.
* [ ] Garlic.
```

```
* [ ] Olive oil.
* [ ] Onion.
* [ ] Rice.
* [ ] Tuna.
* [ ] Wine.
```

You can export this to a TODO-list application and carry it to your supermarket, grocery store, or friendly neighborhood bodega.

The RecipeMark object will be the foundation for additional processing we need to do, for instance, to compute calories (which would hook with the objects and/or routines doing this kind of task in the Raku::Recipes class hierarchy). Once we have all the information in a single object, we can either expose functionality via an API or, if we think it's worth the while, we can add new methods to it. We can also store this data structure in a data store, as shown in Chapter 12. For instance, we could easily add a method to check if a recipe is vegan or not and expose it via the command-line API. This would be the method added to RecipeMark:

```
method vegan() {
    my $data = Raku::Recipes::CSVDator.new;
    return so all self.product-list.map:
            { $data.get-ingredient($_)<Vegan> };
}
```

It's actually quite simple. We use the data store to retrieve all we know about the ingredients (remember, recipes use as *keywords* the name of the products we have in the database). We check one by one if they are vegan or not, and we return true only if all of the ingredients are vegan. The multi that exposes that API will look like this:

```
multi sub MAIN( "vegan", $file where .IO.e ) {
    my $recipemark = RecipeMark.new( $file );
    say $recipemark.title,
            $recipemark.vegan ??
            color("green") ~ " is vegan " ~ color("reset")!!
            " is " ~ color("red") ~ "not" ~ color("reset") ~ " vegan ";
}
```

This is relatively straightforward. The result on two different recipes is shown in Figure 16-3.

```
  raku-recipes-apress git:(      ) Chapter-16/recipemark vegan recipes/desserts/guacustard.md
Guacustard is vegan
→ raku-recipes-apress git:(      ) Chapter-16/recipemark vegan recipes/main/rice/tuna-risotto.md
Tuna risotto is    vegan
```

Figure 16-3. *Checking whether two different recipes are vegan via RecipeMark CLI*

In the next recipe, we will see different ways of processing this into another Markdown document, or even into HTML.

These three recipes, however, show how Raku and its different facilities—from grammars to dynamic-scope variables through roles and powerful regular expression engines and exception processing facilities—can be harnessed to create a well structured DSL language-processing application that is extensible and easily usable through its API. Not only do we have a language processing program, we also have an embeddable interpreter that can be part of a bigger application; this can be done with many different kinds of languages.

Note   Grammars (and their capabilities for defining and processing languages), like regular expressions, are extremely powerful things that you will find infinite applications for, once you get past the first, admittedly steep, learning curve. You have learned about several use cases in this book, and you will probably think of less obvious (and more useful) use cases after you learn how to use grammars in these recipes.

Recipe 16-4. Convert a Grammar Into a Full Recipe-Processing Application That Generates HTML or Another External Format

Problem

The recipes need to be converted to another format using custom highlights for every keyword. For instance, we want to create web pages beyond simple Markdown processing, or even generate a new Markdown document that includes specific markup for keywords.

Solution

Process the recipe as done in the previous recipe and use that generated data structure as an intermediate format or data to use in a template.

How It Works

Actually, the bulk of the decision is what to put in the template and what template engine to use to process the recipe. The data is already extracted to a manageable data structure, so we just need to process it piecewise, giving every part of the document a sensible markup so that if it's converted to another format, it will highlight its role in the document.

Let's take stock of what we have, anyway. A RecipeMark includes a title, description, number of people, and time of preparation. It also includes an ingredient hash and an instructions array. Ideally, the templates should be able to work with them; of course, more ideally it could directly take the RecipeMark object.

We already had a nice experience with `Template::Classic`. Let's work with that now. First, let's create the template:

```
# <%= $recipemark.title %>

<%= $recipemark.description %>

## Ingredients (for <%= $recipemark.persons %> persons)

<%
use URI::Encode;
my %ingredients = $recipemark.ingredient-list;
for %ingredients.kv -> $product, %data {
    take "* %data<quantity> %data<unit> "
        ~ "[ {lc $product} ](/Ingredient/" ~ uri_encode($product) ~ ")"
                ~ (" %data<options>" if %data<options> ) ~ "\n";
} %>

## Preparation (<%= $recipemark.preparation-minutes %>m)
<%
for $recipemark.instruction-list[0][] -> $instruction {
```

```
        take $instruction.key ~ ". " ~ "*" ~ $instruction.value.key ~ "* "
            ~ $instruction.value.value ~ "\n";
}
%>
```

A small reminder of how `Template::Classic` works: it embeds marks within the template, which will be substituted for its value. In this case, it needs a single variable:, which is `$recipemark`, an instance of the RecipeMark class. The title, description, people, and preparation time are extracted directly using the object's public attributes, which is why they are in a `<%= %>` mark that directly inserts the value of what's inside.

We will need a couple of loops to get to the ingredients. We need a loop over the key-values of the ingredients, where we will lay out the ingredient data and insert a Markdown link to the (supposed) website where we describe every ingredient. Here we need to include the `URI::Encode` module to be able to use `uri_encode`. The templates return fragments as sequence elements, we use `take` to "return" them to the rendered template.

We need to use rather strange syntax to get to the list of instructions:

```
$recipemark.instruction-list[0][]
```

The list of instructions is stored as a single element of an array with a single element, mainly due to how it's extracted with the grammar actions. We simply decontainerize this first element by using `[ ]`, which gives us back an array over which we perform the loop. In this loop, we will highlight the first *action-verb*.

We are going to add yet another `MAIN multi` to the RecipeMark CLI to process this subcommand, which we will call simply `md`:

```
multi sub MAIN("md", $file where .IO.e ) {
    my $template-name="templates/recipemark.md";
    my $template-file = "resources/$template-name".IO.e
            ??"resources/$template-name".IO.slurp
            !!%?RESOURCES{$template-name}.slurp;
    my &generate-page := template :($recipemark), $template-file;
    my $recipemark = RecipeMark.new( $file );
    say generate-page( $recipemark).eager.join

}
```

As we did in the previous chapters, we load the template file, create a template routine out of it, and use it later to print the result to standard output.

The result of using it over the document that describes carrot wraps is as follows:

```
→  raku-recipes-apress git:(master) X Chapter-16/recipemark md recipes/
appetizers/carrot-wraps.md
# Carrot wraps

A healthy way to start a meal, or to munch between them.

## Ingredients (for 4 persons)

* 250 g [ carrots ](/Ingredient/Carrots)
* 200 g [ cottage cheese ](/Ingredient/Cottage%20cheese) (or cheese spread)
* 4 Unit [ wheat tortillas ](/Ingredient/Wheat%20tortillas)

## Preparation (4m)

1. *Cut* the carrots in long sticks or slices.
2. *Spread* cheese over tortillas, cut them in half.
3. *Put* carrot sticks on tortillas, wrap them around.
4. *Add* fresh parsley, mint or coriander to taste.
```

This is pretty close to the original, but shows how the document was understood and parsed. Markdown can be converted directly to HTML, but we might want to reuse the template we used before or add formatting or rendering instructions.

An HTML template would be a straightforward translation of this one:

```
<!DOCTYPE html>
<html lang="en">
<head>
    <meta charset="UTF-8">
    <title>Recipe: <%= $recipemark.title %></title>
<link rel='stylesheet' id='style-css'  href='raku-recipes.css' type='text/css'
    media='all' />
</head>
<body>
<!-- This is a Template::Classic template -->

<h1><% $recipemark.title %></h1>

<p><% $recipemark.description %></p>
```

```
<h2>Ingredients (for <%= $recipemark.persons %> persons)</h2>

<ul>
<%
use URI::Encode;
my %ingredients = $recipemark.ingredient-list;
for %ingredients.kv -> $product, %data {
take "<li> %data<quantity> %data<unit> "
    ~ "<a href='/Ingredient/" ~ uri_encode($product) ~ "'>"
    ~ lc $product ~ "</a>"
    ~ (" %data<options>" if %data<options> ) ~ "</li>\n";
} %>
</ul>

<h2> Preparation (<%= $recipemark.preparation-minutes %>m) </h2>

<ul><%    for $recipemark.instruction-list[0][] -> $instruction {
    take "<li>" ~ $instruction.key ~ ". " ~ "<strong>" ~
    $instruction.value.key ~
    "</strong> "
    ~ $instruction.value.value ~ "</li>\n";
    }
%>
</ul>

</body>
</html>
```

We have used HTML markup, trying to come up with the right choices. We use <ul> instead of <ol> in the instruction list since the item number might be repeated. The rest inserts metadata in the right places, with title placed as page title and header, and the rest is more or less in the same place. The MAIN that implements this is mutatis mutandis, pretty much the same as the one for Markdown.

Could we go a step further and try to generate recipes in the MealMaster format? The format is specified on this page: http://ffts.com/mmformat.txt. Let's try to condense that into a template. We can always use the MealMaster Perl module to check if it's been correctly defined. Here's the template we will be using:

375

```
---------- Recipe via Meal-Master (tm) v8.05

     Title: <%= $recipemark.title %>
Categories: <%= $categories %>
     Yield: <%= $recipemark.persons %> servings

<%    my %units =  tbsp => "ts",
                   Unit => "ea",
                   spoons => "sp",
                   cloves => "ea",
                   cup => "cu",
                   liter => "l" ;
    my %ingredients = $recipemark.ingredient-list;
    for %ingredients.kv -> $product, %data {
        my $quantity = %data<quantity> ~~ Rat
                       ?? %data<quantity>.Num
                       !! %data<quantity>;
        my $unit = %data<unit>.chars > 2
                   ?? %units{%data<unit>}
                   !! %data<unit>;
        take $quantity.fmt("%7s") ~ " " ~ $unit.fmt("%2s") ~ " "
        ~ lc $product ~ "\n"
    }
    %>

<%for $recipemark.instruction-list[0][] -> $instruction {
        take "   " ~ $instruction.key ~ ". " ~ "*" ~ $instruction.value.key
        ~ "*"
              ~ " " ~ $instruction.value.value ~ "\n";
  }
  %>
-----
```

The rigid, fixed format of the recipe must be accommodated. It was very usual,
due mainly to the use of COBOL and its simple line-oriented processing format, to use
positions on the line to denote different types of data, as well as specific delimiters. In

this case, the delimiters are at both ends of the file. We use metadata to fill the fixed fields. We will need a new container, called $categories, to create those, since it's not part of the RecipeMark attributes.

But the main transformations are suffered by the ingredients. The quantity of the ingredient needs to be in decimal format in the first seven characters, which is why we convert fractions to a number. Then they are padded to be printed in the first seven characters of the line. The "admitted" measures need to fit in two characters, and there's also a limited amount of them (in the same way we do it in RecipeMark). We accommodate these as well as we can. For instance, there's no equivalent of cloves, so we put "ea" (as in each). The rest of the line will be the ingredient, and we skip the options. This also needs to be contained in 40 columns, so we just skip the options to avoid overstuffing that line. By using fmt("%xs"), we expand (or, as might be the case, contract) the strings to the specified format, so that quantity ends precisely at column 7 and the units end at column 9.

We need to process the filename for this template a bit more. Here's the corresponding MAIN:

```
multi sub MAIN("mmf", $file where .IO.e ) {
    my $template-file= template-file "templates/recipemark.mmf";
    my &generate-page := template :($categories, $recipemark),
    $template-file;
    my $categories = $file.split("/")[1..*-2].join(", ");
    my $recipemark = RecipeMark.new( $file );
    say generate-page( $categories, $recipemark).eager.join

}
```

The main thing is that, as indicated here, we need something to fill the categories. That kind of metadata is included in the filename: the directories where it's included are also metadata. It indicates if it's done with rice, if it's a main dish or appetizer, and so on. The template declaration is slightly changed to include this variable, which is obtained out of splitting the filename and eliminating the first element ("recipes") and the last (the name of the file). The generated file is as follows:

```
---------- Recipe via Meal-Master (tm) v8.05

      Title: Tuna risotto
 Categories: main, rice
      Yield: 4 servings
```

```
  125  g cheese
  0.5 ea onion
    ...
1. *Chop* tuna to small chunks, and stir-fry it until it browns a bit;
   you can do this while you start doing the rest.
1. *Stir-fry* garlic until golden-colored, chopped if you so like, retire
   if you don't like the color.
...


-----
```

According to the MealMaster module, this format is correct; and it's correct since the data needed for a recipe is semantically exposed by the RecipeMark API.

The RecipeMark CLI has eventually evolved to a command with six subcommands, which are able to do transformations and checks and even generate reports. This flexibility stems from Raku grammars and the layers of business logic we created about them, including a class that encapsulates the results of the parsing, the abstract syntax tree, the semantics, and a convenient API. This power can be leveraged in many different ways, but the expressivity of Raku makes it quite easy to work with.

This grammar was written almost from scratch, but many grammars are going to include common language patterns. You don't need to reinvent them every time. We'll see how to reuse them in the next recipe.

Recipe 16-5. Reuse Common Language Patterns
Problem

Many features are shared by many (mini) languages: from expressions to common patterns like email addresses and URLs. It potentially takes a lot of time to rewrite tokens for these common expressions.

Solution

Use Grammar::Common, initiated by the late Jeff Goff and lately maintained as part of the Raku community modules, which has a host of common patterns that you can reuse in your mini-language.

How It Works

One of the insights in the design of the Raku language was the inclusion of grammars as a first-class type. In the same style that modules and classes beget an ecosystem of code, grammars beget an ecosystem of, well, grammars as code. A ecosystem will give you the possibility to stand on the shoulder of giants, applying the DRY principle—"don't repeat yourself." And now we can do the same with grammars.

We certainly stand on the shoulder of a giant with this module by Jeff Goff. He saw the possibilities of grammars to create a foundation of common patterns, patterns that can be easily reused in our programs such as common mathematical expressions using different formats. He also realized that the best way to create that foundation was via grammaroles, so his `Grammar::Common` is a collection of roles for common programming expressions... but also text.

We will need to parse text over and over as long as we get into (semi) natural language processing. A sentence is a sentence, and a word is a word. The first word in a sentence must be capitalized, and there are only so many ways to stop a sentence: question mark, exclamation mark, or a period. This grammar, included in `Grammar::Common`, will help with that:

```
unit role Grammar::Common::Text;

token sentence { <first-word> <.separators> <sub-sentence> <.stop>}

token stop { "." | "?" | "!" }

token sub-sentence { <words>* % <.separators> }
token separators { [","|";"|":" ]? \s+ }

token first-word { <:Lu> <[\w \- \' \.]>* }

token words { <[\w \- \']>+ }
```

We use the Unicode character class `<:Lu>`, which stands for "uppercase letter." A sentence will be a capitalized first word, plus a separator, plus a sub-sentence (sentence without period or first word), plus a character to finish the sentence. Although this approximation is not going to catch all possible words and sentences (quoting and parenthesizing, for instance, will not work), it's a good start that can be overridden in a grammar. But the important thing is that it provides a group of building blocks that can be reused straight away.

We can refactor our RecipeMark grammar using this. Here's the result (with parts that don't change elided):

```
use Raku::Recipes::Grammarole::Measured-Ingredients;
use Grammar::PrettyErrors;
use Grammar::Common::Text;
use X::RecipeMark;

unit grammar RecipeMark::Grammar
        does Raku::Recipes::Grammarole::Measured-Ingredients
        does Grammar::PrettyErrors
        does Grammar::Common::Text;

# No change

token instruction { <action-verb> \h <sub-sentence> <.stop>}

# No change, except for elimination of <words> and <sentence>
```

There's a single change: we use `<sub-sentence>` from `Grammar::Common::Text` in this token and eliminate `<sentence>` as well as `<words>`, which are now in that common grammar. The good thing is that we don't need to change any actions, since they have the same name and thus produce the same tokens. When using any other grammar, we would need to to that.

In the same way it's advisable to check the ecosystem for modules that implement part of the functionality you need, it's advisable to do this for grammars. It can always save you some work.

CHAPTER 17

Fun One-Liners

Raku is a expressive language with functional features. This makes it relatively easy to capture user and system input in one end of the pipeline, and spew processed data or any kind of action out the other end. Contests such as the Perl and Raku Challenge also emphasize short programs, which has given rise to a whole lot of simple scripts that are powerful, albeit sometimes illegible in other languages. However, Raku strives for expressivity, so it's much easier to understand them and create them with Raku.

These one-liners also employ very creative programming patterns. We use them as an ingredient in all the recipes in this chapter.

Recipe 17-1. Write a Guessing Game in a Single Code Line

Problem

As a challenge, you need to write a game that provides players with a certain amount of turns to guess a number and gives them hints every turn.

Solution

Raku uses ; as a statement separator, so you can put as many statements as you want on a single line. Additionally, you can use some techniques to shorten the program and get as few characters as possible: use single-character variables (or no sigil variables), define them when you first use them (or use the implicit variable, no definition needed), use operators instead of control structures (??!! instead of if), and, in general, sacrifice legibility for length.

© J.J. Merelo 2020
J.J. Merelo, *Raku Recipes*, https://doi.org/10.1007/978-1-4842-6258-0_17

How It Works

This guessing game generates a small random number and the player tries to determine the number by guessing. When the players guess a number, the game indicates if the true answer is a bigger or smaller number, thereby allowing the players to narrow their scope of numbers to guess. The game ends when the correct number is guessed. Here's is a non-one-liner version:

```
my $number = 6.rand.Int;
my $prompt = "*";
say $number;
while ( my $guess = prompt("$prompt Your guess>") ) ne "" {
    if $guess == $number { last }
    elsif $guess < $number { $prompt = "<" }
    else { $prompt = ">" }
}
```

The number is generated and we use part of the prompt to indicate if the guess is larger or smaller than the number entered. Then we run a loop that exits (using last) if the guess is correct, and changes the prompt if it is not. The loop runs forever or until we use an empty string in response to it. The command used to write a message and collect what is written is, effectively, prompt.

Let's try to use all we've got to shorten this program to a single code line:

```
my \n = (1..6).pick; ($_ > n ?? ">" !! "<").print while ( $_ = prompt("
Your guess> ") ) != n
```

Note   Okay, so it won't fit into a single line in this book, due to the book's margins. But you can see in Figure 17-1 that it's on one code line in Raku.

This line is 93 characters long (some of which are spaces), and it has two statements; we need one to declare a variable. We use the default variable $_ to avoid declaring one, as well as sigil-less variable to avoid typing $, a shorter version of the random number generation (and probably faster), but it's essentially the same. One-liners needn't even have their own file—you can run them directly from the command line using -e, as shown in Figure 17-1

```
→ Chapter-17 git:(master) raku -e 'my \n = (1..6).pick; ($_ > n ?? ">" !! "<").print while ( $_ = prompt(" Your guess> ") ) != n'
 Your guess> 3
> Your guess> 2
> Your guess> 1
```

Figure 17-1. *Running a one-liner using raku -e*

Note that the script needs to be within quotes. Since we are using double quotes already, we will use single quotes around the entire script.

There are many options if you need to do this in Windows:

1. The latest Windows versions include an Ubuntu subsystem; you can use the shell to install and run Raku in the same way you would do so in Linux. Another option is CygWin, which helps you install many Linux programs. Finally, the GitHub client includes a shell, which is a version of CygWin and where you can install other Linux command-line utilities and run them, should you wish to do so.

2. These last versions also include PowerShell, which has the same quoting conventions as the Linux command line. Use PowerShell to run it in the same way.

3. Finally, you can simply use double quotes outside, and escape all the double quotes inside with \ if you are using older versions of Windows and can't (or don't care to) install the Linux command-line tools.

Remember that Raku is quite liberal in its use of quotes, so if you use single quotes inside the script, you can substitute them for others or simply escape them:

```
raku -e 'my \n = (1..6).pick; ($_ > n ?? ⌈>⌋ !! ⌈<⌋).print while ( $_ =
prompt(⌈ Your guess> ⌋) ) != n'
```

Can we make this even shorter? Well, we can at least make a single logical line and make it functional as well:

```
{ $^b > $^a
        ?? &?BLOCK($^a, prompt("> "))
        !! $^b < $^a ?? &?BLOCK($^a, prompt("< ")) !! "✓".say
}((1..6).pick,0)
```

This is 153 characters; once again, eliminating spaces would make it shorter, but anyway it would be longer than before. But it's a single logical line. It creates a block and calls it recursively. The block has two arguments, the first one is the number to guess, and the second one is the guess. If the guess is bigger, it shows a "greater than" symbol in the prompt; it will show a "lesser than" otherwise. It does a three-way comparison using ??!!; if it's not lesser or greater, it must be the solution, so it prints a checkmark.

The trick here is to call the block recursively: no lexical variables are defined, and the number to guess passes along as $^a (an implicit variable, which you can call anything you want as long as the order of the arguments is also the alphabetical order of the name of the variables), and the guess passes along as $^b. There's no assignment, only the binding of arguments, which makes this purely functional.

The real magic is in the use of the implicit variable &?BLOCK. Raku has many ways to do introspection (which might not always be a good thing, but comes in handy here). For instance, the blocks of code have a way of referring to themselves: this one. &?BLOCK does not care which block it's in. It will always be *this* block, and you can use it to recurse just the way we do it here. Another option, which might use more lines, is to call the routine by a short name and refer to it by name. That, again, could add a logical newline, since sub declarations and code might be thought of as residing on different lines.

So, take your pick. Logically or physically shorter. In either case, Raku has got a way for you to do it.

Recipe 17-2. Compute the *nth* Element in a Sequence Using a Single Line

Problem

You need to compute the *nth* element of a sequence that has been defined recursively, given its first element and a general term to compute *n* given the previous elements.

Solution

This one is easy, since sequences can be defined in a "natural" way in Raku. The position in the sequence can be read from the command line. However, one-liners need to be tested and evaluated, so we'll propose several solutions to do that.

How It Works

Sequences in Raku use a class called Seq, which can hold lazily defined and possibly infinite sequences, but the main way it operates is using the ... (ellipsis) operator. This operator can:

- Generate arithmetic or geometric progressions based on its first terms.

- Define a sequence based on its first terms, and a general term that computes them from the previous ones.

Let's start with an easy one: Compute the factorial of a number, that is, the product of that number and all the preceding ones. (For example, the factorial of 4 is 4x3x2x1=24.)

```
say  [*] 1..( @*ARGS[0]
             // %*ENV<NUMBER>
             // die "Use $*PROGRAM <num> or NUMBER=<num> $*PROGRAM" );
```

Although this solution is shown as several lines for readability, it's a single line logically. The bulk of the script checks for input: it uses the command line or an environment variable, or it dies with a usage message if none of them is present. The // is the defined-or operator. It uses its left side if available, and goes on to the right if not. So we can run this by typing the following:

```
./factorial.p6 225
```

Or by writing the following in the Linux or OSX command line:

```
NUMBER=225 ./factorial.p6
```

It will produce a message like this if none of the arguments is available:

```
Use /home/jmerelo/progs/perl6/raku-recipes-apress/Chapter-17/factorial.p6
<num> or NUMBER=<num> /home/jmerelo/progs/perl6/raku-recipes-apress/
Chapter-17/factorial.p6
```

The path to the program is taken from the $*PROGRAM dynamic variable. This is in a "die" message to produce an immediate exit (and not an additional error), which is typical of an one-liner hack.

However that number is obtained, it's used to generate a range and multiply all its elements using the reduce meta-operator on the * operator. The result is a fast program, but of course there are other ways to do it. For instance, this one:

```
sub MAIN( Int $number = %*ENV<NUMBER>) { say  [*] 1..$number }
```

This is the opposite of the previous approach. It's a single line physically (even shorter than the previous one), but logically it's at least three lines. We use the default value mechanism of signatures to use the environment variable, if available. In this case, the error with no value will be produced by the sub MAIN itself, and it might be less informative, although it makes the program logically simpler:

```
Type check failed in binding to parameter '$number'; expected Int but got
Any (Any)
```

It's not really a usage message, and it obviously omits the fact that you can use the environment variable. On the other hand, we get a helpful usage message if we run it with –help, as follows:

```
Usage:
  factorial-v2.p6 [<number>]
```

This indicates the name of the parameter and the fact that it's optional (in square brackets). There's even a third alternative.

```
sub MAIN( Int $number =%*ENV<NUMBER> ) { my $c = 1; say  (1,* * $c++...∞)
[$number-1]  }
```

We use an auxiliary variable to take into account the index of the position the operation is in; $c will contain that index and will multiply it by the previous value, generating a sequence where the $c element is the factorial. But we're actually generating an infinite (but lazy) sequence to do so. We don't need to do that, so let's try a simple loop, as follows:

```
sub MAIN( Int $n =%*ENV<NUMBER> ) { my $ჶ = 1; $ჶ *= $_ for 1..^$n;
$ჶ.say;}
```

We are using the Georgian letter *phar*, since it sounds like *factorial* and also looks like a little nose with glasses on it. We golfed down the program to occupy the minimum number of characters, and could in fact make it shorter if we gave the environment variable another name. But there's another issue here. Which one is the fastest of all the ones that we tried? If we time how the factorial of 10,000 is computed, using time on the command line, the result will be like this.

```
time raku ./factorial-v4.p6 10000
0,80s user 0,06s system 106% cpu 0,806 total
```

As a matter of fact, this happens to be the fastest on my machine. The previous one is the slowest, with 0.95 seconds. It's the one that uses the simplest data structures, as well as a for loop, that's quite optimized anyway. It's still using a range, but that is not so slow, and in fact the first version is the second fastest; since sub MAIN adds a bit of overhead, this version might, in fact, be quite fast. The result of benchmarking these four versions using the hyperfine command tool is shown in Figure 17-2.

```
→  Chapter-17 git:(master) ✗ hyperfine './factorial.p6 10000' './factorial-v2.p6
10000' './factorial-v3.p6 10000' './factorial-v4.p6 10000'
Benchmark #1: ./factorial.p6 10000

  Time (mean ± σ):     772.9 ms ±  11.5 ms    [User: 812.3 ms, System: 34.3 ms]

  Range (min … max):   764.0 ms … 804.3 ms    10 runs

Benchmark #2: ./factorial-v2.p6 10000
  Time (mean ± σ):     788.9 ms ±  23.6 ms    [User: 837.4 ms, System: 29.2 ms]

  Range (min … max):   776.0 ms … 854.3 ms    10 runs

Benchmark #3: ./factorial-v3.p6 10000
  Time (mean ± σ):     900.0 ms ±  25.4 ms    [User: 946.2 ms, System: 47.7 ms]

  Range (min … max):   865.7 ms … 947.5 ms    10 runs

Benchmark #4: ./factorial-v4.p6 10000
  Time (mean ± σ):     757.9 ms ±  24.1 ms    [User: 803.8 ms, System: 36.8 ms]

  Range (min … max):   735.6 ms … 802.9 ms    10 runs

Summary
  './factorial-v4.p6 10000' ran
    1.02 ± 0.04 times faster than './factorial.p6 10000'
    1.04 ± 0.05 times faster than './factorial-v2.p6 10000'
    1.19 ± 0.05 times faster than './factorial-v3.p6 10000'
```

Figure 17-2. *Benchmarking the four versions, with the last one being two percent faster than the first*

Doing things quickly can take you nowhere very speedily, however. So we need to test, and we need to test these one-liners too. Everything is fun and laughter until that one-liner breaks down when we least expect it.

Fortunately, we can do white-box testing with Raku; that is, we can run tests on scripts written in Raku in the same way we would any other function or module. We do so using the `Test::Script` module that was recently released by yours truly to the ecosystem. Let's test these four modules and check that they effectively work:

```
use Test::Script;
use lib <.>;

for <factorial factorial-v2 factorial-v3 factorial-v4> -> $f {
    my $filename = "Chapter-17/$f.p6";
    output-is($filename, "3628800\n",
        "Output well computed for 10",
        args => [10]);
}
```

`Test::Script` provides a series of functions, one of which is `output-is`. It verifies that the output to the script, which is the second argument to the function, is correct. The arguments to the script are given via the `args` named argument, as an array. In this case, we will try to compute the factorial of ten, which is the indicated amount. Is everything okay? Well, it is not. The last script was wrong. Here's the correct version:

```
sub MAIN( Int $n =%*ENV<NUMBER> ) { my $⍺ = 1; $⍺ *= $_ for 1..$n;
$⍺.say;}
```

I'm not going to ask you to go back and forth between this and the last version: the ^ before the $n was excluding the last element to be considered in the computation, and the result was one zero less than expected. Testing caught the error, and now it's fixed. You see? Testing is important.

Note   I reran the benchmarks to see if this error had any influence on the total performance, and it did not. There's one multiplication more, but that's not too important in the context of 10,000 of them.

We can compute more complicated sequences using a single line. For instance, we could compute approximations to the Neperian logarithm base, e; this is the summation of the inverse of the factorials up to a number. That is, we compute the factorials of a series of numbers up to a point, we take their inverses, and then we add them up. For instance, if the number is 3, the three factorials would be 1, 2, and 6, and their inverses are 1, ½, ⅙, which adds up to 1⅔. The bigger the number, the bigger the precision. This script will do it:

```
say [+] (1,| [\*] (1...∞))[^@*ARGS[0]].map: 1/*
```

The base of this is the infinite succession of all factorials. [*] is an accumulating reduction-operator: It multiplies every element by the result of all the previous ones, but instead of throwing away the result, it creates a series with all of them. It doesn't use 0, which is a special case for which the factorial is 1, but it would break the series, so we put it in front and collate the whole series using the slip operator, |.

The result of that will be the infinite sequence of all factorials. But we just need the n first to compute an approximation of e, so we use the argument given in the command line to cut it where we want. However, to obtain e, we need to invert that series. We map every element to its inverse, and then sum them all to obtain an approximation to e. For 1,000 elements, we will obtain 2.718281828459045, and it's pretty much stuck there for bigger values. Can we go any further? Well, 20! is already a pretty big number, and 1/20! is very small. It goes beyond the capacity to represent floating-point numbers in the system, so why throw all those cycles to waste? Let's just cut the sequence where it can't be improved any further:

```
say [+] (1,| [\*] (1...^max(@*ARGS[0],20))).map: 1.0/*
```

Instead of defining an infinite sequence, which is okay from a theoretical point of view, but not very practical, we cut the sequence of numbers at the argument if it's smaller than 20 or simply 20. Same as above, but we'll get to the result faster no matter what, since 20 terms is all we'll be computing. But then, why are we doing this, if all we've got is crappy precision that we could achieve with a much simpler formula? We need to crank up the precision. And, Raku, again, is helpful in that sense:

```
say [+] (1,| [\*] (1..@*ARGS[0])).map: { FatRat.new(1,$_) }
```

We eliminate the cap for the values, which we don't need any more. But the key here is using FatRat, or big rational numbers of arbitrary precision, to compute every new term. While Rats (or rationals) become Nums (or floating-point numbers) when they exceed a certain size, and are thus limited in precision, FatRats do not. With FatRats, we can keep computing terms until we get tired. For 1,000 terms, it will be as follows:

```
2.7182818284590452353602874713526624977572470936999595749669676277240766630
[...41 lines here...]
2010249505518816948032210025154264946398128736776589276881635983125
```

Raku gives you precision when you need it, but the only two data structures with infinite precision are Ints and FatRats, so if you need to go to the umpteenth position in a number, you need to include one of them in your one-liner (or any other program).

Recipe 17-3. Perform a System Administration Task Repeatedly Using a Single Code Line

Problem

You need to check the logs from time to time, or create an alert, or monitor some variable, if possible with a single line of code. You need to repeat these checks at an established frequency.

Solution

Use supply to create periodic tasks; these should be short if you want to fit them in a single line. If you need to use an external module to perform a system task, you can provide it in the command line using -M.

How It Works

System interaction is not easy, and we devoted an entire chapter to it, Chapter 2. In general, you will need to use an external library to parse logs properly or use the correct command to interact with the operating system API, and that will usually be in an external module.

For instance, say you need to know the evolution of the filesystem and determine how it's being filled up. There are different commands you can use; df and du in Linux and OSX, and probably other kind of commands in Windows. If you don't want to work with all the different cases, you could use a module such as FileSystem::Capacity, which uses these utilities to return directory and volume capacity.

Now you need to do something periodically. Again, you can use the operating system services to do that. This is, however, highly dependent on the operating system, and needs additional capabilities. Let's just use a script to achieve the same, if possible.

There are several ways to achieve this feat in Raku. Promises can be timed, and you can launch another promise with each fulfilled one. However, the simplest way to achieve this is to use a supply. A supply creates a data stream; a live supply will produce values forever or until it's stopped. There are many ways to create these kinds of supplies, but we are going to use .interval, which generates a stream of incrementing integer numbers every number of seconds given as an argument. Supply.interval(2) will produce increasing numbers every two seconds. We don't care about the numbers, but about processing something every two seconds, and this is what we will do in this one-liner.

```
react whenever Supply.interval(@*ARGS[0]) {
        with volumes-info()</> {
            say "Free M ", (.<free>/2**20).Int,
            "- Used ", .<used%>
        }
}
```

Again, 167 characters with spacing and everything. It's a long line indeed, but it's a single logical sentence, wrapped in several control structures. The external one, react, will activate whenever one message is received. The messages it reacts to are included in a whenever clause, which checks when the (periodic) supply emits something. We don't really care about the numbers (which would be in the $_ variable), but we do care about our stuff: volumes-info will return a hash with all the volumes as keys and information on them as hashes and </> will be the root volume (in Linux; this is OS specific and will not work in Windows). We could change the direction of the slash (from / to \) to detect the OS, but that will add to the length and it's probably easier to just change it if you install it onto a different operating system.

Using with helps shorten the script, because it places its value in the implicit variable. .<free> will return that value from the hash, and ditto for .<used%>. We convert the value to megabytes, since by default it's given in bytes (at least in Ubuntu).

We also use the arguments to specify the interval, and we pick it up via @*ARGS. We can then run it this way:

```
 raku -M FileSystem::Capacity::VolumesInfo -e 'react whenever Supply.
interval(@*ARGS[0]) {with volumes-info()</> { say "FreeM ", (.<free> / 2
** 20).Int, "- Used ", .<used%> } }' 15
FreeM 193112- Used 57%
...
```

I really wanted this code to fit on one line, which is why I reduced it so much. Here it is in normal type, in several lines:

```
raku -M FileSystem::Capacity::VolumesInfo
   -e 'react whenever Supply.interval(@*ARGS[0]) {
      with volumes-info()</> {
         say "FreeM ", (.<free> / 2 ** 20).Int, "- Used ", .<used%>
      }
   }' 15
```

The FileSystem::Capacity::VolumesInfo module contains volumes-info and is part of the FileSystem::Capacity distribution. Using -M in the command line is equivalent to the use statement we placed at the front of the scripts. By offloading it to the command line, we have saved a statement in the program, keeping it as a single line.

To make it useful, you will probably want to run it at startup and redirect its output to some log file in the system logging directory, /var/log, for instance. But that's something additional. The single-line script here will perfectly solve your problem.

Glossary

Raku introduces many new concepts into the realm of programming, some of which come with their own words for describing them. This glossary includes a series of words that are of common use throughout the book (and the Raku documentation), as well as others that have been introduced for the first time here.

Dator

Short for *data accessor* and introduced as far as I know in this book. It is a data access class, or an object instantiated of the same class, or a role that describes the (possibly abstract) interface that these classes must employ. Dators are *injected* into other classes to access data stores in a fashion that's independent of the actual data store used.

Distro/Distribution

A functionally related set of Raku modules, classes, and grammars that are published together to the ecosystem or installed in a single action. Equivalent to the classical "library" concept, except that distros might include binary scripts and other artifacts such as documentation.

Grammarole

Also introduced in this book, it's a role that defines part of a grammar and that can be mixed in a grammar, although it can, by itself, be used as such by *punning*.

393

© J.J. Merelo 2020
J.J. Merelo, *Raku Recipes*, https://doi.org/10.1007/978-1-4842-6258-0

Hyper/Race

Auto-threading operators that are used to convert a sequential operation into a concurrent one by dividing the data structure they are applied to in different batches (with batch size controlled by the programmer) and then submitting them to different threads for computation. While *hyper* will return the result in the same order as the original data structure, *race* might not respect that order.

Punning

Creating a new instance of a role, as if it were a full-blown class.

Rakuish

Mythological quality that would make a pattern or statement more adequate than others to solve a problem in Raku. In general, there's no such thing, because in Raku there is more than one way to do it, and Raku is a developer-centered language. However, different programming patterns will result in faster code or in a cleaner appearance. Opting for one over the other is not for the language to say, but really up to you. This also refers to using Raku's features (and specifically those that set it apart from other languages) to express yourself and solve problems concisely. TMTOWTDI also applies to the definition of terms.

Rocket Operator

Used in this book as well as in *Perl 6 Quick Syntax Reference*. This is a "feed" operator that "launches" the result of a stage into the next one. It's the ==> operator, and it takes a list, sequence, or array from the left side, and a mapping/filtering operation from the right side, resulting in an array which can, in turn, be fed to the next stage. For instance, ^3 ==> map(*²) will compute the squares of 0 to 2.

Routingine

Introduced in this book, it's a routing routine, that is, a route block that has the form of a routine in a Cro microservice.

Token

A token, used as part of a grammar and with a expression that is similar to that of a method, which uses the language of regular expressions to extract a part of a string. The main difference with a declared *regex* is that tokens do not backtrack (and are thus faster) and ignore whitespace; rules do not ignore whitespace. Tokens, regexes, and rules are used in grammars, although in this book we have used tokens almost exclusively.

Websocker

Introduced here, it's a websocket server. In other words, an application that responds to messages via websockets.

Index

A

Abstract syntax tree (AST), 215
Adverbs, 193
api attribute, 144

B

BUILD submethod, 144

C

Client-Side Web and API
    check IPs/addresses
        problem, 176
        solution, 177
        working, 177, 178
    download/extract information, website
        problem, 167
        solution, 167
        working, 167–172
    GEoIP database, 165, 166
    get information
        problem, 172
        solution, 172
        working, 172–176
cmark, 307
Communicating Sequential
    Processes (CSP), 321
Comprehensive Perl Archive
    Network (CPAN), 294

Configuration files
    Docker containers, 89–91
    etcd, 91–94
    flags/argument, 80–85
    INI format, 76, 77
    JSON, 73–76
    shell, 87, 88
    YAML, 77–80
Console or terminal user interface
    (CUI/TUI), 270
Cro modules, 199
Cro::HTTP::Test, 223

D

Dangling images, 105
Data parallelism, 316
Data science/analytics
    big files, 55, 56
    cheating roulette/loaded die, 42
    email addresses/user names, 39–42
    random data generator, 52–54
    spreadsheet
        calories.xls file, 45
        sFreeXL, 46
        NativeCall interface, 46
        native module, 46
        Parser, 44
        regex, 46
        regular expression, 46

Printed in the United States
By Bookmasters